'Yaacov Hecht is the father of d[...]
his school of thought emerged th[...]
education programs and significant amount of the educational
communities. Hecht puts in the center the attentiveness to the child and
to his various abilities and needs. In the schools which are influenced by
his ideas, teachers and students alike take responsibility for themselves
and for their shared work, and create an involved learning community.
The Ministry of Education sees in Yaacov Hecht's educational path a
model worthy of studying and implementing throughout the education
system.'

Prof. **Yuli Tamir**
Former Israeli Minister of Education

'Yaacov Hecht guides us through a fascinating human journey, in whose
center is the child and the great power concealed within her. In a road
full of potholes and obstacles, he succeeds in creating a path of sanity
and in shattering the distorted institutional fixation, represented by the
mainstream. This journey symbolizes the beginning of a revolution, and
presents a new and groundbreaking educational outlook.'

Rubik Danilovich
Mayor of Be'er Sheva

'Yaacov Hecht wrote an important book, which expands the concept
of education far beyond the schools' boundaries. He demonstrates
how education can transform whole communities, and how the living
standards of the 21st century enable all, young as old, to adopt the "Life
Long Learning" outlook.'

Prof. **Daniel Greenberg**
Founder of "Sudbury Valley" School, USA

'Yaacov thoroughly understands what freedom is for children. This
understanding enables him to define a free framework with clear
rules and boundaries. His approach to the field of education and to
child raising is free, open and grounded. This is a rare approach. I am
honored that Yaacov drew his inspiration from my father, A. S. Neill, and
from "Summerhill" School, when he founded the Democratic School of
Hadera.'

Zoë Readhead
Principal of "Summerhill" School, UK

'As a student in a normal school, I was considered a thorn to be weeded
out; as a student in the democratic school, I became a rare flower. For
me, this story, far beyond words, is my life story. The tools and the
empowerment I have received in this place accompany me to this day.'

Narkis Sadeh
Graduate of the Democratic School of Hadera

'Yaacov is one of the most fascinating thinkers in the world of democratic education. His ideas are always clear and touching, since they are derived from many years of experience. His articles and lectures around the world have empowered many – students, teachers and educators – wishing to implement the message of democratic education in their countries.'

Kageki Asakura
Dean of Shura University, Tokyo

'The Democratic School of Hadera and the democratic schools network that consequently arose throughout Israel prove in practice that there is a possible alternative, which is significant and attractive to a growing number of parents and young people. This is an unfailing source of hope, both for the message conveyed by democratic education itself and for the potential carried by other external alternatives, that are currently developing in the outskirts of the system. This book was written by the founder of the Democratic School of Hadera, and the one responsible for spreading the message of democratic education throughout Israel. It reflects the outlook which lies in the foundation of democratic education – which, up until now, has been mostly unwritten – in a matter-of-fact, clear and accessible manner. As such it is a must read for anyone anxious for the future of education.'

Dr. Roni Aviram
Head of the Center for Futurism in Education in
Ben-Gurion University of the Negev

'The book describes a moving educational journey of one of the most outstanding educators the State of Israel has encountered – a personal journey which is also a fascinating story of the Democratic School of Hadera and democratic education in general. Yaacov Hecht manages to engage us in his stories and to share with us thought-provoking issues and ideas.'

Prof. **David Gordon** of blessed memory
Department of Education, Ben-Gurion University of the Negev

'Yaacov Hecht's book opens new horizons for the traditional Arab society in Israel, which seeks reform in education and wishes to convey the values of democracy to the next generations.'

Ali Zahalka
Principal of the Innovative-Democratic School of Kfar Kara'a

Yaacov Hecht

Democratic Education
A beginning of a Story

102

183 - 187
testing

193 Boundries ?

213-214 Staff v. Parents

229 Learning Community

319 Social Vision of DE

332 School Refusing children SRCs

345 Brazil + r

Yaacov Hecht

Democratic Education

A beginning of a Story

Innovation Culture

יעקב הכט
החינוך הדמוקרטי
סיפור עם התחלה

Editor: Rona Ra'anan-Shafrir
From Hebrew: Judy Cohen
Language Editor: Shirly Marom

Printed in Israel 2010

To Sheerly

contents

Introduction

About twenty years ago I set out on a journey down an unpaved road, full of pitfalls. I wanted to establish a different school, unlike the ones in existence, in its methods, in its beliefs and in its interactions with the children. I wanted to establish a school in which the protection of human dignity serves as a goal and a main way of operating in the field of education.

At the beginning of the journey I had a clear picture of my destination. I could imagine and describe it in detail – a story with a beginning, middle and end. I didn't know that my story would discover its own independence and life, and would begin writing itself. I didn't know that later on in the story – everyone who took part in it would add or detract lines, shorten or expand sentences. In time I learned that this fact was part of the very foundation of the vision I had created. The original story became old and worn with time, but it became the basis for new, fresh stories. I discovered that I had no interest in justifying my earlier way of thinking, the one I had when I had set out. Expressions I frequently used at the beginning, such as: "the truth is..."; "without a doubt..."; "the mistake is...";

"the correct answer is..." – all these gradually lost their value.

I realized that I had to suggest a different point of departure – one that did not know things in advance, give directions or leave a legacy; one that assumed that every child, and every individual, has his own story and his own way of advancing the plot of his life. As a result, over the years, as more knowledge and experience were accrued, I found myself returning again and again to the most basic questions and deliberations. With no single truth or set formula, we live in constant examination of the idea of promoting human rights and the individual's ways of self-fulfillment.

The story before you describes parts of this journey I have taken since the establishment of the Democratic School of Hadera, through the founding of other democratic schools, and till the establishment of public and educational systems underlined with the ideas of democratic education.

As I have said, at this point in time I am at a certain place in the plot, which has developed in fascinating directions, different from all I would have expected at the beginning of the road. I don't know how this plot will develop in the future. Therefore, this book is not a conclusion or an end. You might see it as a "picture album" from a journey of searching, undertaken by myself and by my friends, for a different life – a life at whose center stands the concept of "human dignity" and the ability to live with and through change and creativity.

The creation of this book is in many ways a parable on all the concepts which I wanted to describe in it: Many people I met on the way asked me to write down what I have said in my lectures. I was asked to describe democratic education, and mainly to explain the theoretical concepts underlying this world outlook. I also felt that writing this book would release me from a heavy load and enable me to move on more easily to new territories.

I tried. I wrote a number of short articles, I sat for hours facing the screen, but I couldn't write what I myself had said. I felt blocked.

As a child, too, I had had great difficulty in reading and writing. Today I would no doubt be diagnosed as dyslectic; in the past I was defined simply as a "problematic child". I had never finished high school, and the long winding road I traveled to become manager and consultant for education systems is described more in detail in this book. I managed to overcome my difficulty in reading, mainly because it is a central tool I use in the study of the world that so fascinates me; but I have never truly gotten over my difficulty in writing.

At some point I decided to record my lectures, transcribe them, and edit them as a book. But then it became clear that this was a problematic task. My speech is not only the sum of all the collected words - it is too multi-dimensional and associative to be "translated". I often felt like a failure. I wanted so much to describe in writing things that had happened, to convey my thoughts to others, to share with them all that fascinated me. But I did not succeed.

I waited for my opportunity, for someone or something that could make the impossible possible. And the opportunity arrived, in the form of the hands reached out by Ronit Tal (who offered to promote and organize) and Rona Shafrir (who took on the role of editor), former students of mine and present friends, who came to me and offered/demanded to publish this story. Yael Schwartzberg, the director of the Institute for Democratic Education, joined them with full intensity.

For long months we climbed, Rona and I, over mountains of words, pictures, ideas and stories. Rona gathered my words boldly and tied up the ends. Later on we were joined in our almost impossible task by my friends from the Institute for Democratic Education and by my wife Sheerly.

Thus, in a slow and difficult process, I found my way to the words. Hesitant, unsure, leaning on people I loved, I at last found my own voice. I found the story I could tell, and even – write.

I believe that every person, and every child, encounters throughout his life blocked areas: places of mistrust, despair and feelings of void. Some of us surrender and retreat from those places. But sometimes, when there is belief in one's self, and one lets things happen, believing that even a setback is part of the course of one's life – then exciting and fascinating surprises occur.

One of these exciting surprises is the very existence

of this book. And so, although this book is the story of the Democratic School of Hadera, and of the formulation of the ideas of democratic education and their implementation in various walks of life, this book is mainly a proposal to look at the world differently: a vision that assumes that all people were born equal but unique, with a special gift that is important and significant, with a story that only they can bring to the world.

Yaacov Hecht

Chapter One
The Beginning

At the age of five, in the dark shed of kindergarten, I thought for the first time about education. The teacher would lock me up in there often, as punishment for my behavior. I remember clearly that I was not angry at her; on the contrary, I felt mostly pity for her. I decided that she, too, must have come from "there", from the Holocaust, like my parents, and so I mustn't be angry at her. I would sit in the familiar darkness, listening to the children's voices and think. I felt that there surely must be a better way to educate children. A way without dark sheds, without arbitrary punishment, and with respect. I didn't know then, at age five, that I would devote most of my adult life to the search for this way.

Twenty-four years later, in 1987, the Democratic School was opened in Hadera. In the yard of a small community center we celebrated its opening, after two years of hardship on the way to its establishment. During the week preceding its opening we received three closure orders from the Ministry of Education, and we succeeded in canceling them three times. Our joy was great, but we also knew that we had embarked on a journey into the unknown. We had many fears for the future. And yet, there was something in the air – which I called "the fire of life" – the feeling that we were doing the right thing.

This book tells the story of the Democratic School of Hadera and the education systems founded after it. But these are in fact background for the central story, which is to be found sometimes between the lines and sometimes up front – the story of the journey of myself and my friends. This was a journey in which surprises became par for the course. The concepts of success and failure ceased to be as clear-cut as they had been, and likewise knowing and not knowing, which stopped being contradictory. From studying the relationships between adults and children we moved to studying relationships between people and thinking about human existence in general, and from there we returned to examine ourselves...

Today, some twenty years after we set out, I believe that we are still only at the beginning of our journey.

Childhood

When I began first grade, it became evident to me that I could not learn to read and write. I had two options: either to join what the children called "the retards' class", or to conceal my condition. I chose the second option and summoned up all my natural talents and energy to carry it off. I learned all the right answers by heart, I pretended to be chronically absent-minded and forgetful, and I copied on exams.

By sixth grade I had managed, through tremendous efforts, to acquire basic reading (to this day I still can't write without mistakes). At school no one knew – outwards I was an average student, a bit absent-minded, forgetful and prone to illness around exam time, and yet good at math and sports, a reasonably good student.

However, deep inside I felt horrible. The huge gap between what I knew about myself and what others knew about me was almost intolerable. I lied systematically, copied, constantly watching my back, trying to keep all the stories I had told to different teachers straight. I remember asking myself what was wrong with me. I could beat adults at chess, I was a national champion in broad jumping, I had fine achievements in sculpture, and yet, at the end of eighth grade, I still read like a kid who had barely learned to read. The letters refused to join together into acceptable words. How could it be, I asked myself, that in some areas I was strong and successful, while in others – the ones most important to my parents and my school – I was a total failure?

My parents saw my difficulties as the result of laziness. I had innumerable private teachers, and I was required to sit for hours every day practicing my handwriting.

Fortunately, I didn't believe them. I knew that I was neither lazy nor stupid. I rebelled against my parents, disobeyed them and fought tirelessly for all the things that were important to me, the ones that helped me survive (the Scouts, my friends, the Chess Club, the Model Planes Club and more). However, my story would not be complete without my mentioning that my parents' love and the feeling of security they gave me, despite all our struggles, contributed greatly to my journey in life and to my ability to fulfill my dreams. My mother never shouted or scolded. She was a kind of guardian angel, and taught me about the good that is in humanity. My father was a very creative, resourceful person. He sold radios that he had built himself, and was the first person to bring electricity to Arab villages using wind mills. There are several registered patents in his name. His original way of thinking, and his ability to find solutions where most people only see a solid wall, were a great influence on me, and in fact continue to be today.

In school too, in the midst of tiresome routine, shone one ray of light – Victor Halbani, the art teacher. He himself hated the conservative school system and suffered from it. He would often "save" me by taking me out of lessons to help him. Moreover, he put himself at risk by going to the principal to tell him that I was very talented in sculpture and should be allowed to develop in that field. The principal thought that Victor had lost his mind, but he allowed him to continue his special relationship with me. Thus we spent the last half of my eighth grade studies together, preparing sets for the graduation ceremony. I learned more in that time than I had learned in all my years at school.

Some years ago I heard that Victor Halbani had left teaching and become a famous sculptor whose works were exhibited throughout the world. I wanted to meet with him, but was afraid that he had forgotten me. Yet I was totally wrong – he remembered! Not only did he remember me, he also remembered some of the work I had done with him, things I myself had completely forgotten.

This relationship with Victor opened a door for me to the world of adults. Despite the cracks I had discovered since kindergarten, I had considered adults the ones who knew "the right way". All my life adults had led me to believe that they had knowledge which was not held by children, that they knew something I didn't know. Once, when I refused to go to the dentist, my mother called my father to show me that dental treatment was not painful. He sat in the dentist's chair and opened his mouth, and there was not even the slightest spasm of pain in his face. This led me to an additional astounding conclusion about adults: Not only did they know what was right and wrong – they suffered no pain. As a young child I was disturbed by the question – when would I be able to receive their knowledge; when would I be impervious to pain, when would I know what was right and what was wrong in life? At some point I believed that at my Bar Mitzvah ceremony the rabbi would give me a book that explained everything...

Later, when I understood that that little handbook didn't exist, I decided that somehow I had to get through these difficult years of childhood until the much-desired adulthood. Victor was the first person to show me that it could sometimes be hard for adults, too, like for children, and that there could be an alliance of trust and respect between a child and an adult.

Youth

Meanwhile, the huge gap between myself and the world of adults continued to widened. When I reached high school, a huge school of some 2000 students, I realized that no one really cared about me or my private world. The only thing that was important was the grades I got. After my ninth grade homeroom teacher claimed to my parents that I was smoking drugs (to this day I have never smoked anything including cigarettes) because I used to fall asleep in class, I realized that I had to play the game in order to get through the next years.

I quickly joined a group that would steal all the exams. Together we broke into the teachers' room, prepared copies of perfect exam papers, and passed them in at the end of the test. Later we broke into the health clinic and stole doctor's permission slips for our absences. I convinced myself that these thefts were moral and that there was no other way to beat the predatory system. In physics and math – the subjects I was good in – I tried to take exams without stolen test papers, but I discovered that crime has its own side effects: I could not answer even the questions I understood. I had gotten used to not thinking during exams, and so the next time I stole those papers as well. My school grades were high and even the principal knew me and treated me kindly. At the same time I was giving lessons on morality in my homeroom class and was active in the Scouts movement, but behind my successful façade I was in fact a criminal. Only I was aware of this harsh truth, and I was very much alone with it.

At times I wonder: is this how normal children turn to criminals? Children that no one sees, whose human qualities no one recognizes, as they are required to do educational tasks that are cold and valueless to them, ones they can't cope with? How many of the "bad kids" in the education system are actually the miserable products of its requirements?

At age 15 I did not ask these questions, but I felt unclean. I became entangled in the web I had woven around me, and even now it isn't clear how I would have ended up, were it not for the war.

When the Day of Atonement War broke out, almost all the men around were called up for many months. We, the youth, began to run the city. I worked nights at the Hadera bakery, in charge of distributing the bread as well. In the mornings I worked with my friends, the Scouts leaders, in elementary schools, where we ran activities for kids who were left without teachers. In the afternoons I delivered mail. After a few weeks the Hadera municipality set up a strong, active Youth Headquarters, which ran the entire city with the full backing of the leaders of the community.

This activity went on for half a year, and during that time I felt needed, successful, enterprising, surrounded by people who appreciated me. Later, when I returned to school, a teacher saw me in the schoolyard and scolded me for my absence. For me, it was like a kick in the head - all that time they had all been studying and taking tests! A blood-filled war had been going on in the State of Israel and at school – nothing. Business as usual.

From my shock, an understanding began to flower. I suddenly realized that true learning comes from doing. In the Scouts we were learning; in our volunteer activity we were learning. School, on the other hand, was a tool to measure grades and a workplace for thousands of teachers. "That's why they have schools," I said to my friends. "Perhaps we should move the schools to the Ministry of Labor and leave the real educational work to the youth movements."

In addition to this shock, I had undergone an internal change. I could no longer go back to the lying and the theft. The positive activity of the last months had changed me; or perhaps it would be better to say – brought me back to myself.

I decided not to go back to school. My parents were appalled. "If you don't go", they threatened, "you will become a degenerate... you'll never be able to succeed in life". The school principal called me in for a chat. "You are only 16," he said, "you don't understand what you are doing and you will ruin your life. With no matriculation, nothing will come of you".

My father sat there, silent and withdrawn. I knew he was praying that the principal would be able to convince me. I knew, too, that if I stayed one more day at that school, my life would be ruined. Going back to school meant going back to thievery, and I wasn't willing to do it.

I stuck to my guns, though it wasn't easy. During my adolescence I had begun to change my views on the adult world, but my old doubts were still gnawing away at me, deep inside. When the principal informed me that I didn't understand anything and that I was ruining my own future, I indeed believed that I was taking on a great risk by discontinuing my studies in the tenth grade. Fortunately, I felt I had no choice. The price I was paying (stealing and lying) was clear to me, and I was not willing to keep paying it.

The Forest

The day after my conversation with the principal I went to have a conversation with myself, in the place I loved best of all at that time – my true field of learning – the Hadera Forest.

When we were kids, in the suburb of Givat Olga, we would take trips with our parents to the forest on Saturdays. We always walked along the paths surrounding the forest, and never went inside. The question of what went on beyond those paths, in the thickets, fascinated and frightened me. In the seventh grade I summoned up enough courage to take a few steps inside. Every day I took a few more steps. I could visit the forest every day of the week. My friends would say, "Oh, we've already been to the forest", but for me every time there was a time of new discovery. It was there I tested my courage, there I discovered that I knew how to learn.

Actually, during my early adolescence, the forest was the only place where I truly learned. I felt like an explorer discovering new countries: I found rare flowers in the forest, iris and rare ophrys, and I discovered water fowl. The ducks fascinated me, while the lapwings and herons held my attention like magnets. Through a process that I could not then understand, I found myself checking and searching books to find out more about the birds I had discovered and the plants I had encountered. For the first time in my life I was looking in a book of my own free will, to find significant answers on subjects that interested me.

During the next two years, the forest continued to be an anchor of searching and finding. I would arrive there alone, to observe the birds and to map the forest. I came there with my young Scouts, to let them have their first encounter with wild nature. There are plants that to this day I go to see, as they blossom on a particular day of the year, and we have been in close contact for over thirty years. The ducks still fascinate me, even after I have discovered all their hiding places. In time I became an expert, on a relatively high level, on the natural life of the entire region. Because the forest interested me I learned its history, all about the draining of the Hadera swamps. I returned to the library, now a new and challenging place for me – out of my own desires.

I learned about a group of young people, who over 100 years before had set out against all conventions of their period and fulfilled a dream in the midst of swamplands and malaria. These people's dream had been strong enough to overcome all their obstacles, though they had seemed insurmountable at the time. Learning about these first pioneers, who had come to Hadera and planted the forest, was my first meeting with people who had gone against the mainstream. My encounter with their story, and with the forest which gave testimony to their existence, gave me the strength to persevere and go my way for the two years preceding my passage into "the adult world", the passage I had been waiting for all these years.

Adulthood

The first choice I made as an adult was to be the leader of the Hadera Scouts Troop, in parallel to the last part of my army service. Within a short time the number of Scouts grew from 200 to close to 1000. We were considered a particularly active and special troop. We had many activities outside in nature, and also in the city in its various neighborhoods. My fantasy was to create a community with a close relationship among its people, not based on judgment or criticism, but rather on caring and common interests. And indeed, it was not long before a very special atmosphere of cooperation and friendship was created. A large part of the troop's activities was devoted to the group leaders themselves, as the group became an increasingly central part of their lives. This was a place where we struggled to fulfill even the wildest of our dreams. As I had imagined some years before, the activities of the Scouts did replace the school from the aspect of significant educational activity.

For a certain period of time I was happy, but after a while there began to be cracks in my satisfaction. I would say to the leaders: "The Scouts are you". But in time I understood that this was not accurate. As time went on I began to feel that I was lying – they were merely realizing *my* plans and initiatives. The Scouts were *me*. The important lesson I learned from this touched upon the connection between charisma and cooperative activity: a cooperative act requires more compromise and the ability to step aside in time. I thus began to seek a way in which the desires and skills of every one of the participants would be expressed.

After the Scouting episode in my life was over, and on completion of my military service, I decided to study education at university. This decision contradicted everything I had believed in, in my youth, as well as my feeling that I already knew everything there was to know about education. New worlds had opened up to me during my time in the Scouts, and in the framework of my acquaintance with the methods of Alternating Facilitation, which I will shortly explain. I thought I already knew all there was to know about "other education". And yet, just as I was drawn to enter the forest, and not only to walk around it, so I felt the need to examine what was hiding behind the walls of the academic world.

Between May and July of 1981 I completed 9 matriculation examinations. At the same time I was holding persuasion sessions with the Ben Gurion University admissions committee (the only ones who agreed to meet me for a personal interview) and I promised to complete my matriculation in time, before the beginning of the academic year. My matriculation grades were actually quite low, and I had to promise to complete my English exam during my studies; but by the end of the summer I had been accepted to the university.

I know this story sounds problematic, and would seem to indicate extraordinary skills. But no, my academic skills are not high, and in every diagnosis I have been defined as dyslectic and dysgraphic, with average academic capabilities. Yet I believe that anyone who truly wants something, and is focused on his true goals, can overcome obstacles that would seem insurmountable. I have seen things like this happen dozens of times with my students at the Democratic School. They faced obstacles much greater than matriculation exams, and they easily jumped over the hurdles – whenever they really felt connected with their true goals.

Rotations

In the time I had left before I began my studies, I wanted to realize all my dreams – then and there. I was burning with the need to experience the world in my way. I thought that my leadership in the Scouts, and the personal lessons I had had in the forest, had given me rare knowledge of education, knowledge I had to apply as quickly as possible.

Together with two of my friends, Yossi Katz and Roni Anavi, I made a proposal to the Emek Hefer Regional Council to open a unique summer camp. The camp would operate according to an original idea we had heard of from Haimke Rosenblatt, and which suited perfectly my ideas at the time: "Rotations" (later Haimke changed the name to "Alternating Facilitation"). The idea, which dealt with group work, was to create a rotation in which at each session a different group member would be an advisor of the circle. This was a revolutionary approach, because it took the leadership out of the hands of one individual – "the advisor" – and presented the entire group with the challenge of leading and being led, each time by someone else.

We decided to try out this method with the children of the summer camp – kids in grades 1 – 6. At first we tried the rotation method for an hour each day, and by the end of the term the kids were leading an entire day of camp. We set up "corners" and filled them with materials according to subjects (e.g. a paper corner, a plant corner, a sports corner), and when a group of children would come to one of these places, one of them would take responsibility for the activity going on in that particular area. After the child had completed an activity, he would pass the responsibility on to another child.

All in all, the experiment was a success. Within two

weeks the day camp had filled up with visitors who came to see the "wonder" – children managing themselves and each other. One of the most moving – and influential – events of my life happened there. This was a child we accepted to the day camp despite all the warnings we had had concerning his violent behavior. He was a second grader and was handicapped, a deaf-mute. For two weeks he participated in the activities, slow and dragging after his older sister. On the last day of camp one of the adult leaders called me over urgently. I hurried to see what was going on and stopped, stunned. I saw this child signing, with his sister translating his words for a group of 15 children, who sat there listening intently to his instructions– and performing.

Right then and there I thought I had discovered the secret of education, the true deed of the educational encounter, from a new perspective.

I set out to lead "rotation" workshops all over the country, and again I thought that I already understood enough to establish an educational agricultural farm which would operate according to this method. I didn't know then how little I knew and what a long way I had yet to go.

Be'er Sheva

I began my studies towards a B.A. degree in Education and Geography. I was living in "Daled" neighborhood, the one considered the toughest neighborhood in the desert city of Be'er Sheva, but for me it was a warm, welcoming home. It was in that empty Negev desert that I discovered the most fascinating panoramas of the soul. I felt that every day I discovered a new person, a book I hadn't read, a subject that I thought of and suddenly realized that others had been dealing with for thousands of years before me. The library became my second home. There I met for the first time A.S. Neill (1883-1973) and his book "Summerhill". I read Tolstoy, Bertrand Russell, Dewey, Rousseau and Januscz Korczak. I felt like someone who had been traveling for years through internal deserts, and had suddenly come upon an oasis. And here I found that not far from this oasis were vast green plains offering opportunities for exploration and discovery. Basically, I felt that I was no longer alone in the world.

This great experience was hampered only by the examinations. In my first education exam I got a 40. The lecturer had asked us to write only what he had taught, and I had also written about things I had read in books. I got the point, and when I took the retest I got a high grade. Gradually I learned to make the distinction between the rites of examination and the real process of learning.

Because of the remote desert location of Ben Gurion University, a community of learners was formed which, given the lack of alternatives, turned the study together into a fascinating social event. We were a group of inquisitive lecturers and students, who had come together around fascinating subjects. We spent all the time we could in significant learning.

Summerhill

In Neill's book "Summerhill" I found the answer to a question which had troubled me since I was a small child: Can there be a happy childhood?

He claimed that the answer was positive, and presented dozens of examples of productive and fascinating lives of children and adults together.[1]* Even earlier I had come to the conclusion that one could reach the zone of happiness only in the framework of a journey made out of free choice. I already knew that I was better at learning subjects that interested me – in the Hadera forest, or in the field of education. However, as I read "Summerhill", the parts of the puzzle, which I had tried to put together all my life, began to come together into a whole, coherent picture.

When Neill wrote about growing with the children in their directions, or about human dignity for all human beings, or that diversity was good, and that contrary to my mother's opinion one didn't have to be "like everyone else" in order to be happy – I felt that he was talking to me and about me.

In the summer, when my first year of studies was over, I went to England – to find Summerhill.

At the university I had been told that Summerhill was long gone. That Neill was dead. That the place had burned down. No one had any address for me. But I took the trip anyway, and in England I discovered that

---

* See Bibliography at end of book.

Summerhill was very much alive, and that Neill's wife continued to run the place in the same spirit.

For the first time in my life, I met children who loved to learn. I saw children for whom all options were open – to go to the swimming pool, to study math, to play tennis, to learn history, to climb a tree, etc. And they could choose. To my astonishment, the swimming pool and the tennis court were not always preferred over the math or history lesson. But it was obvious that every choice was made out of free will and with enthusiasm. When I was a student at school, as I have already mentioned, I loved to play ball and I hated to learn in the classroom. But even the good students in my class saw learning as a chore, or at best "something important to do". Not one of my friends had experienced learning as something he loved. We saved our feelings of love for games or boy-girl relationships in class.

At Summerhill, for the first time, I saw kids who **loved** to learn. I sat in on a "meeting", the weekly general assembly at Summerhill, and I saw kids speaking their minds – without fear and without trying to humor the adults around them.

This visit was a milestone in my thinking, although I did have some reservations, mainly concerning the place's management as a boarding school, without any involvement of parents. The structure of the school I was aiming for became clearer to me: a democratic structure as in Summerhill, which would include the influence of the nuclear family on the processes going on in school, with the understanding that in the center of the entire process was the free choice of the child.

When I returned from Summerhill, I began exploring around Israel. I decided to search for open schools, with the intention of becoming affiliated with one of them after I had completed my studies. There were then such schools in Haifa, Maagan Michael, Bat Yam, Rishon LeZion, Rehovot and Jerusalem.

From reading the literature I realized that in the 1960's, a large wave of open schools was created in Israel, but most of them had disappeared within a few years (see Chapter 6).

The vision of a democratic school was only in its very early stages, but the main components of what I wanted were already clear to me:

- A choice of areas of learning; the students choose what they want to learn and how.
- Democratic self management.
- Evaluation focusing on the individual - without comparison with others and without tests and grades.
- A school where children grow from age four till adulthood (eighteen and over).

In Israel, I discovered, there was no school that included all of these principles that I was looking for: There were schools that had creative and active education, which allowed for the students' choice within a lesson, but with mandatory presence in the class. Others did not have the democratic system of decision making, and still others allowed for choice and did have a system of democracy, but didn't have the continuity from kindergarten to high school graduation.

Pregnancy and Birth

During my first year at Ben Gurion University I met Sheerly, my partner. Our main topic of conversation as a couple was about raising and educating children, years before our first son was born.

Our relationship helped me to consolidate the way I would go after graduation. It was clear that I was going to make a change, but for some time I deliberated between focusing on the education system and on the university itself.

Eventually, through ongoing dialogue with Sheerly, I realized that in order to raise our children in the way we believed in, and in Israel, I would have to found a school that suited our concept.

I put notices up at universities and colleges, inviting people who were interested in thinking about establishing a different kind of school, which would operate according to the four principles that I previously described, to come to the first meeting in my home. About 20 young people came to that first meeting, most of them students. We began a process of learning, which continued on a weekly basis for an entire year.

At first we studied the ills of the existing system. We

read articles and met with people from within the system. We became familiar with the gradual but constant process of a system that was failing to function. Educators we met, and students, reported similar experiences of alienation, irrelevance, boredom and violence.

When we analyzed these problems, we realized that they did not only characterize the system in Israel, but were happening throughout the world, turning into an ever deepening crisis.

We diagnosed three main reasons for this situation:

1. The lack of connection between the labor market and the education system.

Assuming that the education system is supposed to prepare the students for the world waiting outside the school fence, and to serve as a microcosm of reality, the "school" that was founded in the framework of training and preparation for work in the factories of the Industrial Revolution is unable to adapt to ongoing and predicted changes in the labor market.

This "industrial school" tries to preserve the frameworks in which it was created, in a world where the successful worker is an "improved robot" (like Charlie Chaplin in Modern Times). Accordingly, the main mission of a student in such a school is to drill obedience and following instructions.

The "relative" of that school (which continues to function today with very minor changes) finds it difficult to adjust education towards initiative, creativity, development of imagination, thought and creation, which are the current and future needs of a progressive labor market.

2. The revolution in human and children's rights and its expression in schools.

Traditional schools were established in a world whose perception of human rights was significantly different from today's. The 20th century was marked by far more awareness and recognition of women's rights and minority rights from various populations, and recently we have become much more aware of children's rights. Almost all over the democratic world, the modern family is different from its counterpart at the beginning of the 20th century. The main difference is that we now hear the "voice" of children and the "voice" of women. The modern family shows great difficulty in adapting to the new situation, in which the child's place is different, complicated and ambiguous. School has not yet undergone that vital change that is demanded by this revolution in human rights. It is, then, a complicated and difficult encounter, that in these days can hurt many of those involved in it. Just see, as evidence, the growing number of schools in which there is conflict between parents and teachers.

3. The revolution of information and computerization and its encounter with schools.

The traditional school, which sees as its main goal the

impartation to children of knowledge which they lack, is rapidly becoming superfluous, as new technological advancements enable us to receive information in ways that are far more efficient and effective than schools.

The education system is trying to deal with the crises at its gates in three basic ways; Watzlawick, Weakland and Fisch in their book "Change", define them in basic models of inappropriate treatment of problems:

a. Denial that the problem exists – action is needed, but is not taken: "We don't have it in our school"; "let's not exaggerate, we're products of that system ourselves"; "whatever was, is what is now and will be; we have no control over it".

b. Attempts to make changes in problems that can't be changed or problems that don't really even exist – action is taken when it is not needed. Changes are made in schools as part of an unfocused race after new educational fads; innovations sometimes even contradict each other. As a result we see a flood of projects overwhelming the schools.

c. When the solution is actually a problem and we try to solve the problem by "more of the same": **more** authority, **more** discipline, **more** exams, back to the old familiar solution that brought us to where we are now.[2]

The system is trying to deal with crises with tools that it recognizes as "creators of change in the past" – with "more of the same". That is what led to the present situation; in other words, the assumption that the solutions are known and we just have to do them "better" or "more correctly".

The results that we can actually see are merely an increase in the ineffectiveness and irrelevance of the system, and harsh feelings of frustration among many who deal with education – teachers and designers of educational policy.

One could use the parable of the "cooking frog" appearing in the book by Peter Senge "The Fifth Discipline: the Art and Practice of the Learning Organization", which is brought as an example of "learning difficulties" of organizations; it describes how the education system gradually "cooked" itself crazy, in the last hundred years, and hence the difficulties of gathering up its energy for the needed change: According to this parable, if we put a frog into boiling water, it will immediately try to jump out. But if the water is at room temperature, it will splash about at its pleasure. If the pot is put on a source of heat and gradually warms up, the frog will remain sitting in the water and cook although nothing is preventing it from jumping out. Why? Because the internal mechanism of the frog, which is supposed to recognize threats to its life, is designed to identify sudden changes and not slow and gradual ones.[3]

Like the frog, so the education system was not prepared for the social and cultural changes that have slowly evolved over the last hundred years, and today it finds itself irrelevant to its own purposes.

Thus we arrived at the understanding that a new education system needed to be created - a system whose considerations would be suited to a new conceptual world, an updated and democratic one. The order of the day was to stop the failing attempts to improve the "old education system", which was based on values of a past world, without democratic awareness. In order to be relevant, the system had to undergo a significant change in the definition of its purposes and in the definition of the ways and the tools at its disposal. This "new definition" had, in our opinion, to lead to the appearance of a new interpretation of the concept of "school".

The "old education system" is aimed at preparing the student for a reality which is perceived as "the only one" and unequivocal. The purpose of a school, after its redefinition, would be to develop in the child the power to choose and create the reality in which he wishes to live, and the ability to see today's reality as multi-faceted and multi-purposed.

After this "redefinition", the student's passive place in school would change. If the "old school" defined the student's goals, objectives, required production and exact ways of carrying all these out for him, the future school which we have described would be a testing and training ground, with the student as an active, operating factor in the system.

In school, the student will focus on the selection and identification of his personal and social goals,

and will develop his strengths so as to be able to direct his life in accordance with those goals.

In addition, the school will direct and educate towards values of "human rights" and will see that they are applied on its premises.

We deliberated at length what to call the school – experimental, open, free, innovative, humanist...At last, after lengthy examination, we chose the name "democratic". We realized that democracy was a way of life, a way in whose framework we had chosen to live. Many see in democracy a mere governmental procedure, thus missing the point. Democracy is first of all a set of values. It is an entity whose purpose is to promote and implement human rights in society.

Churchill claimed that this was the least bad form of government. We agreed that if the intention is not the respect for human rights, one could think of better administrative models than the democratic process. However, it was clear to us all along that it would be worth bearing the hardships and disadvantages of democracy. Worthwhile – if respect for humankind and human rights were put above all and served as the purpose of the entire process.

It should be remembered that our main profit, as citizens in a democratic government, is expressed not so much in democratic procedures such as participation in elections every four years, or the utilization of the court system (which most of us never need). For example, right now as I am writing down my thoughts and beliefs with no fear, my rights to free thought, opinion and expression are being implemented. Many other rights, expressed in daily life, are not self-understood in other parts of the world.

Democracy did not suddenly spring into being, or come out of an arbitrary decision of leaders, but rather evolved through lengthy processes of thought and struggle. The first of those who began discussing it intended mainly to protect the rights of the white male aristocrat. These same white elitists did not take into account the fact that they were knocking over the first domino that would later affect the white woman, the non-white person, and eventually the child as well.

When we were sitting and thinking about the new school, we of course could see many differences between adults and children in a number of areas – physiological and psychological – but it was clear to us that these differences did not contradict their equality in the right to respect. The girl and boy, like the adults, have the right to be treated with respect.

The model of addressing students in a regular school was built in a world that was not yet democratic. Therefore, the changes that led to the democratic society that most of us live in today, must also be expressed in the area of education.

The school that was to cope with this challenge therefore received the name: the Democratic School.

From this we derived the two goals of the Democratic School:

The first goal is **education towards independence**. Already today, people change professions during their lifetime, and in the future this will increase. But even if an individual remains in the same profession for all of his working life, he will have to study and train constantly (Life Long Learning). In this kind of reality, one's ability to study independently, and the quality of his independent study, becomes a key factor in his economic and social success. The ability to study independently becomes possible when the individual is able to set his own personal and authentic goals and carry them out.

We defined this goal as follows: **"to assist the student in creating and acquiring tools which will help him to fulfill his own goals."**

I believe that people belonging to the old education system would correct our definition thusly: "to direct the student towards knowledge and the acquisition of tools which will help him to fulfill the goals **which others have set for him,** or **the goals of society**".

Why have we chosen the term "tools" and left out the term "knowledge"? Because in a world that changes rapidly, specific bits of knowledge have no long term significance. On the other hand, emotional intelligence, which a student develops in the learning process, has significance that transcends time and place. This is what will continue with him, towards coping with the next goal (see also Chapter 3). In other words, we can encounter two students of identical age and background, with similar cognitive knowledge, who in an old school would be given equal scholastic evaluation. But a look at them from a different perspective would show that the process of acquiring knowledge seriously harmed one of them (for example, hurt his self-confidence), and strengthened the other. Thus, when we examine the two children from the aspect of emotional intelligence, we can see huge differences.

The term "tools" addresses, therefore, the strengthening of emotional intelligence which will help the student to find out what his goals are and achieve them. The role of the adult is assistance in creating and acquiring these tools, thereby strengthening the student's independence and reducing his dependence on a teacher or other accompanying factors. In other words, the traditional role of passing on information alone no longer "fills the bill".

The key question which will accompany the teacher in democratic education is: In my interaction with the student, am I strengthening his independence?"

The second goal is **education towards human respect and dignity**. In a rapidly changing world, where the powers of the free market have great importance, there is always the danger of the compass of values being tilted towards the strong and the worthwhile. In such a world education plays a central role in reinforcing the anchor of values. We must focus on humanist and democratic directions and take care to promote human rights.

We defined it as follows:

"We wish to create an educational framework which sees as its main goal the education towards human dignity, as it is defined in the Declaration of Human Rights". Democratic education considers the protection of human rights in school as a necessary and basic condition for the beginning of work on education towards human dignity.

These educational intentions take place in three spheres:

One – "my" and "our" human rights

Two – the rights of "the other" or "the different"

Three – the rights of the whole of humanity

The basic assumption of a democratic school is that a young person, living in an environment which respects him and protects his rights, will know in the future to protect human rights in all three of these spheres. Such an environment will try to create a model of life in a democratic culture in the framework of the school.

Yanusz Korczak wrote, already at the beginning of the 20th century, in a collection of articles "The child's right to respect", about attempts to improve the education system by thinking in terms of "educating the child towards respect....rather than focusing on how to improve us...", "...we have given up on the struggle with ourselves, and have put all our load on the shoulders of the children. The educator is eager to adopt the rights of the adult. It is not himself he must watch, but the children, it is not his transgressions he is to list but the children's.".

Korczak proposes school mechanisms that will make the school a place that protects human rights. For example, "the "peers' court" which Korczak writes about in his book "How to Love a Child": "If I designate a lot of room, with no proportions, to the court – I do this out of awareness that the court can be a link leading to giving a child equal rights, to a constitution, to the mandatory application of the declaration of children's rights. The child has the right to serious and just study and treatment of his affairs. Till now everything was dependent on the educator's good will, on his good or bad mood. The child had no right to protest."[4]

At the end of the group's first year of work, we looked for a place for the practical application of the ideas we had formed. After a search all over Israel I found myself returning home, to Hadera, to my "extended family". Here there were many people, loved and loving, from my past, and later many more who joined in the task of establishing the new school. The idea of a democratic school gave many of them the light of hope for new creativity. Some 300 families joined the non-profit organization that was established to advance the school. The great experience of our evening meetings, and the intensive work, brought me back to the stories of the social pioneering that had taken place on the land of Hadera, more than 100 years ago. I thought about this wonderful opportunity to make a dream into reality, and I understood that the return to

Hadera must not be accidental, at least not where I was concerned.

At the end of two years of exhausting labor, we stood at the gates of the school feeling that we had "done it". Actually, we were only at the beginning of a long, hard and wondrous way. The way of the Democratic School of Hadera.

Chapter Two

The Democratic School of Hadera

Part One
Making Our Acquaintance

About our Location

The school is located in a thicket of eucalyptus trees, on a hill at the southern point of the town, among fields and citrus groves, in an open, green area. We moved there about three months after the school was opened.

In our tenth year, among our many visitors, arrived a group of students of architecture from the Technion (i.e. the Institute of Technology in Haifa). I wondered what could be the reason that motivated architecture students to visit the school, and when I asked, their leader told me that she had brought them to us in order to teach them the relation between beliefs and ideals, and their physical application.

I was very surprised. I told her that the only principle in building our school was the principle of the arbitrary. We had looked for the cheapest structures possible (because we had never received a budget for building) and set them down in the area.

She informed me that what we had done was called,

in professional terms, "evolutionary architecture". People build a path only when they have gone that way dozens of times, and they then feel the need for the path. Thus one builds a place that expresses the connection between beliefs and the physical area. "Look," she added, "We have been walking around here for over an hour, and we still have no idea where the principal's office or the teachers' room is. In ordinary schools, it is very easy to recognize those buildings, because they are usually different and prominent compared to the other school buildings. And here, we just can't find them. The whole school is built in a circle, and there is no distinction between the place of the older children and the territory of the little children. It also isn't clear what is more "valued" in your eyes; the library isn't especially conspicuous, the laboratories are no different from the art workshop. In this school we can find the expression of the circle of equality that is part of your ideology, a circle without any hierarchy".

I thanked her for making this distinction and gave it additional clarification: "The principal's office and teachers' room, which you were looking for, are not small or less prominent. They simply do not exist".

The First Years

In the school's early days, the parents valued the freedom of learning but claimed that "it's all very well and good, as long as the children have a few basic compulsory subjects, like arithmetic, English and Bible." So it was within the school's staff; only one person out of a team of 25 believed that one could open a school with no compulsory subjects.

Things being as they were, I chose to begin where most of the staff members and parents could agree, in the broadest area of agreement that we could find. From there, I thought, we could continue. And if the free system worked well, then the idea of freedom would take root and grow naturally, in the direction of the students' free choice in all areas.

For a school like this to be strong enough to make changes, we decided to operate as a system that made decisions in a democratic way. In our first stage, we set up a Parliament – a general assembly of all the school's community: students, staff members and parents. I believed that if the elective courses proved themselves, we would have a majority willing to change the way of learning in the school, and it would be possible to pass the decision in the Parliament.

We opened the first year of school with a curriculum that was divided into two: half a day of compulsory studies and half a day of electives. The compulsory subjects included Bible, English, arithmetic and Hebrew. Within one half year we had a clear picture: During the hours of compulsory study we functioned as an ordinary school, with disturbance and discipline problems and shouting, while the elective studies were pure enjoyment for both students and teachers.

Gradually the students, teachers and parents

developed strong opposition to the compulsory lessons, and raised the subject for discussion several times in the Parliament. At the end of the year, by a decision of the Parliament, we changed the curriculum so that it had no compulsory subjects. It was decided that the students could learn whatever they wanted; however they had to have at least 24 hours of set study a week, in the framework of lessons, a personal agreement, or a learning center.

In the second year of the school, there were heated debates regarding the 24 compulsory hours. In a gradual process we reduced them to 12 hours, yet the tension continued even then. The students didn't understand why they had to enter a lesson that did not hold their interest, or to make promises they couldn't keep.

They had a slogan: "Coercion does not encourage creativity". But the parents, and part of the staff, persevered with their idea that without the framework of compulsory lessons the system would "fall apart" and the children "wouldn't learn anything". The arguments were many and the atmosphere was tense.

An Alternative in Boston

The event that led to the change actually occurred abroad. In the middle of our second year, Sheerly and I took a trip to visit a friend in Boston for a week during the Passover break. I had with me a list of alternative schools in the area, hoping to discover that we were not alone in the world, and to get support from the experience of older schools. I was acting out of the drive to find something that would provide a point of reference for all of us. The parents, and some of the staff, told me: "We are the most radical school in Israel. Why should we go to any more extremes? We have only 12 hours of compulsory studies! That's really minimal". But my feeling was that we could go a lot further, and that what was stopping us was understandable fear. In other words, I needed some proportions.

The year was 1989. The Internet was a distant dream, and all the information that I had gathered came from friends and rumors. In Boston we went from school to school, but we found no schools that offered freedom. We certainly didn't find anything that resembled what we had. It was only on our last day of vacation that we were told about "some strange school that might be worth your while to see," about 10 minutes from our friends' home. It was "Sudbury Valley".[5]

The moment we arrived in the parking area, we realized that we had arrived at the place we were looking for (years later I tried to solve the riddle: how could we have felt what we felt from 100 yards away? The answer is related to the way the children were moving in their surroundings – like free people, at home). We saw a large stone building, huge green lawns, and a beautiful lake beside them with a dam that had created a kind of waterfall. It was a dreamlike panorama, and I had an inner sense of entering my most secret dreams.

Inside, the building looked like an ordinary house,

with a large kitchen, a living room and many small rooms. At first we saw no adults at all, and then we were sent to the office, where we also saw mainly children. From under one of the tables came an adult with a screwdriver in his hand, and said hello to us in Hebrew. In Hebrew?!

This was our first meeting with Daniel Greenberg. Danny and Hanna, his wife, had established the school, and they still work there today. Hanna, originally from Jerusalem, had met Danny Greenberg, an American Jew, when he came to study at the Hebrew University, and they both developed academic careers in the US. But after their eldest son Michael was born, the question of education became central to their lives, eventually leading them to leave the distinguished cathedral of the university in 1968, in order to establish "Sudbury Valley".

As we toured the school, we saw that there were no set lessons, and in fact, there was no school curriculum. On the other hand, there were wonderful places like libraries, lakes, and play areas. There were sympathetic adults – and children who were learning from everything going on around them.

Our visit went on for hours, magical hours during which we created the first connection towards a close friendship that later developed between our families. At the end of our tour Danny and Hanna "loaded us down" with books and articles that Danny had written, and invited us to their home.

The moment that I began to read the books, I realized that someone had already written all that I was supposed to write. Someone else had actually fulfilled **my** dreams. For a moment I felt redundant. But at the same time, I could see the great opportunity before me, the one I had been looking for throughout this journey – the opportunity to "skip" twenty years forward, by learning from the experience of this veteran school, and mainly to derive the courage to continue following my innermost thoughts and feelings about learning. This meeting with "Sudbury Valley", with students and adults who had been learning all their lives in a world of free choice and self-management, charged me with new powers.

When I returned to Israel, equipped with books and articles and strong impressions of my visit to Boston, I knew that now everything was going to change. The following year I sent a delegation of students and staff members from our school to Boston, and at the same time we hosted a group from there. This was in addition to long discussions within the staff, about the significance of the experiences of the "Sudbury Valley" people.

A few months later, on the third anniversary of the school, the Parliament passed a decision to cancel all compulsory studies.

The Structure of the School

As we began our fourth year there were 350 students in the school, and this figure remained the same in its tenth year. The number of students was determined from a fundamental decision not to grow any more, and to maintain our atmosphere of intimacy and personal connections. The youngest students at the school are four years old, and the oldest are eighteen-nineteen years old. The staff is made up of 45 teachers, 30 of them full-time teacher-advisors.

The students arrive at the school from all over the country. We have had students from the Golan Heights, from Tel Aviv and even from settlements in the Negev (until other democratic schools were founded). Today, the school population is mainly from the Sharon area: Hadera, Pardes Hanna, Binyamina, Zichron Ya'acov, the Heffer Valley and even the more distant Ra'anana and Tel Aviv.

There are no homeroom classes at the school. Each student has a **personal teacher-advisor**, whom he has chosen from the staff. The advisor is the liaison between the student and the school, both from an organizational aspect (for example, checking attendance) and from the personal aspect (e.g. the student's feelings in school and outside of it) and also from the aspect of learning. The advisor's role is to help the student along his "learning journey" in school.

Officially the school is divided into three large divisions:

- Ages 4 – 8 - the Youngest Division. In this division there are three "houses", that is structures resembling small houses which contain children of all ages. The children of this division are in the area of the houses, with two teacher-advisors for each house. However, these young children can also take part in all the school activities. Throughout most hours of the day, one can see the older children, even the teenagers, coming to the youngest division and playing with the younger children.

- Ages 8 – 12 - the Elementary Division. The elementary school children have a central building that looks like a large house. They must register with their advisors daily, to inform them that they have arrived. The activities they take part in afterwards depend on them.

- Ages 12 – 18 - The Secondary Division. Activity here is similar to that of the elementary division, except for a separate social club for the high school students. Both elementary division and high school division students choose a personal advisor at the beginning of the year.

- All options of study for elementary and secondary school children are according to the students' choice, thus most of the classes are multi-aged, and one can easily find a class in which ten year olds study alongside fifteen year olds.

The school operates as a sort of microcosm of a democratic state, with two main pillars:

One – the aspect of democratic values: giving respect to every individual, child or adult, and general conduct according to the declaration of human rights.

Two – the procedural aspect: operation of democratic

mechanisms for the management of the community of the school.

Part Two
Ways of Learning

When a student at the democratic school, whether in the elementary or the secondary division, arrives at school, he can choose what he will be doing from five official options. In addition, he can initiate and act in a number of informal frameworks.

In the democratic school, every activity – playing, moving or conversing with a friend – is defined as learning. The five options which are to be mentioned now are only the formal ways that the school offers.

1. Choosing a lesson from the school's curriculum

At the beginning of the year, a curriculum and schedule are offered to the elementary and secondary students, made up of elective subjects (there are no compulsory subjects). Actually, at every hour of the day there are twelve different options for lessons. These lessons are given mostly by the teaching staff of the school, but students and parents are also invited to teach lessons. The subjects of the lessons are determined partly by the teachers (who have chosen a subject that interests them, and that they wish to learn together with the students), and partly by students. It should be mentioned that the lessons at the school are not given according to age, but in certain cases have prerequisites such as previous knowledge and familiarity with the material. There are various conditions to one's participation in each lesson, conditions set by the autonomous teacher teaching the lesson. Whoever wishes to participate in a certain lesson, must meet the conditions. These might be, for example, regular attendance, handing in papers, or just the obligation not to disturb the lesson. However, exams cannot be included among the conditions. In lessons which prepare students for matriculation, there is practice in taking tests; however these are only part of the preparation for matriculation, not compulsory exams.

In 1997, the last year in which I was principal of the school, I took part in facilitating a "search lesson". We worked as a team of three teachers: Idit Eisen, the movement teacher, Miri Spector-Tczernitz, the art teacher, and I, who come from the world of words. We had a study group of students of whom the youngest was in fifth grade and the oldest were in eleventh - twelfth grade. We worked cooperatively with tools of art, movement and texts, in order to deal with questions of the significance of life. At the beginning of the year we set rules for the work in the group, which were the conditions under which the students could participate.

Setting rules for the lesson was always done before the opening of any new activity in school, and these rules were strictly obeyed.

That same year I participated in an additional lesson, which was called "The Human Rights Club". Here, too, we worked as a team of three teachers, and together with the students we studied various issues in the area of human rights. We demanded of ourselves to do in-depth study of a particular area in which there was a violation of human rights, and we set out on an actual struggle for this right. That year we chose to fight for the rights of foreign workers and their children.

In the two lessons which I have just described, and in many others, I had the privilege of unusual learning experiences – as I both taught and learned, and while sitting in class with my students was also involved in my own personal development.

Because I was teaching at various academic institutes in parallel to my teaching at the Democratic School, I can say that the democratic learning experience is essentially different. This is an experience that does not deal with results that are irrelevant for the student, such as "will this be on the test?" or "do we have to write this?" but rather initiates a different kind of class discourse, critical in its character, deriving from curiosity and interest. One of the expressions of the uniqueness of this learning experience at school is that many times, my students brought learning materials into class that I was not familiar with as a teacher. Another expression of this was the fact that many students did not accept the viewpoints that I presented in the lesson as something to be taken for granted, and fought for their own views, while leading the entire class to new, unknown areas of learning.

That year I also taught "regular" lessons in the school. For example, I taught a class in civics towards matriculation. Matriculation classes are different from the other classes in the schedule, because their goal is clear and uniform – success in the matriculation exams. From this goal, the way of learning is derived. We spent less time dealing with civics and democracy, and more time on methods and ways to pass the test well. Students who still asked to study the subjects in depth could go to other frameworks in the school. In the matriculation class I set clear rules regarding participation, tardiness and reading requirements. A student who wanted to study for the matriculation exam in the framework of this lesson was obliged to abide by its rules. Students who wished to study for matriculation, but not in the framework of the lesson, came to me, and together we created individual ways of learning.

2. Learning centers

There are various learning centers scattered throughout the school: an art center, a language learning center, a music center, computers, science laboratories, a library, a kitchen, a video center and more. Every child can come to these centers even without scheduling it in advance, and experience what the center has to offer.

One of my favorite centers was the art center. Every time I felt weak, depressed or tired, I would go there to "gain some energy". The art center is located in a large space on the edge of the school, at the end of a path that winds along between the trees. In it you can find various work areas: painting, sculpture, photography and more. Every student in the school can enter the center any time he chooses, to do artwork in the way that suits him best. Four to six different teachers have worked in the center through time, and each had his/her own unique teaching methods and personal viewpoints regarding the world of art. As a result, the students at the school could also choose the teacher who best suited them. The art center has a gallery, where there are always changing exhibits of the students' work, as well as a social club which is chiefly for the use of those working in art.

My visits to the center deepened my understanding of the uniqueness of the experience that the school offers its students. Actually, people, particularly when they are defined as "students", do not have the opportunity to deal intensively and exclusively with a work that fascinates them. In regular schools of the arts they must learn all the subjects in parallel; and after military service, like anyone else in Israel, they are concerned with problems of making a living that make it difficult for them to be able to do in-depth work in art. Here, however, the art center at the school was a place that was open and "alive", where for the first time in my life I saw children working in art every free moment they had, sometimes for months or years. I saw wonderful creations made there, and true progress of young artists who could take themselves completely seriously.

In every time period new centers were created at the school, according to the needs of the children. At one particular time there was a strong group of children who wanted to work with video, and at whose initiative a center of editing and directing was created, and an appropriate teacher found. In a joint initiative of students and teachers, a movement and theater room was created, as well as other centers.

3. Personal agreements

The third way of learning in the school is through personal agreements. When a student wishes to learn a subject that is not being taught in the regular school schedule, or in any of the learning centers, he can initiate a personal or group lesson. This kind of learning is possible both for a group of students, like the group that came to us asking to learn about business initiatives, and for a single student, like Amir, an eleventh grade student who asked to study in depth the brain and its functions.

When we are approached like this by students, the school coordinates between the student or the group and one of the staff members, who takes interest in the requested area. In certain cases, we had to hire the services of a special teacher, who was familiar with the required subject.

Two stories can well demonstrate this kind of study and its consequences: One year we received a request from a group of children and adults who wanted to learn Japanese. At the same time, a different group asked for French lessons. In both cases there was no suitable teacher at school, so we suggested purchasing language learning tapes. It was decided that if these proved unsatisfactory, the following year we would try again to find a suitable teacher.

Both groups posted the opening of these two new areas of learning on the notice board, and additional teachers and students joined them. After a few months each group went a different way:

The "Japanese" group didn't last and eventually broke up. On the other hand, the "French" group turned their cooperative study into the central event of their year. They would bring coffee and croissants in the morning, prepared French meals together, and at the end of the year they demanded we bring a French teacher for the following year. And so it was.

By the way, this group also disbanded eventually, again creating change. For the ten years when I was principal – and to this day – there has been constant change.

4. The school's surroundings

When we founded the school we reached an important understanding: one can't learn everything in school, even in a place like ours, with its broad frameworks for different kinds of learning. This understanding led to deliberation: Do the boundaries of school have to be the boundaries of the students' learning? What should we do when a student requests to study in depth a subject that we don't have in the school; must he do it "at his own expense" outside of school hours?

We did not believe so. We thought that the student's choice of an area that didn't exist in our school would be an opportunity to discover our surroundings – our immediate surroundings, the community in which we live, as well as our more distant surroundings.

There was one year when several of our students wanted more than anything to practice surfing. We had neither seashore nor a sailing teacher in our school. However, there are surfing clubs a short ride away. We met with the parents, the students and a surfing club representative, and we made an arrangement for a yearly learning plan, for students who chose it, during school hours and with the full cooperation of the school.

At another time, a student came to me asking to get some experience in auto mechanics. Within a short time we had drawn up an agreement with a garage owner near Hadera, who agreed to let the student become his apprentice in auto mechanics. The student's advisor was also deeply involved in this arrangement.

Another student, one of mine, was interested in marine biology. In a joint process we arranged for him studies at "the Institute for the Study of Lakes and Seas" in Haifa, and afterwards he joined a course on the subject at Haifa University.

During the years we turned to many people and factors

in our area, asking them to help our children on their journey towards the goals they had set for themselves. Children studied music outside of school, with our help and backing, while others became apprenticed to a variety of professionals such as veterinarians, artists, filmmakers, doctors and more. We saw our role as one of assisting the student in the coordination and creation of agreements with external factors, and in safety backing and supporting them throughout the process.

At the heart of the learning process, outside of school as inside it, was the student's process of choice. Because of this the student himself would lead the making of the connection with the outside, and in many cases, after he had gotten over his initial anxieties, he was pleasantly surprised to discover how happy people were to help someone who took a genuine interest in their line of work.

This way of study created deep connections with people in the community around us, so much so that professionals with whom we worked were disappointed if there was a year in which we didn't come to them.

5. Study in workshops
The fifth option for study in the school is through workshops. Every person at the school can announce, through the notice board, that he is interested in opening a workshop, and can invite others to join him.

Among other things, a custom developed of "white nights" – a study workshop that began in the evening and ended the next day. We began this once on the Feast of Weeks, following the Jewish custom of Tikun Shavuot (all night study of the law on the Feast of Weeks), but the next white nights dealt with a variety of subjects: There was a night of feasting in the style of Plato, a night in which we discussed love, an evening of Zionism, and another that dealt with physics and quantum theory, as the students decided to study the theory in depth and try to understand it.

There were also workshops of a week or more in length, which were built in accordance with the needs of the participants in the school. These included an art workshop that formed around a visiting artist from abroad who agreed to spend an intensive week with the art students, or a week's workshop in ecology, archaeology and other subjects.

The study in workshops derives from the concept that a weekly lesson is not always the best way to arrive at an in-depth understanding of the subject at hand. Sometimes, intensive study for a week or an entire night, in a field of learning that one finds fascinating, can give the learner a significant learning experience.

The Child at Play

Even after describing all the above, I have still not described two additional and very significance ways of learning at our school. Actually, my descriptions are in accordance with the (more or less) familiar concepts of the act of learning: There is a subject or a field, and there is a learning plan, e.g. a lesson, a workshop, outside advisory etc. But a child is a learner by nature, and he is constantly engaged in learning about himself and about his surroundings, using two natural tools: play and free conversation. He does this without need for learning programs.

I don't know who decided, or why, that play and learning are two different experiences. In most schools I have known, they are treated as separate. During the break the kids play, and in a lesson, on the other hand, they learn. "Stop playing during the lesson", say the teachers to the children in the lower grades, who are still expressing their learning nature, "and listen to what I am saying". This automatic determination, which separates play form learning, distances the adult from the understanding of **natural learning that goes on without direction.**

In the democratic school, adults are asked to try and observe what children do naturally, instead of asking what they don't do yet, according to the proper square for their age.

This determining which says that one can play till age six, and then one must learn reading and writing, and afterwards English at age ten, and so forth, creates stations without checking if they could suit all children. We tried to look anew at the children, and to understand what they were doing and why.

We discovered that, as Danny Greenberg writes in

his book "The Sudbury Valley School: Growing Up in Another Place", children want to play most of the time. Their next choice – is to talk. The proportions change as they get older: around early adolescence, when their cognitive skills are maturing, children generally want to talk more and play a little less.

We realized that play is a complex learning process, deriving from the child's free choice, as he sets himself clear goals – and stretches his skills to their limit in order to succeed. The game can be imaginative, sport-like, social or otherwise. In any case, it is a process which requires the child to utilize all his strengths.

If we compare a math lesson to a play experience, we can see that during the lesson the child is activating a particular area of his brain, and developing a particular capability. The game, on the other hand, is a "multi-tool" which develops many broad skills simultaneously: social, logical, intuitive and physiological.

In a study which researched animals that play (dogs, cats & wolves) as opposed to animals that don't (sheep, cows & chickens) it was found that the greater the animal's capacity for play, the more easily it can adjust to its surroundings. Thus it becomes apparent that there is a biological connection between play and the capability for learning and adjusting to changes.

About Football and Success in Life
During one of our first years, Yossi A. joined the school. He entered the third grade after two years in a regular

school. After some time Yossi became addicted to the soccer field. Actually he spent most of his time there. He barely entered any lessons or workshops, and he didn't even check what was going on in classes. The field became his chosen and exclusive territory.

Yossi made great progress in the game. During the first days I watched him play with his eyes fixed on the ground, not paying attention to other team members, never passing the ball on. Gradually he learned how the game was based on team cooperation. He began to lift his head and make good passes. Eventually Yossi A. became the undisputed leader of the players on the soccer field. However, our meetings with his parents were not easy. His mother was a teacher and his father a professional, and they were both deeply troubled. "What is happening with Yossi," they kept asking, "What does he do all day?" I reported to them on Yossi's progress on the field, on the constant improvement in his social position, on the leadership capabilities he had revealed.

They looked at me as if I were an eccentric, but since they were nice, tolerant people, they agreed to wait a bit longer and see what would happen.

Yossi never left the soccer field, not that year and not during the fourth grade. He improved constantly. He had a great capacity for planning, and was a natural leader. He still was barely entering any classes, not history, not Bible and not math. He was mainly on the field.

The next year, fifth grade, was the same. Yossi remained on the field and continued to improve his skills. His social status was by then well-established and he began to give soccer lessons and to organize the school league's tournaments. The lessons in the school curriculum didn't interest him.

At the end of fifth grade the parents broke down. "Yossi feels great in school," they told me sadly, "he has become a confident child, smiling all the time, surrounded by friends, but we are very concerned. He can't go on like this. We've decided to take him out of school".

In a concluding conversation I had with his parents they expressed anxiety for what awaited Yossi in the regular school. "He finished his regular studies in the second grade, he has played soccer for three years, and now he is going into sixth grade, when actually he knows nothing" they claimed.

I usually do not tend to predict the future or make promises. However, this time I felt differently. I told the parents that within a few months Yossi would be an excellent student in his new school and a leader in his class.

After two months the parents arrived at school, holding a big bouquet of flowers. "We came to tell you that you were right," they said. "Yossi is an excellent student, a leader in his class, popular with both students and teachers. We don't understand how it happened."

The process Yossi had undergone was understandable and logical. He had become an expert at setting and fulfilling his own goals. On the field, he discovered his many and varied talents: planning, organization, leadership, perseverance. The game had been a significant tool of development for him, and when he found himself in a new situation – he easily succeeded in both applying what he had learned and in achieving.

From Play to Talk

As children grow the interactions of games gradually give way to conversations (as the world of play continues to exist in parallel, at other levels). At school we discovered that children converse a lot. They are interested in what others think, and try to learn about the world through the eyes of their friends.

The discourse among children is multi-age, and throughout the day one can see groups of children of different ages sitting together in the sun and talking. My impression is that these conversations fill a role as important as that of play. Whereas at play a child learns about the world from his own personal experiences, in conversation he learns about the world through the eyes of another. He discovers that one can learn from talking or reading without experiencing everything personally. He learns to understand the other's messages, both explicit and implicit ones. He learns to share his thoughts with others and to listen patiently to what the other says. He learns to argue and to resolve arguments. Through conversations, children can promote projects, raise issues and ideas and examine them, and allow themselves intimacy and friendship.

Parallel to the conversation among children there are

also adult-child conversations. These can occur with the child's personal advisor, whom the child has chosen at the beginning of the year, or with another staff member. The advisors, who have regular conversations with their charges, try to deal with the child's world, with things that bother him, and not with things that are important to adults. If the process is successful, the advisor becomes a sort of older sibling, and the child can share his life, his choices and his deliberations with the advisor.

One can learn about the importance of these conversations from the story of Oded, who arrived at the school in the third grade from a special education class, with a recorded IQ of 85. When he was in the fourth grade he still could not read or write. I watched him from a distance over the years. It seemed that he was doing very little. He barely managed to read and write, and spent some time working with video, but he spent most of his time under a tree in the yard. His parents were very dissatisfied with his lack of activity at school.

When Oded was already in the eleventh grade, we were visited by principals of various schools from Tel Aviv. I would usually ask a random child from the yard to join us on the tour. This time I asked Oded. We sat together and explained the principals about the school.

After a while Oded claimed that the conversation was boring and left. One of the principals rose immediately and asked me: "tell me, Yaacov, are all the kids at school like this one? Is this kid representative of your school?"

"What do you mean?" I asked.

"If you deal only with gifted children, everything is easier" he said; "give me kids like Oded and I will be able to do miracles in my school too". I quickly inquired and discovered that most of the principals thought the same. They believed that Oded was gifted, with unusual talents. This was all because he had spoken to them in a matter-of-fact tone, without fear, at eye level. As school principals, they were not used to seeing children speak in this way with adults, easily finding their own natural place in the conversation. By the way, by the time he had finished school, Oded had focused on work in the video room. Later, he completed his matriculation after his military service and became a popular tour guide.

Part Three
A Democratic Process

The school's community conducts itself as a complete democratic structure, including four authorities: legislative, executive, judiciary and review.

The legislative authority is the general assembly – the Parliament – which meets once a week. All decisions regarding school laws are made there.

Our meetings are held every Friday morning, and are open to the participation of students, parents and all staff members. The Parliament team, which is elected in general elections at the beginning of the year, runs the Parliament. Every person at the school can raise suggestions for discussion at the beginning of the week, after which the Parliament Committee puts a notice up on the notice board, and sends an e-mail to the community, as to what will be the subjects for discussion in the coming meeting.

People who wish to influence decisions on the subject to be discussed can come to any Parliament meeting. As a result, there may be Parliaments with considerable attendance, on subjects that are important for everyone, or Parliaments that interest only a limited number of participants. The decisions of the Parliament regard the school's way of life, including: setting rules for play in the schoolyard, decisions about the structure of the school's curriculum, new building, the annual budget, and more. Students' and staff's personal issues are not up for discussion in the Parliament. The three members of the Parliament team include: a chairperson who runs the discussion, a person responsible for discipline, and a clerk who writes a protocol of the discussion and notifies the community regarding decisions and laws that have been passed.

I am often asked if it doesn't bother me that the Parliament has a definite children's majority. My replay is that the distribution typical of a regular school, in which children and adults are always in opposite camps, does not exist in our school. I cannot remember a single Parliament, during all my years at the school, when there were any coalitions of adults against children. There were always mixed groups of students, staff members and sometimes parents, who got together on a particular subject, and separated on the next subject.

As adults, it is important to us to show the students that we, too, are individuals who are different from one another, with diverse viewpoints and outlooks. The school has no "adult brotherhood" that automatically supports one another's ideas, but rather different opinions and coalitions that are not age-related. It often happened that I did not agree with another adult, and our argument went on in front of everyone during a Parliament meeting.

Another question that I am often asked is whether the Parliament isn't a clever cover under which I and the other adults can express our dominance. The thought behind this question is that the powers of the principal (and the power of staff members as adults) bend voting results so that the school will, after all, be run according to our viewpoints.

I believe this is a potential danger – adults do indeed have the power to express a dominant standpoint and the charisma to change results. We must take care that this does not happen. Here I am happy to share with you the hard feelings I experienced when the Parliament, for the first time, did not accept a single decision that I tried to pass. I came out of that meeting angry and hurt, announcing to whoever wanted to hear that the school had just "shot itself in the foot".

During the years I learned that many of the decisions I had tried to promote were wrong, and many that I had opposed worked beautifully. During my last year at the school, about half of my proposals were rejected by the Parliament. I learned that this was an important measure of a working democracy.

The executive authority works through our committees. Committee members are also chosen by secret ballot in democratic elections at the beginning of the year, and also include parents, students and staff members. The committees are the main institutions in which one can see multi-age activity in the school. Unlike the Parliament, in which the participants occasionally change according to the subject, the activity in committees is in small groups of some 4-10 committee members who work intensively together. This activity includes meetings outside of school hours, so that the relationships which grow out of the committees create a unique and important dimension of the adult-child relationships in our school.

At the beginning of their work, the committee's members choose a chairperson and a meeting schedule. Then they read protocols of the committee's activity during the previous year, and meet with the former representatives for a period of overlap. Next they determine their objectives for the year, a work plan is built, and tasks are distributed among the committee's members.

There are committees which work on ongoing subjects, such as the following:

The Teachers' Committee deals with relations

between teachers and students, and with hiring and firing teachers.

The Admissions Committee accompanies the process of admitting new students to the school, from organizing the registration phase, through conducting evenings of explanation about the school, to personal conversations with families who are interested in their children's enrolling in the school, so that each family can examine its decision in depth. All the families are put on a waiting list, and after the committee conducts a survey in school of the student distribution for the coming year, and determines the number of vacant places for each age group, a draw is conducted among the waiting candidates.

The Field Trip Committee organizes the school's trips throughout the year. The Budget Committee defines in advance how many days of trips the Field Trip Committee can afford that year, and a varied curriculum of trips is designed. This includes day trips, week-long trips, camps, "wandering camps" (that go from place to place), trips for expert hikers, etc. When the schedule is ready, each student can choose what trips, if any, he would like to participate in.

The Field Trip Committee is responsible for the execution of all phases of the trip, from ordering transportation to organizing equipment and food. Activity during the trip is also organized by the committee, sometimes by bringing in an external guide and sometimes by providing the school's own independent guidance.

In the framework of the school trips, students of different ages, staff members and parents create a magical world of democratic experiences; for example, if I join a trip as a school principal, I may take instructions from a young student who is in charge of supper. Adults who are less familiar with the school's ideas, and who take part in our trips (drivers, guides, etc.), report that our trips are an extraordinary experience for them.

The Events Committee organizes the year's events schedule. This includes regular events such as holidays and ceremonies for the beginning and end of the year, as well as special events such as conferences or other events that the community members are interested in organizing.

The Physical Committee is in charge of planning, building and maintenance of the school's buildings and facilities.

The subject of cleanliness in school comes up at least once a year for discussion in Parliament, and almost every year the organization of cleaning at school changes. Sometimes the entire school is cleaned by staff members and students, and at other times workers are hired from outside. In my conversations with school alumni, they claimed that the time when I, as principal, was in charge of cleaning the bathrooms (literally!) was most significant for them than any other time at school.

Besides cleaning, the committee also deals with various initiatives, and with the esthetic design and the physical planning of the school.

The Budget Committee is in charge of accepting budget requests from all school members and organizing them into a budget proposal subject to the Parliament's approval. After approval is given the committee is responsible for follow-up and execution of plans, while remaining in the framework of the school's budget.

There are other committees responsible for operating rooms and learning centers in the school, such as the **Music Room Committee**, the **Video Room Committee** and so forth. There are also *ad hoc* committees set up to carry out decisions of Parliament.

The Judiciary Authority is made up of the Mediation Committee, the Discipline Committee and the Appeals Committee.

The members of these committees are elected in the general elections, and they may be adults (staff members and parents) and children of all ages. The committee members go through special training in their various areas of activity. The judiciary authority deals with the students' personal issues, complaints about violence, other disputes or any case in which a student or an adult feels that he has been hurt by another student or adult.

The judiciary process begins in the **Mediation Committee**, when one of the members of the community feels injured and summons the other party to mediation. Three mediators preside in the committee, whose goal is to help the two parties involved find a solution to their difficulties. If the Mediation Committee does not succeed in its task, the controversy is transferred to discussion in the **Discipline Committee**.

In the Discipline Committee, three members preside as "judges". They must listen to the two parties, summon additional witnesses as necessary, and then decide whether to accept or reject the claim. When necessary, the committee may decide on punishment, and one of its members must follow up its execution. If either the plaintiff or the defendant does not agree with the decision of the Discipline Committee, they must appeal to the **Appeals Committee** and their appeal must be discussed within 24 hours. 5-7 members preside over the Appeals Committee, and their decision is final.

It should be mentioned that while in a regular school laws are determined and applied only towards students (and only students can present a "discipline problem"), in a democratic school the laws are made for everyone, and therefore most of us, both staff and students, have violated laws, were brought up before various judiciary committees, and were punished. I myself have been punished several times by the Discipline Committee, mostly for recurring postponements and cancellations of lessons. In such situations, I have always seen before me the image of Januscz Korczak, who, when he violated any of the laws of his orphanage, would submit himself to trial in the "court".

The Review Authority consists of a Review Committee and an exterior comptroller who is at the disposal of the school. Its role is to review the executive system (all the committees and the school administration) and to check if all decisions are properly carried out, while implementing proper standard procedures and preserving the basic rights of everyone involved.

The Review Committee can carry out its review independently, and every person in the school is welcome to give a proposal for review of any one of the different areas of activity at school.

Every three months, a "reviewer's report" is to be handed in, which indicates any problems and ways for improving the school's activity.

The school's constitution is basically the declaration of human rights. In retrospect we realized that we had been wrong not to determine a constitution before the school was founded. For ten years we set up many committees to create the school's constitution, but we did not succeed. The arguments over every word and idea created a dead end situation. Therefore, in 1994 the school Parliament decided to declare the Declaration of Human Rights as a substitute for a school's constitution. It was further decided that the Appeals Committee would, when necessary, act as a school's constitutional court. Every person in the community, who felt that his rights had been infringed on by a majority decision of Parliament, could appeal to the constitutional court for an inquiry, and when necessary even for a cancellation of the decision of Parliament.

An Invitation to a Frightening Game of Democracy
One of the questions put to me again and again is, doesn't the inclusion of the students in the democratic process of the school frighten me? Those who ask usually go on to describe the dangers expected for the children who take part in the democratic process.

The game of democracy is indeed frightening – but not only because of the student participation. Adult participation is just as dangerous, if not more so.

Let us imagine for a moment a different reality. Let us say that all the schools are democratic, and all the countries are dictatorships. Here are a few of the things that would probably be said about democracy:

- Democracy is good when you are talking about small groups of people, but it can't work in countries with millions of people.

- Democracy is suitable for schools, because they are working with children's affairs there, but it would be irresponsible to give ignorant and uneducated people, who have just arrived from developing nations, the right to make decisions about the fates of countries, or about matters of life and death.

- Democracy is good in theory, but how could a professor and someone who can't read or write have an equal voice?

- How could just anyone be a candidate for Prime Minister, and what if someone evil or stupid or hypocritical wins the elections?

- Do you really believe that millions of citizens can

remember and understand all the laws? That everyone can understand the principles of democracy? They're really only for intellectuals!

- If everyone in the country chooses his own occupation, no one will be willing to do the "dirty work", and the really hard work. With a government like that – the country will fall apart.

- If every person decides where he is going to live, where he will go for entertainment and what he will strike or demonstrate for, and if every newspaper can publicize what it wants – anarchy will take over.

- Democracy is suitable for school. There everything is small, and not dangerous. But in reality, in the lives of nations, it will never work!

In other words, why does democracy in a school frightens us, while our lives as citizens in a democratic country do not cause us concern? In school the children experience democracy, with all it involves, but they are protected. All of our decisions concern only the school. We do not deal with life and death issues as do democratic countries.

Of course, in the democratic process as it occurs in school, we experience all the "evils" of political democracy as well. Sometimes children vote against their own opinion, out of social pressure. There are children who are not considerate of minorities, and there are sometimes infringements on the rights of various groups. But all these are opportunities for learning. After Parliament meetings, we find ourselves discussing the process that has taken place, opening once again discussion of human dignity within the democratic procedure. This is an important and central role of the adults, in the multi-generational dialogue in school.

Is it right for us to send our children to schools where they experience dictatorship, and then to expect them to be model citizens in a democratic country? Or should we give them active experience in democratic life in the framework of the school's community – before they become citizens participating in elections and decisions on life and death questions?

Young Children in the Democratic Process

Many times people ask me if the younger children at our school understand what democracy is, and if they are ready to act in a democratic system at such an early age.

In my opinion, most of the youngest children and some of the elementary school children do not understand what democracy is, certainly not in its theoretical aspects. But they are growing into a democratic culture. Even before they know what a "Parliament" is, they know that it is where the school's laws are determined, and before they understand what a "judiciary authority" is, they know that the school has an institution where situations in which children have violated the laws are examined.

In parallel, most children in regular kindergartens and schools do not know what a dictatorship is. But they gradually learn that adults make the rules, watch over them, punish them and oversee the punishment.

In other words, the legislative, judiciary and executive authorities are one – one authority which is in the hands of the adults. They do not learn about dictatorship – they grow into it.

Students in democratic schools grow into a democratic culture. Slowly and gradually they begin to ask questions about the process. At first – about their surrounding world: why did they decide to build the swings here and not there? And who decided? Or – how is a child "brought up" before the discipline committee? (I once heard a little girl ask how high the discipline committee was, and if one couldn't fall off).

The rules of the democratic game are not clear to the children, but they know that it is in Parliament that what is allowed and what is forbidden are defined, and they understand from a very early age that there are "votes" and then "decisions". They don't generally attend the Parliament, and the discussions there do not interest them. But they live in a democratic environment, and internalize its values in a natural, developing way. Later on they will learn to act in a democratic framework, and in this way they will eventually understand the principles underlying the democratic mechanism. Through this they will understand the importance of social involvement; they will learn to confront bureaucratic systems; and they will not be afraid to act towards the stopping of corruption. When they leave school, the big democratic world will be a familiar arena of activity.

It may be that the explanations and descriptions

I have put forth until now raise more questions, rather than answer them. In the next chapter I will explain in more depth the philosophy behind the practice, and in the fourth chapter I will answer a set of questions. But before that, to conclude this chapter, I would like to tell a story, one of many which can demonstrate the exciting dynamics which have been formed in the democratic school.

Jimmy Jolley – How to Make Dreams Come True

At the beginning of our fifth school year, Limor (a teacher) and several students came to the Parliament and told us about a landscape architect who was traveling around the world and setting up special playgrounds. They proposed we invite him to come and help us improve the appearance of our school grounds. There was no real discussion of their proposal. Actually, no one believed that anything would come of it. I told them they could try and locate the architect, talk to him about a budget – and then we would see. We thought that that would put an end to the story.

A week later Limor and her students returned and told us that they had spoken with him. His name was Jimmy Jolley, and he was "turned on" by the idea of our school and was ready to come as a volunteer. All he needed was a place to stay, living expenses and materials. According to their calculation, the total cost would be about $20,000.

The Parliament was racked with laughter. "We don't have any money," said some of them, "the budget has been closed. We could never raise a sum like that."

During the years I have often said in the Parliament: "every time a new idea is blocked by the arguments "there's no money" or "the insurance doesn't cover it" or "it's against the laws of the Ministry of Education" – you should know that someone is trying to manipulate you".

This was an excellent opportunity to test that very message. "No money" – money can be raised. "The insurance won't cover it" – one can talk with the insurance agent about expanding the policy. And in the Ministry of Education – there is always a possibility of talking to them and trying to find an opening for change.

Bureaucracy does not necessarily block ideas. On the contrary, one can look for creative ways that will enable bureaucracies to support new ideas.

In this spirit, Limor and her students also asked for the opportunity to try and raise the money within a month. Jimmy Jolley expected an answer within that time, so that he could arrange his visit for the following month.

After Parliament, other students and staff members joined the group who had made the proposal, and they succeeded in organizing the entire school around their idea. Everyone worked to raise money: they sold potted plants, washed cars, worked in gardens, sold cookies and other foods on Fridays, ran a special "Grandparents' Day", asked nearby factories to donate money and equipment, and even got the municipality involved.

By the end of the month, the school had at its disposal some $100,000 worth of merchandise, equipment and cash. It was enough to put up all the school's playground facilities, as well as a new library.

Close to Jimmy Jolley's arrival a large amount of equipment was collected. Some of our classrooms turned into storerooms. Electric poles, screws and ropes were sorted and organized. Different groups sat and planned the playground. Every group built a scale model of the facilities they were interested in building. Then there was a stormy Parliament in which the facilities to be built were chosen, and a work plan was set. Some of the upper grade students, who were studying for their matriculation exams, claimed that even during the building period, for which everyone, staff, parents and students, were being recruited, they would have to keep studying, otherwise they would fail their exams. Thus a special Parliament decided to set up a learning center, in which all the matriculation teachers would work in rotation, and where the students would receive assistance and also study independently.

During work days the entire school became an intensive workshop. We wanted to use this opportunity to build everything we had not had time to build since the school was founded: trellises, a playground, fences, playhouses, an amphitheater and stage for shows, and various other facilities. Every day school opened at 6:00 in the morning, and stayed open till late at night. Almost all the parents came there (some with technical equipment) before they went to work, early in the morning, or late in the evening. Some even took a vacation and spent all their days and nights at the school. Staff members and students worked all day. With time, a makeshift kitchen was set up to provide food. The circle of activity kept expanding, and every day more and more people came to join this celebration of creativity in school. These were ten most exciting days, and the entire process added great momentum to our becoming a close-knit community. We completed the activity of building the playground at the end of November 1991. One week later the heavens opened and we experienced together the rainiest winter the country had ever seen.

The story of the building of the "Jimmy Jolley" playground is a major milestone in the building of the school. We saw, before our very eyes, how the dream of a few individuals – who had fired the whole school with their determination and enthusiasm – became a reality.

Chapter Three

Pluralistic Learning – Learning in a Democratic World

Part 1
The Journey to Personal Uniqueness

Getting lost

When I was about seventeen years old, I went on one of my many hikes over the sand dunes north of Hadera. I took along a pair of binoculars and planned to do some bird-watching in the area. It was a hot, exhausting day. Grains of sand stuck to my skin, sweat poured down my face, I was thirsty, and found none of the usual pleasure I took in bird-watching. Disappointed and upset, I resolved to go home and turned westward, making my way towards the highway. I knew the way well, but irritated by the combination of perspiration, impatience and the scorching sun, I got lost.

I searched for what seemed like a long time, but all the sand dunes suddenly looked exactly alike. For a moment, I imagined that I would be stuck there forever, when I suddenly noticed a hill that I hadn't climbed before. A spark of curiosity awakened in me. I knew the dunes well, but I couldn't remember seeing that one before. I climbed it, cursing myself for my foolish curiosity, till I reached the top. I will never forget how it felt. A lake the size of a football field sparkled with blue right in the middle of the dunes; clear, inviting water surrounded by greenery. Whooping with joy, I scampered down the sand dune, tearing off my clothes as I ran, and dived into the cool water. I swam for quite a while, splashing about and roaring with pleasure, amazed by the discovery of this unknown lake. Then I got dressed and easily found my way back to the highway.

A week later, I invited a few friends to share my discovery. "You won't believe it," I told them. "Wait until you see how amazing this lake is". This time we drove there, approaching the lake by the nearest access road, and walking quickly, we climbed the hill. We stood there, looking over the clear water, I – with mounting excitement, and my friends - with surprising disappointment. "What, that's it? You're so excited by this little lake?" they said. "Don't you know that just a kilometer away from here, there's a huge water reservoir right in the middle of the dunes? What's so special about this tiny lake?" I tried to explain to them how special the place was to me, but to no avail. Since then, I have brought other people to the lake, but have discovered each time that I am unable to recreate among others that same sense of excitement and interest that the lake holds for me.

This story epitomizes, in my eyes, what happens to a

person during the learning process. Learning is a story of searching and discovery, of great excitement and intimacy – all of which are difficult to convey to others. I believe that all learning is the discovery of something new. The experience of discovery, the moment when something new is discovered – to find a plant that I have been seeking for a long time, to come across a book I have never seen before... or any other discovery, whether about the world or about myself – is one of the most powerful and moving experiences there is.

But what happens in conventional, conservative schools? School should be a place where children discover dozens of new and exciting things every day, but instead a strange thing happens – the kids become bored and are constantly looking for ways to escape from the discoveries and experiences that come their way. Even the word "school" awakens in most of them a feeling similar to the reaction my friends had when I told them about the small lake: "It's that pest again with his weird lake..."

It appears that in order for the experience of discovery to take place, each individual must first go through his own "personal wilderness", so that he can search for and find his own "personal lake". This experience cannot be transferred because it is unique and individual. But those who have experienced it once thirst for the experience of it again and again. There will always be those who have never savored the exquisite sensation of discovery, so they miss out on the desire for it, too…

In order for every child to discover his or her own "personal lake", a school must allow children to wander "in the wilderness". They must choose their way by themselves – even if they discover that they have made the wrong choice and were searching in the wrong place – because this personal discovery will be far more meaningful than any attempt to take a shortcut by having an adult "show them what's right" or where "their mistakes" are.

Some might understand from this that I am opposed to learning from other people's experience, but that is not the case. In fact, I am convinced that we can learn most things from other people's experience. I too have learned, and still learn, from the experience of others – those whom I have chosen to learn from. I believe that other people's experiences are fascinating to everyone and especially to curious children. But at the same time, I believe that if we enable these same curious children to learn without coercion, they will be fascinated by the world of those people that they choose to learn from at that particular moment. Therefore, any attempt to impose my experience, or that of anyone else's, on children will be sterile and lacking in any connection to their personal journeys.

Pluralistic Learning

I had a great deal of difficulty deciding what to call the learning process that occurs in a democratic school. I finally chose the name "pluralistic learning" because it goes to the heart of the concept of democratic education. It is a learning process that recognizes the diversity among learners – learning based on the equal right of every individual to express his or her uniqueness.

We are all human beings, and consequently we share numerous characteristics that set the human race apart, and yet - we are all different. We do not exactly resemble one another, physically or otherwise. Most of us have different goals in life and different ways to reach those goals: some people love caring for animals, while others have an aversion to them; some of us like to work with children, while for others it would be a nightmare; some people find it easier to study in the morning, while others are at their best at night; some like to study mathematics, while others are bored to distraction by the subject; some people learn best by listening to lectures, while for others they are a sleeping pill.

I could go on and on, ad infinitum. The point is this: every individual on earth has a unique learning profile.

Human diversity is one of the most beautiful things in our world; it is the fuel that runs the world. It should thus be the basis for every learning framework. Human diversity means that the learning framework must acknowledge the fact that I am different and unique. If it does not, then it does not acknowledge me: It may acknowledge people who are similar to me, who resemble me, but it is not interested in getting to know the unique me.

I am not the sum of the qualities that resemble me.

While it is true that there are many characteristics I share with other people (e.g. male, over the age of 40, Israeli, having a college degree, etc.), these characteristics do not draw my unique picture, that unique "something" that connects all the routine characteristics with the individual nucleus – the whole that is greater than the sum of its parts.

The answer to the question "who am I" can be found in the "unique and multifaceted me" that connects all the infinite elements: The "I" whose main interest at this time is to write down my ideas on the subject of education; the I who is currently involved in the question of "how to get myself into a state of writing"; the I who knows how to write in the early morning hours, but not at night; the I who knows how to tell stories but less so how to cite others; the I who thinks in images and pictures; the I who has unique loves, personal memories and certain individuals to whom I am attracted. All these and more are the "unique me". That is the "I" whose existence is not represented by an orderly list of data that can be found in government ministries or school files.

The learning framework that acknowledges me sees me as a human being with a multicellular genetic code that has no human equivalent. This learning framework is founded on the perception that all human beings are unique and that each one makes a unique contribution to the world. It will help each participant acknowledge, accept and express his or her own uniqueness.

That is the meaning of pluralistic learning. But before I

describe how this learning occurs, I would like to clarify some relevant terms.

"The Square"
For the purpose of this discussion, this shape will represent the world of knowledge.

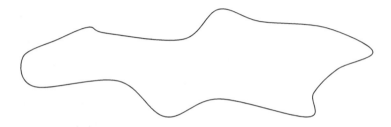

To be more precise, let's call it "the world of encoded knowledge" (i.e. human knowledge), because the world of "unencoded" knowledge is unlimited.

"The square" represents the knowledge that the education systems in the world have decided that students need to learn in school (while it is true that different countries include different specific knowledge in their square, the volume of each square is similar in all the various cultures).

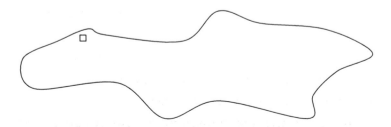

For example, the square contains some knowledge of science, but most scientific knowledge is found beyond the limits of the square. The same goes for literature, art and all the other subjects studied in school. Entire worlds of knowledge exist outside the square. The working assumption of those who create the square is that concentration of the basic elements of all the "important" subjects and exposure of children to them will enable the children to expand and deepen their knowledge in the areas of their choice in the future.

Carl Rogers, one of the founders of humanist psychology in the United States, criticized the concept of "the square" over 40 years ago. In his book "Freedom to Learn", Rogers writes:

Not long ago, I became much interested in the Australian Aborigine. Here is a group which for more than 20,000 years has managed to live and exist in a desolate environment in which modern man would perish within a few days. The secret of the Aborigine's survival has been teaching. He has passed on to the young every shred of knowledge about how to find water, about how to track game, about how to kill the kangaroo, about how to find his way through the trackless desert. Such knowledge is conveyed to the young as being *the* way to behave, and any innovation is frowned upon. It is clear that teaching has provided him the way to survive in a hostile and relatively unchanging environment. Now I am closer to the nub of the question that excites me.

Teaching and the imparting of knowledge makes

sense in an unchanging environment. This is why it has been an unquestioned function for centuries. But if there is one truth about modern man, it is that he lives in an environment which is continually changing. The one thing I can be sure of is that the physics which is taught to the present day student will be outdated in a decade. The teaching in psychology will certainly be out of date in 20 years. The so-called 'facts of history' depend very largely upon the current mood and temper of the culture. Chemistry, biology, genetics, sociology are in such flux that a firm statement made today will almost certainly be modified by the time the student gets around to using the knowledge.

Rogers writes further:

We are, in my view, faced with an entirely new situation in education where the goal of education, if we are to survive, is the facilitation of change and learning. The only man who is educated is the man who has learned how to learn; the man who has learned to adapt to change; the man who has realized that no knowledge is secure, that only the process of seeking knowledge gives a basis for security. Changingness, a reliance on process rather than upon static knowledge, is the only thing that makes any sense as a goal for education in the modern world.[6]

Rogers casts doubt on the notion that there is a basic reservoir of general knowledge independent of humans, situation, time and place. I share his opinion. "The square" has no advantage over any other point in the expanse of knowledge. Every point is connected to every other. And the basis for all learning, as our sages said, is not found in the general domain; it is in the human heart: "A person does not learn Torah except from the place his heart desires" (Babylonian Talmud).[7]

Consequently, throughout the learning journey we take in our lives, we can encompass only a minuscule percentage of the global knowledge that is constantly increasing. The truth is that we will never know what we have missed.

Viewing students as a uniform audience leads to the creation of curricula that are dependent on age and content rather than on the unique individual. The world of "the square" is given yet another definition by the adult world: the "well spent time" zone. The adults (e.g. parents, the educational system) maintain that when students are involved in activities within the square, their time is well spent, whereas when they are active in areas outside the square, their actions are defined as being in the "wasted time" zone.

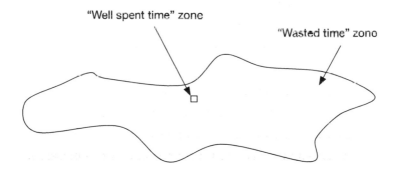

"Well spent time" zone

"Wasted time" zone

These definitions lead the vast majority of school-aged children to crowd into the area of the square. I believe that this overcrowding has catastrophic repercussions: First, as in every crowded area, no one can see himself or the others clearly. Second, because education experts are convinced that the evaluation of the individual student is a vital process, the overcrowding has forced them to create a system that categorizes the children inside the square by means of tools that bypass individual evaluation. These tools include a division into age groups ("All children at a certain age are..."), systems of uniform tests ("All those that receive a mark higher than X are...") and other tools that assess the group inside the square instead of the individuals.

Additionally, the overcrowding and categorizing motivated the development of an ideology that places non-personal acknowledgment at the center of the process. This ideology is termed "objective", an intriguing concept that turns human beings into objects - i.e. things - and as such makes them much easier to compare. As we know from evaluation theory, the systems that "objectively" test students (and, later on, adults too) do not describe an existing reality – they create it.

To the matter at hand, the great industry going on inside "the square" tries to measure us all relative to an ideal objective model. It teaches the students to aspire to the ideal model – in other words, to resemble one another.

The problem is that we are not similar. As I have already

noted, even if we share certain characteristics, we do not resemble one another in the details of which we are composed. Placing all learners inside a crowded square and measuring them with "objective" tools create what we know as a "normal curve", within which the children are measured and placed into clear categories: the ones that are "average", the ones that are "excellent" and the ones that are "weak" – all relative to the ideal object.

Presumably, most of those reading this book were categorized in school as "average", a few as "excellent", and a few, like me, as "weak".

Sadly, because "the square" is perceived as a "preparation for life", most of its graduates tend to accept the categorical rating that measured them for the 14 years of their education. Most of us, indeed, categorize ourselves as average. Where does that inner voice, the one that determines for most of us (including those among us that are successful) that we are "not good enough", come from?

I believe that it is the culmination of the voices we heard inside the square:

- Your uniqueness is not relevant to life. What is important is how close you get to the "ideal mode", i.e. if you have high marks and are "excellent".
- There is no significance to the value you attach to yourselves. In order to prove your value, you must receive authorization from an outside expert (the teacher, the system, etc.).

- Only a few of you can excel. On the normal curve, most of you will always be average.

In many cases, there is a constant fear, even among those who have been defined as "excelling in the square", that they are really "average", or perhaps even "weak", and that they have been defined as "excellent" only because they know how to "fool the system" and make it see them as such.

Some might respond and say to me, "Sorry to wake you up, but welcome to the real world. It's time you came down from the heights of your theories and landed on earth for a moment. Open your eyes, look around and you will find that most people *are* average, that there are very few people that are brilliant and others that are weak. Say, where were you during statistics classes?"

This is the point where, in my view, the conservative school system has its greatest "success" – by turning us all into "squaracists", by teaching us to categorize people according to their degree of success within the world of the square. Even when our occupation with the square ends, we continue to preserve its principles of categorization automatically and, consequently, continue to believe that those who have "made it" inside the square (i.e. got good grades in school, finished their doctorate, etc.) are more successful, more important and better individuals.

The statistics classes are correct only when one measures human beings on a single scale – the scale of "the square", the scale of the ideal model. But the situation changes when people are allowed to choose the area in which they want to develop.

Areas of Strength

I believe that the potential areas of pursuit and interest are greater than the number of people living on the face of the earth, and that every single person has "genius quality" in at least one area of life. I believe that all human beings, not just a talented few, can excel. We are all talented and we can all excel, but each of us excels in a different area.

An education system which accepts this outlook cannot give up its main resource, which is the natural talent that every student brings with him. The democratic education system is committed to enabling all students to discover and develop their individual areas of strength: the areas in which each person's individual nature excels relative to others. It is of paramount importance that at the beginning of our lives we be allowed to grow in those areas in which we have the interest and capability to learn on a high level and the ability to experience success. Interest and success are essential experiences for a growth-enabling childhood.

The Perception of Humankind in the Democratic World

The perception of humankind in the old, stratifying and undemocratic world (which unfortunately has been adopted by most democratic countries) is that the population can be divided into three groups: the "excellent" group (the geniuses), the "average" group, and an additional group of "weaker" people.

The new model, suggested by democratic education, is one in which **every person** (and of course every student) has areas in which he excels and others in which he is average or weak. This is a way of thinking which sees the whole person as composed of many and varied capabilities, and does not see him as belonging to one particular stratum of society.

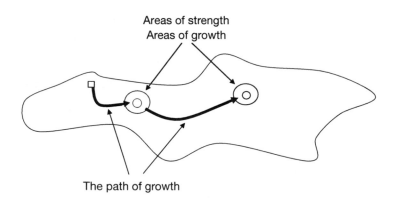

Areas of strength
Areas of growth

The path of growth

The purpose of democratic education is to provide students with the conditions that will encourage them to step outside "the square", to begin a process of searching for the areas of strength where they can enhance their belief in their own abilities.

The rules of the normal curve only "work" inside "the square". When we are placed inside it, most of us can only be average or mediocre. Only a small proportion of us will have any real success in the areas of knowledge that are inside the closed box (and another small proportion of people will clearly fail and be thrown out of the system).

But when we get outside the square, every individual can excel. Every individual is a genius in at least one area of endeavor: human relations, caring for animals, long jumping, geography... The possibilities are endless.

When we do not define a given "square" of desired knowledge, but rather open up the entire world of knowledge, the normal curve loses its validity. When we do not determine a differential value for different achievements, e.g. saying that a professor of mathematics is more important than someone who cares for horses, we will find that every human being has within him the ability to be a genius in his or her own area of strength.

Area of Growth

The area of growth is the field which fascinates the learner, at the present time, more than any other area. It is the subject, area of interest, or pursuit which causes the learner to feel the greatest attraction and curiosity.

The area of growth is characterized by intense emotions, such as enthusiasm, excitement, challenge and an acute desire to return to that area of interest again and again. When children or adults are in their area of growth, even for long periods of time (days, weeks, months or years), they do not experience any diminishing of energy; they receive positive feedback, which revitalizes them.

It is easy to identify these areas in young children who have not yet been steamrollered by conventional social judgment. When toddlers discover that they can walk, they will try again and again to repeat the experience. They continually present themselves with new challenges and will be excited by every step – even if they keep falling down. Kindergarten children can spend hours on games of the imagination that excite them, even if none of the adults around understands what they are about. Note what happens to a child who discovers the game of marbles, for example: See how many hours he can sit and try again and again, trying to hit the target, with an enthusiasm that may appear to us to be a little exaggerated. "Don't you want to do something else?" the parents sometimes ask, but the child is happy to remain where he is.

In the area of growth, failure does not cause withdrawal; instead, it represents the challenge of new experience. In the area of growth, learners use their optimum skills in order to succeed at challenges that often seem beyond their current abilities.

The area of growth is necessarily our greatest area of strength. From observations of children that grow up in a free environment, it sometimes appears that they choose to grow in the areas that are most difficult for them. I know a nine-year-old child for whom physical prowess is not his strongest suit; he was born with considerable motor disabilities. For months, this child practiced handstands, cartwheels and many other activities that were particularly difficult for him. He worked for hours on end on a single movement. Observing him from a distance, he looked involved, deeply concentrated and enthusiastic, although he fell often and his movements were not smooth.

When children (or adults, for that matter) are allowed to remain in their area of growth without being disturbed or forced to leave it, they acquire considerable emotional and cognitive skills. The child who did the handstands succeeded, thanks to a belief in his own persistence; he learned about overcoming difficulties and about courage; he drew conclusions from his falls, and his learning ability grew. The next time he wishes to enter the learning process, he will be able to use the tools he gained from doing the handstands. The ability to draw conclusions from failing, an understanding of the importance of persistence and patience – all these will serve him well when he tries to contend in other areas of learning. I call this process "*transfer*".

Pluralistic learning, as defined here, occurs within areas of growth. This is not learning about what is done, but rather about how processes occur. The specific contexts in which the growth occurs are not important. It is not the knowledge about handstands or marbles that is meaningful. What is important and meaningful is the growth of inner strengths that enrich and enhance the repertoire of learning tools.

When students, or any other individuals, are involved in a subject that fascinates them, they are at their highest possible learning level. In this state, their physical and mental abilities are at their peak.

Areas of Growth and Emotional Intelligence

Daniel Goleman begins his book "Emotional Intelligence" with the intriguing question of the correlation between success in school and success in life. Goleman investigated a large number of studies on this subject and, to his surprise, discovered that there is no correlation between academic success in school and the indices used to represent success in life. However, when he searched for some kind of statistical anchor to connect abilities during childhood and adolescence with success in life, Goleman arrived at the concept of "emotional intelligence", which, unlike good grades in school, can serve as an instrument for the prediction of success in life.

According to Goleman, emotional intelligence is made up of four competencies:

1. Self-awareness

In this category, Goleman includes emotional self-awareness, which means the ability to read one's own emotions and those of others, appreciation of the impact of these emotions, and the use of "gut feelings" when making decisions.

Self-awareness also includes an individual's ability to

assess himself as accurately as possible, and involves an awareness of one's strengths and weaknesses. Self-confidence, that is a reasonable sense of self-worth and abilities, says Goleman, is also part of the awareness component.

2. **Self-management**

This component includes:

Emotional self-control: control of feelings and urges that disrupt order.

Transparency: Being honest and trustworthy and having integrity.

Adaptability: The ability to be flexible in changing situations and in overcoming obstacles.

Achievement: The drive to improve one's performance to meet inner standards of excellence.

Initiative: Being ready to act and seize opportunities.

Optimism: The ability to see the positive in events.

3. **Social awareness**

This component includes:

Empathy, defined as "sensitivity to the feelings of others, understanding the other's perspective and taking an interest in his concerns".

Organizational awareness: the ability to sense the politics and networks of the organization.

Service orientation: the ability to understand and fulfill the needs of subordinates.

4. **Relationship management**

This component includes leadership ability, as expressed in the ability to initiate and coordinate the efforts of a network of people; conflict management, expressed in the ability to resolve disagreements; the ability to create close interpersonal ties; and the ability to sense the feelings, motives and concerns of other people and to understand their nature.[8]

Reading the ideas in "Emotional Intelligence" led me to the conclusion that democratic education, and especially pluralistic education, cultivates the development of these characteristics. When Goleman describes the learning systems that foster the development of emotional intelligence, he describes the learning process as "*flow*", and argues that the ability to enter into a state of flow is the development of emotional intelligence at its finest.

This is how the concept of "flow" is described by Professor Mihaly Csikszentmihalyi of the University of Chicago, a major scholar of the concept of flow for the past 25 years (quoted in Goleman's book):

Flow is a state of self-forgetfulness, the opposite of rumination or worry: instead of being lost in nervous preoccupation, people in flow are so absorbed by the task at hand that they lose all self-consciousness, dropping the small preoccupations – health, bills, even doing well – of daily life. In this sense, moments of flow are egoless. Paradoxically, people in flow exhibit a masterly control of what they are doing, their responses perfectly attuned to the changing demands of the task. And although people perform at their peak while in flow, they are unconcerned with how they are doing, with thoughts of success or failure – the sheer pleasure of the act is what motivates them. (Csikszentmihalyi 1996)[9]

These words are an amazingly precise description of what happens to students in a democratic school, although, to the best of my knowledge, Csikszentmihalyi has never visited one.

At the end of the chapter on flow, Goleman proclaims: "Learning and flow: A new model for education", and goes on to explain:

The flow model suggests that achieving mastery of any skill or body of knowledge should ideally happen naturally, as the child is drawn to the areas that spontaneously engage her – that in essence, she loves. That initial passion can be the seed for higher levels of attainment, as the child comes to realize that pursuing that field – whether it be dance, math or music – is a source of the joy of flow. And since it takes pushing the limits of one's ability to sustain flow, that becomes a prime motivator for getting better and better; it makes the child happy. This, of course, is a more positive model of learning and education than most of us encountered in school. Who does not recall school at least in part as endless hours of dreary boredom punctuated by moments of high anxiety? Pursuing flow through learning is a more human, natural, and very likely more effective way to marshal emotions in the service of education.

Indeed, Goleman's model finds daily expression in the context of democratic education, in which the emphasis is not on the "what" (those areas the students are supposed to study at school), but rather on the "how" (improvement and control of learning qualities at the highest level, enabling the student to study any area he or she takes an interest in).

The connection between the area of strength and the area of growth

The goal of pluralistic learning is to bring students into their area of growth, where the students' abilities are at their peak (flow). The process, shown by Csikszentmihalyi, is found to have a very high correlation with the various definition of variability of happiness and creativity. The transition through the areas of growth charges the students' batteries with belief in themselves, filling them with the realization that they are "worthy" and "able". This charging comes in addition to the natural charging that occurs in the area of strength. However, because the areas of strength are mostly fixed, and the areas of growth are dynamic and dependent on time and psychological condition, a unique situation is created: In order to reach an area of growth, learners must first leave the areas of strength that no longer interest them. In certain situations, when difficulties in the areas of growth "sap" their energy, they must return to their areas of strength to recharge themselves with energy for a new journey into an area of growth.

In other words, the learner channels his or her learning process between areas of strength and areas of growth, with the areas of strength serving as "refueling stations" for the growth journey.

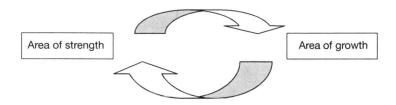

After the learner has completed the refueling process in the area of strength, he or she can set out on a learning journey in a new area of growth.

In most cases, while on the new journey of growth the learner exploits the strengths and skills acquired during the first journey; s/he then uses these skills in order to expand his or her ability to contend with the difficulties and obstacles that await them during the second journey.

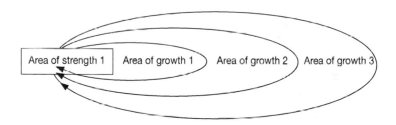

At this point, it is important to note that most students have more than just one single area of strength, and during the journey within the areas of growth, they find new areas of strength that can serve as additional reserves of learning energy.

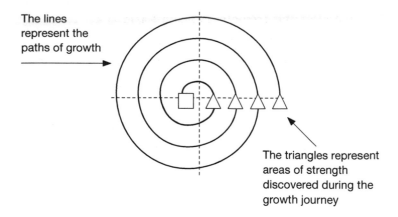

The lines represent the paths of growth →

The triangles represent areas of strength discovered during the growth journey

The spiral, which depicts the journey between the areas of strength and the areas of growth, represents how pluralistic learning gradually expands the learner's emotional intelligence and enables him or her to set out on deeper and farther growth journeys. The learner acquires more courage and new tools to study those areas that fascinate him/her.

Part 2
The art of "not knowing" – The journey to the discovery of diverse uniqueness

The concept of linear learning

The difference between pluralistic learning that occurs in the "wasted time" zone and learning that occurs in the "well spent time" zone is not expressed only in the way and manner of learning, but also in the perception and expression of the world of knowledge.

In traditional schools, the emphasis is on the study or acquisition of knowledge: processed knowledge, prepared knowledge, correct knowledge, knowledge devoid of doubts. The knowledge served up to the students is not the result of a question that was asked or of a personal quest; it is knowledge that is bestowed as a gift by the authorities to the student.

The knowledge is learned in a hierarchical fashion, meaning that all knowledge serves as a basis for further knowledge. A journey in the traditional world of knowledge is a journey from ignorance to enlightenment; a journey to satisfy the authorities.

Allow me to represent the journey as follows:

Not knowing ————————▶ Knowing

Then additional arrows are added, creating what I call "linear learning":

$$\text{Not knowing} \quad \xrightarrow{a} \quad \xrightarrow{b} \xrightarrow{c} \quad \xrightarrow{d} \xrightarrow{e} \quad \xrightarrow{f} \xrightarrow{g} \quad \text{Knowing}$$

On this journey, which occurs inside the square, the students learn that:

1. There is "correct" knowledge and it is in the hands of the authorities.
2. Their personal quest is of no significance because it is not relevant to their learning.
3. Their personal position is not relevant because the correct knowledge was discovered by unique and

rare individuals and lies in the hands of the "right" people.

4. Any discovery that does not comply with "correct knowledge" is in error.

5. One is expected to avoid making mistakes (because making mistakes causes the learner to lose points from his final score).

6. It is highly important to prove that one has the right answer.

When a learner is exposed to an answer that is not on the line (as in the following diagram) a "wrong answer" light goes on – and, in more extreme cases, an "individual disqualification" lamp may light up.

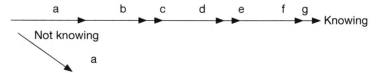

I encountered a typical example of this when some students in our school expressed contempt about an earth-shaking discovery they had made: "We met some religious Jews, and you won't believe how stupid they are. They actually believe that God created the world".

I asked them how they thought the world had been created.

They looked at me in astonishment and replied: "Come on, Yaacov, are you kidding us? Don't you know? Everyone knows that the world was created in the Big Bang!"

I said to them: "So how are you any different from those ultra-Orthodox children? Just like them, you know how the world was created. And, like them, you know that any other answer is wrong. You even know all about those daring to present any other answer: they're idiots..."

Knowledge that is "on the line" does not come only from the field of scientific knowledge. One may find incontestable knowledge in many areas: "There is no life without matriculation exams"; "reading and writing are the basis for all knowledge"; "university is the gate to life"; "money is the means to attain all things in life"; and the list goes on and on.

In order to find out if you belong to the linear learning school, check to see how threatened you feel by encountering views that are opposed to yours – whether such views rouse you to fight against the "traitors", or if opposing views stimulate you to set out on a new learning journey.

The story of the rope and the abyss

To most people in western society, life is like walking on a tightrope tautly stretched over an abyss. Being able to walk the rope from one end to the other is considered exceedingly important, the true test of success, and consequently people focus mainly on the danger posed to those who are unsuccessful at the task – the danger of falling into the abyss.

Walking the tightrope begins on the day we are born, and some say even before that. The rope has many different stations along the way, for example: reading and writing in first grade, matriculation exams between the ages of 16-18, university in your twenties, marriage, children, food, health, professional success, family, nation, and the list goes on.

I do not take the stations lightly; I have visited some in the past and am staying in others at the present. And there are yet others that I plan to visit in the future. Yet I have an urge to stand up and shout: "There is no abyss under the rope!"

Then I would add that there isn't really any rope at all and there is no danger of falling into an abyss (except for those that believe that they are walking a taut tightrope over an abyss).

Additional Thoughts regarding the Rope and the Abyss

Technical details about the rope:

- The rope is a very crowded place. This overcrowding causes a great many problems, and many unnecessary falls bring on disaster.
- The stations along the rope are constructed so that not everyone can pass through them. The overcrowding near the stations creates a situation in which nearly everyone falls at some stage.
- Professional alarmists stand all along the rope, to remind anyone who has forgotten about the dangers of falling into the abyss.

Reminders and Recommendations

- In areas outside the rope there is plenty of space for everyone.
- Outside the rope's range one can find or create stations that will interest him, stations we can pass through and find gratification and success. To arrive at these stations one needs the courage to look beyond the rope.

Learning in the "wasted time" zone or learning "lack of knowledge"

What really exists "away from the rope"? What happens to those who "fall into the abyss"? These are significant questions in the field of pluralistic learning and I would like to examine them by first seeing what I *know*.

For example, what do I know about momentous questions such as: How did we get here? What happens after death?

My answer to these questions is clear: *I don't know!*

Because these questions intrigue me, I have asked numerous people about them. I have received many answers which gave me no sense of new "knowledge", but made me feel that many of us make no clear distinction between our beliefs or thoughts and our knowledge.

Naturally, I also have numerous beliefs and thoughts about life; but it would be arrogant of me to think that my beliefs embody the absolute truth for all humanity. In their book "The Unfinished Revolution", John Abbot and Terry Ryan maintain that ninety percent of what we currently know about the brain has been discovered in the last ten years. They assume, therefore, that in three years' time, ninety percent of the knowledge in this field will be new – the result of research carried out in the next three years.[10]

Believing that my thoughts are the absolute truth is tantamount to declaring myself God, and I don't even know if there is a God...

This is the source of my position on the concept of

freedom: I do not have the right to force my lack of knowledge on others and they do not have the right to force theirs on me. Some might claim that I am encouraging ignorance, because if we never really know anything, what is the point of learning?

So let me make myself clear. Let's say the physicist Stephen Hawking and I are invited to participate in a debate about astrophysics, and the question is: How was the earth created? My answer, which would get full marks, would be that I don't know, and to this day, no one else does either. Hawking would give a similar answer. So why has he studied so much, when anyone could give a similar answer to just about any question?

The reason is this: Hawking's lack of knowledge in the field of astrophysics is greater than mine! And that lack of knowledge is the result of a great deal of learning and extensive study of knowledge and discoveries in that field. In other words, as many have already said, and many more experience daily, the more you learn, the greater your knowledge is; and the realization of your lack of knowledge grows accordingly (in other words, learning knowledge is a pre-requisite condition to developing a "lack of knowledge" in the chosen field).

This is a common situation, especially when one becomes involved in a process of in-depth and meaningful learning.

The following spiral illustrates the relationship between knowledge and lack of knowledge in a particular field.

At the beginning, knowledge is limited and, consequently, lack of knowledge is too:

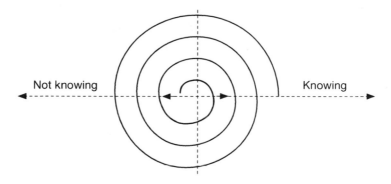

Later on, as acquired knowledge increases, the individual's awareness of his lack of knowledge increases too:

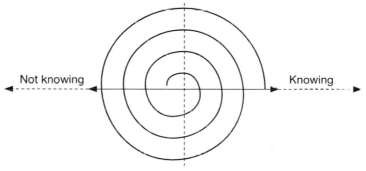

The spiral model expresses the concept that at every stage of learning, I remain connected both to my present ideas and to questions and doubts that fuel my quest for knowledge.

Life that combines the world of knowing with the world of not-knowing creates conditions that encourage growth.

In a state of growth, the questions and doubts that exist in the lack of knowledge zone are not swept under the rug; they are the engine that drives the quest for knowledge onto its highest levels (flow and opening). In this state, different views become an opportunity for learning and no longer represent a threat to the learner.

The growth of the spiral also represents the *increase in the learner's emotional intelligence competencies,* in accordance with the indices set down by Goleman:

1. Self-awareness: The reciprocal state between "knowing" and "not-knowing" creates a constant perspective of criticism and scrutiny.
2. Self-management: The learning quest is driven by curiosity and personal responsibility.
3. Social awareness: Staying in the not-knowing zones invites different perspectives, and a multi-cultural and multi-perspective society is viewed as an opportunity rather than a threat.
4. Relationship management: The other is not "judged" on whether he is "for" or "against" us. The other represents an opportunity for new discoveries and personal development.

"Living knowledge" versus "dead knowledge"
Let me touch on the tension which exists between not-knowing and knowing from another angle.
Try to imagine or draw a tree.

I assume that most of you pictured a tree made up of a trunk, branches and leaves that schematically looks something like this:

But this of course depicts only part of the tree, the part that is visible. Trees also have a root system. The tree in the above picture is only half a tree; or rather, a chopped-down or dead tree.

The depiction of a living tree should look something like this:

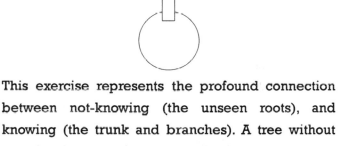

This exercise represents the profound connection between not-knowing (the unseen roots), and knowing (the trunk and branches). A tree without roots is a dead tree. Knowledge that is unconnected to the roots of lack of knowledge (i.e. questions, doubts and curiosity) is dead knowledge. Sadly, the hobby of collecting "knowledge dummies" has become a popular one.

An argument that can be raised against the spiral model is that since any current discovery may turn out, in the future, to be either wrong or faulty, this approach could cool the passion of the quest and discovery, which are the core of our motivation to search and explore "new worlds."

I found a moving answer to this question in an interview conducted with the Swiss artist Alberto Giacometti in 1961:

I find it increasingly difficult to complete works. [...] I look at my statues. All of them, even those that appear to be completed, are a fragment, each is a failure. Yes, a failure!

But in each of them, there is something of what I am striving for, a certain thing exists in one, and something else in another, and in a third, there is something that is lacking in the other two. But the statue I have in mind contains everything, and in that dwarfs everything that appears in the other statues. That is what spurs the powerful desire to continue to work.

Giacometti describes the two extremes of creation and, perhaps, one of the secrets of the human existence: On the one hand, absolute knowledge; and on the other, a painful quest, fraught with failure and doubt. When I am told: "For someone who claims not to know, you sound pretty sure of yourself", I think of that statue that has everything, and of the artist who will never succeed in sculpting it, but who will always be on a journey to it, always searching.

There is no alternative but to try to have it both ways – to have the absolute knowledge, the faith that enables us to act within reality and make decisions, on the one hand; and to remain with that feeling that we do not know, that helps us cast doubt, change direction and renew ourselves, on the other.

In his book "How to Love a Child", Janusz Korczak describes the experience of his own not-knowing:

How, when, how much – why?

I observe many questions that are waiting for answers, doubts looking for clarification.

And I reply:

– I don't know.

'I don't know.' – In science, this is the haze of formation, the appearance of new thoughts, which each time are closer to the truth. "I don't know" for a brain that is not subjected to scientific thinking is disturbing emptiness.

I would like to learn to understand and love that wondrous "I don't know", so full of life and brilliant surprises – that same creative "I don't know" of contemporary science in its approach to children.

I would like it to be understood that no book, no doctor or scientist can replace alert independent thought and attentive discernment.

About fifteen years later, in the introduction to the second edition of "How to Love a Child," Janusz Korczak continues to describe the experience:

Fifteen years have passed; many more questions, assumptions and doubts have been added and the lack of faith in previously determined truths has increased.

The truths of the educator are a subjective assessment of experiences, one single, final moment of considerations and feelings.

His wealth – the number and weight of problems that concern him.

Instead of correcting and completing, it is preferable to note (in small letters) what has changed around and within me.[11]

The Journey in the Spiral of Not-knowing

What happens when a child or an adult seeks his/her area of interest and examines his/her path inside the area of growth?

Very often I have heard people say: "Children in democratic schools have an easy time of it". The argument is that since we do not compel children to study certain subjects, and they choose for themselves what and how to learn, their lives are much easier than those of their counterparts in the conventional school system. I would say that just the opposite is true: Seeking out an area of interest is a very formidable task, and the learning process inside the area of growth requires enormous reserves of inner strength.

For years, I tried to understand if there was any particular organization or order in the situation of learning that was presented to me in the environment of the Democratic School of Hadera, and in the other democratic and free schools that I visited. The task is seemingly impossible because there is such great diversity among the students.

Only recently have I succeed in formulating a model that, in my view, expresses the seeming chaos that one encounters in the environment of the democratic school. This model may not make sense to all those in the field, but I hope that it can serve as a basis for a study on new learning fields, which so far have not been the subject of research in the field of education.

The Dynamics in the Circle of Pluralistic Learning

The known journey of learning moves from not-knowing to knowing.

In accordance with the linear learning processes, this journey should continue throughout one's life, with the student (and adult) involved in a continuous journey of discovery. However, a close look at a democratic school, as well as at a conventional one, will reveal other situations: there are students that are resting, others that are fearful (not only during tests), some are in a state of crisis, others are bored, etc.

At the same time, one may also find students that are in more than one of the above situations, and some whose feelings towards learning change. For example, a child is deeply involved in a particular pursuit for a few months; it is his entire world. Suddenly, he finds himself in a period of boredom; he lacks interest in anything and does not want to touch his previous area of interest.

I will use the spiral model to explain what, in fact, has happened to that child.

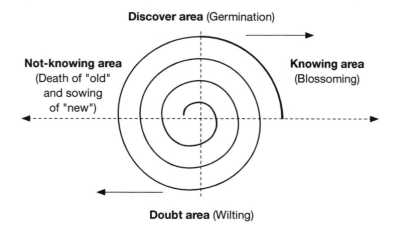

Discover area (Germination)

Not-knowing area
(Death of "old"
and sowing
of "new")

Knowing area
(Blossoming)

Doubt area (Wilting)

The Four Basic Parts of the Spiral of Not-knowing

The process I will be describing here is a spiraling process, and consequently I have to decide exactly where to begin to describe it.

The innovation in the description of spiral learning, in contrast to linear learning, is that spiral learning is a multi-directional journey. It does not involve mere linear progress from a state of not-knowing to one of knowing, to be followed by yet more knowing, and so on. The spiral process is cyclical: One direction moves from not-knowing to knowing; I call it "a constructive journey of growth". At the same time, there is another path that moves from knowing to not-knowing; I call it "a deconstructive journey of growth". In other words, both construction and deconstruction have great importance in the journey of personal growth that the student undergoes.

This journey within the world of learning is not a cognitive-quantitative one, as many learning theories hypothesize, but rather a multi-dimensional journey that includes both the psychological and philosophical levels of the process.

We will start the description of the journey somewhere in the "area of not-knowing". When in this state, I begin to take an interest in a particular subject, which leads me to a high level of learning (i.e. a state of flow), until the stage when I consider myself to be an expert in the subject that I am pursuing. At this point, I reach the "area of knowing". I have chosen to describe this station as the first of the four.

The Area of Knowing – Blossoming

In this area, we feel that we have arrived at that which we have been seeking for a long time. And not only have we "arrived", we feel "at home" there. When we have mastered the skills of performing in our area of interest, it can be described as completing all the parts of a puzzle to create a single, complete picture.

At the higher levels of this stage, the learner discovers that he has reached his area of strength and can attain new insights in this area. At this point, the learner experiences a feeling of achievement and personal satisfaction of the kind one feels at the end of an arduous journey - there is a sense of elation, a rush of energy and power.

But it is precisely because of these emotions that this stage is fraught with danger. It is this stage that could bring the learning process to an end instead of launching a journey of new learning.

The danger at the first stage is that the experience of achievement will inflate the ego to the point that the claims of others appear to be unimportant or irrelevant. The individual starts to feel that he has mastered everything, that he "owns the truth" and that everything is "beneath him".

I call this the "*arrogance trap*", which is rather common at the blossoming stage. Learners at this stage tend to avoid learning from others and rely only on their own experience, which in turn reduces the level of their learning.

The second trap is the "*safety trap*", a situation in which the learner has gained a respected position among his colleagues and earned the admiration of his peers. His expertise brings in a comfortable income, but he has ceased to take a real interest in his field. The "safety trap" will confine the learner to his "area of strength" (his success), which is no longer his area of growth.

As I noted earlier, the area of strength remains fixed, while the area of growth changes. Consequently, the discovery of the area of strength can serve as an incentive to set out on a new quest, but the "safety trap" could put an end to future areas of growth

**because it compels the learner to give up control
and mastery over the situation and enter into a place
of uncertainty.** When an individual avoids the trap, he
no longer takes an interest in what he has pursued until
now, and is willing to allow himself to go ahead with the
process; then he arrives at the next stage of the spiral.

The Area of Doubt – Wilting

At this stage, the area of strength changes. The learner
feels that cracks are beginning to cause the perfect
puzzle to fall apart. The cracks could be a lack of
confidence in the discoveries made at a previous stage,
or a frightening feeling that his level of interest in the
area is diminishing.

This stage makes it necessary to give up positions
of defense and self-justification. The learner must give
up past discoveries and make a transition to a state of
attentiveness. What is required at this stage is the courage
to listen to the voices of doubts, and to challenge the self-
evident.

The learner then enters a stage of deconstruction –
the cracks in the puzzle grow increasingly wider and the
state of uncertainty burgeons.

Those that manage to overcome all the obstacles enter
into a learning process in the area of doubt. Learners
may initially feel bitterness, distrust and even anger.

Gradually, especially if they are able to understand
that this is a natural stage in the growth process, new
experiences arrive – such as the realization that "this is

the first step towards the beginning of a new path".

The stage of doubt requires great reserves of inner strength, because it means that one must leave a comfortable and rewarding place in order to attain growth in an unknown and dangerous one. Moreover, this process often compels one to relinquish a previous perception of the self. This is why a number of different traps may appear at this stage:

- Denial of the flow process ("I have to get this nonsense out of my head"; "I have to be realistic and get my head out of the clouds").
- A "return to the fold", which involves a consecration of the previous knowledge, a lack of desire to give up that which has been achieved.
- Adoption of a single, clear knowledge – Instead of enabling the process of deconstruction, the learner adopts a single knowledge without first going through a pluralistic learning process, i.e. without first making an in-depth examination of personal doubts.
- In order to go through the stage of doubt, the learner must have the courage to lose control and to believe that the process of personal growth will lead him to the discovery of new worlds.
- This stage requires deep faith in one's personal abilities on the one hand, and on the other, a willingness to give up the motivation of the ego, which will probably lead the learners into the previously mentioned traps.

The Area of Not-knowing – "Death of the old" and "Sowing of the new"

This area is located around the line of not-knowing. It is an area of chaos in life, the stage at which the learner feels totally lost. The pieces of the puzzle appear impossible to put together; there is a complete undermining of one's entire previous world view and the learner swings from total despair over the death of the "old", to a feeling of tranquility, time-out and "recharging" in preparation for the sowing of the new field.

Students, at this stage in the democratic school, report feelings of boredom, a lack of interest in all the goings-on in school and, in extreme cases, even depression.

The importance of the passage through this area is enormous. A person that learns to make the transition through these areas discovers that they represent a guarantee of renewal and personal creation that is directly connected to the individual's unique personality.

This period resembles the final stages of pregnancy, which – although sometimes unbearable – are essential for birth.

I have seen students who, at this stage, exhibited enthusiasm and did not pressure themselves to continue. They used the time to rest, in the knowledge that they were moving in the direction of creative learning and the discovery of new places (although they had no idea what those places would be). The expectation was accompanied by a feeling of great elation. Other students fell into the traps.

At this stage, the traps are of two main types:

1. Avoidance - A desire to skip over the tensions and fears while giving up the "birth of self uniqueness"; in other words, to cut short the attentiveness to inner voices. At this stage the learner "automatically" returns to his previous area of strength, a move which is unrelated to feelings of current interest, only to a need to gather the strength to survive.

2. The chaos leads to "adoption" rather than "birth" - Learners experience total helplessness and cannot find comfort in previous achievements. This helplessness does not allow the engine of creativity to start and the only lifebelt that can save the learner is the "adoption" of whatever appears adoptable, although unrelated to the area of personal interest, and motivated only by survival factors.

These traps result in dependence upon external factors and in "locking up" the "unique self", and eventually in the learners' growing lack of confidence in their abilities.

The Area of Discovery – Germination

The area of discovery is the area of germination and growth that leads from the crisis of not-knowing to the area of knowing.

This is the stage at which the various parts of the puzzle come together to create a new picture. At this stage, the learner does not require external support, because his energies are at their peak. He enjoys a feeling of completeness and satisfaction, and experiences meaningful learning at its best.

The learner enters frequent states of flow and has a strong feeling that he is discovering new worlds almost every day.

The trap at this stage is of getting stuck in an area of strength that does not serve as an area of growth: During the journey into the areas of discovery, there is a strong likelihood that the learner will encounter previously unknown areas of strength. These encounters could bring about changes in the learner's direction of growth, and any such change is welcome. However, an encounter with an area of strength that does not interest the learner could quickly cause him to get stuck in a "talent trap" or "safety trap."

This is, in very general terms, the spiral model, which illustrates the process of pluralistic learning. This does not only refer to learning within the confines of a school or in a particular area; all individuals at any stage in their lives can find themselves at any of the spiral's stages. There are people who during their entire adult lives will complete a single round of the spiral (or will spend many years of their lives in one of the traps), and there are those that move from wilting to germination to blossoming and back again to doubt, at varying rates.

Naturally, the model is more complex than presented here, because in life, processes tend to work in tandem; processes are not isolated, and we may be going through processes in a number of areas at the same time. That is why, when in one area, we are in an area of strength, while in another, we may be in an area of not-knowing, and navigation between the various areas is of singular importance.

Democratic education enables the spirals in different areas to coexist and supports them. It does not compel students to move to the next stage or to remain where they are. It enables them to experience in-depth learning of all varieties and with all its components at a young age.

The child learns to love the experience of walking through the wilderness, getting oriented and finding one's way, and to view the experience of getting lost as an opportunity to splash about with rapture in the waters of the tiny lake he has discovered.

Part 3
The Results of pluralistic learning – A Democratic Culture

Conventional learning focuses on the assimilation of the concept of "linear learning", learning what the "right answer" and "wrong answer" are, who a "person that knows" and a "mistaken person" are, and how dangerous it is to make a mistake.

The results of this learning are that:
– We continually check where we are on the normal

curve to see what our worth is and what society expects of us.

- We continually place all those around us on the curve, too, so that we don't – heaven forbid – become involved with people who are "not on our level".

In other words, all this leads to social stratification.

The individual effects of pluralistic learning that occurs within the spiral are quite different. They cause us to:

- Find our areas of strength, in order to recharge our batteries so that we can be active in our areas of growth (interest).
- Gain the insight that we are on a "quest" and, consequently, that we must relinquish old knowledge in order to grow into new knowledge – which if we continue on our quest will also eventually change.
- View a different perspective as an opportunity to speed up the learning process that we are involved in.
- Find the unique aspects of other individuals and thereby boost our own individual development.

There are four criteria in a school that are indicative of the success of pluralistic learning:

1. The school changes – new voices lead to new creation. This is expressed in all aspects of the school: the buildings, the organization of the classes, their

design, the subjects that are studied; everything is subject to change.

2. Different voices are heard in the school – the school is not concerned with marketing its success, but rather with encouraging the different voices heard within it as an opportunity for the growth of the school as a whole. Different voices are not hidden or shunted aside; they are moved to the front of the stage. In his book "Real Education", the English educator David Gribble describes fourteen unique schools throughout the world. One of them is the Democratic School of Hadera. One of the characteristics that contribute to the school's unique nature, says Gribble, is the fact that just about every aspect of the school is open to debate, and the debate is completely transparent to everyone, including visitors from outside the school.[12]

3. Violence quickly diminishes – I view violence as one side of the scales, with the other side being individual creativity. When students are filled with faith in their own capabilities (i.e. they have discovered their areas of strength), and are involved in processes of flow on their journey to realize their goals, they have no need of violence or destruction to declare their existence (see Chapter 8).

4. A large number of spontaneous group organizations for activities – prolonged observation of students' and teachers' activities shows many instances of groups organizing spontaneously. This is done by students and teachers to achieve a wide variety of goals.

These may include the organization of a team to produce a video magazine, the performance of a play, running a summer camp in school, the organization of study teams in various areas; the list goes on and on. Teachers get together to give multi-disciplinary classes. There are also mixed teams of teachers and students. The amount of spontaneous team activity in democratic schools is far greater than that which one usually finds in other schools (including those that define "team work" as part of their declared goals). A more in-depth look at the school shows that the longer students and teachers remain in the school, the more teamwork they become involved in. In my view, this spontaneous organization into teams is the main indication of the success of the pluralistic learning process.

When people discover their own uniqueness, it is only half of the journey. Gradually, they discover that they are living in a society made up of unique individuals. Because most of the tasks they have to deal with are multi-disciplinary, it is easier in a society of this kind to find people who possess the skills that they lack in order to create a winning team.

Many students have noted that, in their view, what makes the Democratic School of Hadera unique is the unusual gathering of so many people that are gifted in so many different areas. I respond that it is likely that most of the children studying in the Hadera school are no different from children all over the world, except that most children study in conventional schools that do not enable the students to see one another as individuals because of the overcrowding inside the square and the intense pursuit of "making the most of their time".

The bottom line is that a pluralistic learning process creates a **democratic culture**, a culture that advances every individual to the place where he or she can discover and express the unique individual inside, and also becomes aware of the enormous importance of discovering and expressing the uniqueness inside other individuals and collaborating with them.

In his book "Democracy and Education", John Dewey defines the concept of "culture": "Culture means at least something that is cultivated and grown, something ripened; it is opposed to the raw and crude". According to Dewey, this process occurs when: "...what one is as a person is what one is as associated with others, in a free give and take of intercourse".

When Dewey talks of the development of that person/ associate and the maintenance of a democratic culture, he arrives at the following insights:

An individual would not be an individual if there were not something incommensurable about him. Its opposite is the mediocre, the average. Whenever distinctive quality is developed, distinction of personality results, and with it greater promise for a social service which goes beyond the supply in quantity of material commodities. For how can there be a society really worth serving unless it is constituted of individuals of significant, lofty personal qualities?[13]

In other words, the main outcome of pluralistic learning is the creation of a democratic culture. The central pillar of a democratic culture is the ability to find the unique in every individual and to collaborate with him or her, to create something together.

Chapter Four

Life in a Democratic School – Students in the Pluralistic Learning Circle

A Look In from Outside

Visitors to the school tend to express two different main opinions, which actually contradict one another:

"You must admit," they say to me, "that life in a democratic school is easier, because everyone does what he wants". On the other hand, they feel that children are unable to meet this harsh demand of freedom of choice, or believe that coping with this issue of choice should be postponed till a later age, when they approach adulthood.

Regarding the first opinion, in order to "do what they want" the children are constantly deliberating how best to spend their time, what they would consider a waste of time and what would be time well spent. The need to choose their way every day (despite certain formal decisions made at the beginning of the year) requires mental resources and great strength, and like in the adult world, it is sometimes very difficult, sometimes boring, sometimes joyful and wonderful and sometimes depressing and sad. But it is rarely "easy".

As for the second opinion, I believe that a person who is "freed" from choice during the first twenty years of his life, will find it difficult to clarify what really interests him and what is important to him in his life. This difficulty has many well-known names, such as "post-graduation crisis" or "midlife crisis". These are crossroads where one stops and

asks himself: how did I get here, what am I doing now and what did I really want to do?

Democratic education believes in posing these questions from an early age: What do I want to do? How would I like to do it? When? With whom?...

This doesn't mean that we would have a four-year-old deliberate about his future profession, or about what will be important to him in his adult life. We offer him the chance to deal with issues related to his present life: Will he spend today in the mattress room? Will he stay outside all day or will he play with a friend in the games room? How will he deal with a complex social situation? And so forth. Such decisions involve significant choices for him. The child acquires, through these choices, the ability to choose, to decide, and to give practical expression to his ideas. As his age changes, his fields of interest and the goals that drive them also change, but his ability to be a self-propelled person will accompany him in his adult life as well.

I opened this chapter on the life of our students in the Democratic School with the answers to two questions that represent the complexity of life. If one tries to paint the picture in black and white, words like happiness, joy, curiosity and fellowship, might show up alongside words such as anarchy, hedonism, disorder and neglect. The picture, it would seem, is much more complex, and is made of many shades of color.

A Personal Journey to Choice and Responsibility

A student at a democratic school, living a life of searching and learning, has a varied and changeable daily schedule. It has some permanent parts ("the curriculum") and other parts that are spontaneous and change from day to day and from moment to moment. These include games, interactions with friends and with the staff, and a variety of activities that grows and changes from day to day.

The daily schedule of a democratic school reminds us of our lives as adults in a democratic world – every day we must make decisions. We must determine what we want to do with our lives and how to realize these desires. Then we are required to take responsibility for the choices we have made, and of course – to cope with our successes or failures. The lives of the children at the democratic school are no different. Every day they must choose what to do, and decide how to do it. Through this process they learn to take responsibility for their lives.

In the framework of the democratic school, each

student manages his own daily schedule. Still, I will try to describe my own personal viewpoint of the lives of the students, through the spectacles of the pluralistic learning circle. At this stage, however, I need to emphasize that this particular angle is one of many. One cannot predict through theory the life of any particular student.

The concept of "responsibility" is at the center of the learning process at a democratic school. The student is directed towards taking responsibility for his life. He is supposed to choose his goals and his path, and to face the results of his actions. He does not have the option of putting responsibility for the outcomes of his actions on the system ("school is a grade factory........") or on adults ("my teacher is......").

The journey of independent learning leads the student to the pluralistic learning circle. He begins in an area of not knowing – a condition which obligates him to set out on a journey of searching and examining the direction of his actions and their content; he continues to the area of growth, characterized by a learning and deepening process in a subject which the student has chosen; he arrives at the area of discovery, where he fulfills his goals or fails; and then the area of doubt is developed – where the student examines and evaluates the place he is in now.

It is very difficult to create a uniform picture of a child's day at school, from the moment he signs in in the morning until the end of the day. He may play soccer, visit various lessons in the curriculum, or build a path out of concrete. The picture varies greatly from child to child, but one can clearly see that it depends on the stage he is in, in his individual circle of learning.

If we are speaking of a new student, his day is affected greatly by the way he enters the school.

"Welcome to the Democratic School"

When a child joins the Democratic School, he must deal with a new experiential, stormy, and at first glance, disordered world. In our absorption process we notice three kinds of common situations:

- students who experience a "freedom shock" on entering the school
- students who are trying to succeed "more than in their former school"
- students who slip into school smoothly and easily

Freedom Shock

A child's first feeling as he encounters the school is that he has come to a magical place. He feels dizzy, flooded with the many possibilities the school offers him, and tells everyone that "there was never a place like this". But this first feeling disappears quickly, and is replaced by what we call "freedom shock". This experience of freedom causes the collapse of all the child has known previously, both about himself and about his roles within his surroundings.

Let's look at the example of Rami, who came to us at

age thirteen. His encounter with the Democratic School began as a celebration. He set himself some serious goals: to complete all the matriculation exams within two years, to become the Chairman of the Parliament, and to promote connections with children from democratic schools all over the world. In fact, things turned out otherwise, but for the first time in his life Rami was unable to use the usual excuses for his lack of success (school or teachers). On the contrary; he got help from the establishment, but he discovered gradually that the scenario was not working out as planned. He found it difficult to meet the requirements of the matriculation, discovered that it was not easy to be elected Chairman of the Parliament, and that the students from other countries were not cooperative. He felt there was a large number of possibilities, but no real practical options. Freedom – like a giant mirror – required him to face himself. This is a frightening difficulty, hard to describe for anyone who has not faced it himself. Rami was unable to stand in that complicated place. He tried to act in illegitimate ways, for example handing out candies to the younger children so that they would vote for him for Parliament Chairman. As his frustration increased, his methods became less refined, resorting at last to verbal and physical violence towards his opponents.

There are children who skip the stage of magic and fall right into the freedom shock. They have no idea where to begin, after years in which they never really examined by themselves what interests them and what they want to do. They feel bad about themselves and don't know what will make it better.

This feeling that "everything is falling apart" pushes the children touched by freedom shock to a radical examination of the boundaries of this new place. They check if "we can really do everything". Are the teachers really on their side? Can one really spend the entire day in the yard, without entering any of the classes? And so forth. Sometimes, feeling "drunk on freedom", as they examine their limits, they arrive at experiences that are harmful (to themselves and their surroundings), and even at criminality. This process of examination may last some time, and its end varies from child to child. Some will finish their examination within a month, while others may take a year or more. The child's emergence from freedom shock usually occurs when he finds within the chaos an area that truly interests him, devotes himself to it – and reaches his areas of growth.

In the context of learning processes, which were described in Chapter 3, in the condition of freedom shock the child is quickly swept into the realm of not knowing and the feeling is that he has no tools to deal with it.

One of the incidents that I experienced with Rami demonstrates this stage:

One day I saw that Rami was attaching a rope to the branch of a tall tree, sitting children on it, and "swinging" them while pushing them forcefully into the tree trunk. I ran over there and told them the "game" was dangerous and asked him to stop it. Rami refused, claiming it was not in my authority to stop him, and that if I wanted to I had to refer him to the Discipline Committee. I told him that that would indeed happen, but also explained that meanwhile, in my capacity as the one in charge of school safety, I was stopping the game. Rami refused, and therefore I took the rope off the tree myself. I told him that if he thought I had broken any of the school rules, he had the right to bring me up before the Discipline Committee. I thought that the matter had ended and I turned to leave. It immediately became evident that I was mistaken. A few seconds later, as I was leaving the place, Rami began tying the rope again. I returned and explained again that this was forbidden, but he referred me to the Discipline Committee, saying that it was his right meanwhile to continue the game. All my attempts to explain that "meanwhile" a disaster could happen failed. Then, the only time in all my years at the school, I used my authority as the one in charge of school safety to remove a child before his review by the Discipline Committee. I sent Rami home.

He reacted immediately. Dramatically upset, he went into every room of the school to tell everyone about the "dictator" principal. When he finished he went home.

In the Discipline Committee, Rami accused me of breaking the school rules, while I accused him of endangering the lives of students. After a difficult discussion my standpoint was accepted.

Surprisingly, this incident improved our relationship. We became much closer, and Rami began to share with me more and more of his thoughts and plans to "conquer the world". From that moment on his life at school began to change as well. He gradually became a central figure at school. In time he did develop the connections that he had planned with schools around the world, organized delegations, and was even invited to various schools around the world to present to them the ideas of democratic schools.

Rami eventually studied medicine and works in his field today.

At those times (of freedom shock) the adults surrounding the child play a critical role, especially with older children who come to our school from a regular school. These children know that in similar situations in their former schools, the adults reacted with anger and negation. They are expecting the same reactions in their new surroundings as well, and thus it will be difficult for them to initiate relationships with the adults around them.

The role of the adults/advisors is multidimensional and not at all simple. On the one hand we cannot give up the school boundaries, while on the other hand we cannot give up the child or our relationship with him (see more on this topic in the next chapter).

I would put the message the adult must convey to the child in this way: "Look, I know that right now you feel like you are in the middle of the ocean, seeing nothing till the horizon, but there is a beach near you and you will reach it. I will be with you on this journey, and even if it is hard for both of us – you can come to me at any time. Still, you must remember that our journey is **on** the water. I will never let you either drown yourself, or drown anyone else around you."

Through the years I heard from children that meetings like this with advisors in the democratic school caused changes in their views about the adult world.

One of my students told me in a final discussion:

"This was the first time I ever got any support from an adult – not when I succeeded in doing what I was told, but when I was in a really difficult place, a place of failure." When an adult believes in a child and accepts him, one can get to the shores of safety.

The experience of freedom shock is not unique to children coming from other schools. Even a younger child, coming to the first grades, can experience a sense of shock when entering the school. For the most part this shock takes the form of aimless wandering about the schoolyard, with the children unable to find anything to grasp onto. They will complain that they are bored, they may cry, and might even not want to come to school in the morning. Of course in the case of these young children as well there is great significance to the role of the adult advisor. It is his job to meet the child from a close and supportive standpoint, despite the difficulty and the "I'm bored". Here, too, the goal is to contain the child without fear of his boredom, and without trying to fill it with contents.

We, the adults, remember chiefly impressive creative processes that the children underwent at school. But surprisingly, many of our graduates claim that the stage of freedom shock was the most important experience they had undergone in all their years at school.

"More than in a regular school"

Children in these circumstances will try to prove that, although they have arrived in a world of freedom, they can achieve more than they could in a regular school. In the youngest age groups we will see five and six-year-olds going into older children's classes and studying subjects that in a regular school would be learned only years later. It is important to say that there are children who choose these subjects not because they are "achievers". The difference is in the goals. With the "achievers" there is the sense that they go into English class (for example) not because of a real personal interest but because they want to be "the first ones to learn the language", and to catch up with others – mostly friends and relatives who are studying in other schools.

At a later age there are children who choose to complete all their matriculation exams, in all subjects, and take upon themselves classes that don't exist in other schools. They study for many hours every day, and often request to take the matriculation exams at an earlier age than usually accepted.

Usually, a child who belongs to this group will experience an initial period of success and enjoyment. It can be assumed that he will receive considerable support from family and surroundings; his parents may tell others about his success: "Our child goes to a democratic school, he is enjoying school life and also doing his matriculation, and all this in ninth grade"; or they may be proud that their six-year-old is going into classes with the twelve-year-olds and even learning English.

From our experience, in most cases, this feeling of achievement passes and is replaced by a fall. In the case of the younger child, we will see that he no longer enters the English lessons, and doesn't even want to hear about the subject. The older children may undergo an even more difficult experience, feeling they have nowhere to turn. In these cases, the families often cannot cope with the difficulty and remove the children from the school.

If they "hang on" and let the process continue naturally, with the help of the advisors and other adults in the school, then the "fall" – the collapse of the whole glamorous school schedule – will open the way for new possibilities. Eventually the child will create a balanced learning schedule for himself, one based on his true interests. This case also requires the containment of the adult, to help the child get through this period with patience, out of faith that he will eventually find his personal path.

During the years we have seen other cases, too, in

which children with tremendous will power continue down the path of achievement throughout all their years at school. These children succeed in their path thanks to the support they receive from their homes and surroundings. They are not connected to the idea of searching for areas of growth, and prefer to create a system of normative achievement. These children also need a containing adult who will not judge them, but rather reflect for them the difference between what captures their interest and what they "must do". In a final discussion I once held with Shuval, a graduate of the school, he said: "I was here for four years, and actually I never let myself go free to experience the school for even one day."

"Born at School"

There are children who seem to have been born in a democratic school. What characterizes them is that after a month, it seems as if they had been living there for years, and this sense is common to the children and the teaching staff alike. Their conduct in school is free of both freedom shock and achievement frenzy. They quickly connect with what interests them and begin to act. The younger children will show a variety of interests: in social interaction, independent play or a realm of learning. They will seem busy all day, with almost no areas of boredom, and they are, in fact, in a daily process of flow and progress. The older children quickly find their areas of interest and enter a long-term learning process.

Thirteen-year-old Orli, in her first month at the school, got the video room "back on its feet". She continued leading the whole subject of filmmaking in school, until she graduated.

Narkis's story is particularly interesting, because according to all the early signs she should have been the perfect example of a difficult adjustment period to the school. According to the people on the kibbutz where she lived, she could not be controlled in any framework. She was described as a violent girl, with no boundaries. Well, from the day she entered the schoolyard for the first time, we saw nothing of the phenomena we had been warned about. Narkis became a social leader, filled a central role in the activities of the school committees, and gave help and support to children in need. Although we were expecting a crisis of freedom shock – it never came. Years later, when I tried to clarify with Narkis how she explained her easy entry into the school, she said that for her the school had been "the beginning of a new life". She felt that people believed in her, and for her this was a very primal feeling. She felt that everything was open, anything was possible, and that in any event she would have support. Today Narkis is a teacher at a democratic school.

Students in the Waves of Pluralistic Learning

After the stage of entry, the children enter the circles of learning described in the previous chapter. This is of course a complex process, which varies from child to child in accordance with personality, age and other factors. For a single child, too, the process is not continuous and consistent. One could also describe the spiral of pluralistic learning as a wavelike movement. At the beginning of the learning process, the waves are frequent and not very powerful, and as the learning goes on, the waves grow in power as their frequency lowers.

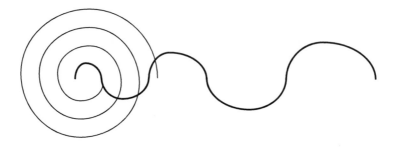

With younger children (in general, not necessarily for every specific case) I can distinguish short-range waves. The child may show interest for a week in a particular subject (getting to know a new friend; spending days digging holes in the sandbox; drawing for days on end, etc.). Later the interest dissipates, and for a few days he seems to be wandering about aimlessly, and then again – gets into another field of interest. The spiral representing the movement between not-knowing and knowing exists for short periods of time.

Sometimes the waves continue for longer, when it seems the new field of interest excites the child, filling him entirely. For example, a child may be learning to read very intensively, and his parents report that at home, too, he asks to read every brand name on a box, and every book title; or a child who is working all day in the animal compound. In most cases, this wave will also pass.

For the parents, this can be a frustrating experience. They have already told the world that the child is deeply interested in reading and progressing at amazing speed, and here their child completely abandons the reading and transfers his interest to the football field. The parents fear their child will never return to his former interest, and their anxiety increases when it regards fields considered important or prestigious, such as reading, math or English.

My oldest son, from age four till ten, would devote a month out of every year to drawing. During that same month drawing would fill his entire world. After a month he would abandon the drawing as if he had never done it, and return to it the following year. I discovered that the quality of his drawings improved from year to year, as if internal processes had taken place even during the "empty" months.

From observing many additional children, I can conclude that this seems to be a natural way for humans – to become engaged in a subject in depth, and then to let it flow naturally, with waves of deep interest and periods of little interest.

One can identify similar waves in older children. However, the time range is longer. For example, a particular child might deepen his interest in writing for the school newspaper and producing it. For several months, or several years, the newspaper in all its aspects will be at the center of his activity. The child may expand his interest – from writing for the paper to producing, editing and even advertising and selling it. He may even move from writing for the newspaper to writing in general. In this case, he may go on to drama lessons, in order to specialize in play writing, or ask the literature teacher how to write screenplays, short stories and more.

This wave will also pass, and it will be followed by a period of emptying, whose length we don't know. Despite the difficulty, this situation does not resemble what was described before as "freedom shock". When children reach this period, they seem like people who are coming up for air and gaining strength. At any rate, the "pause" is not an easy experience for the older children, and they sometimes fear that they have exhausted their abilities, and may not find a new challenge at school. In other cases, they may examine the possibility of expanding their former field of interest in another school (for example, to move to an arts school). Usually, after a period of rest, and with the support of the adults around them, they find a new area of growth. For the most part, the new area of growth is associatively connected to the former field of interest. When the children describe this feeling, they say that "it connects inside". They say this even when they seem to be describing a change that is hard to accept, for example from football to physics.

The Journey from "Recharging" in an Area of Strength to "Coping" with an Area of Growth

When a child arrives at a new area of growth, he needs considerable strength to cope with frustration and lack of success. I have seen dyslectic children who began writing in our newspaper. I have seen a child with speech problems who strived and succeeded in becoming the head of our Parliament. I have seen a child with serious problems in simple arithmetic, who was attracted to the sciences and eventually studied at the Technion. I have seen many other examples of children who were attracted, as if pulled by magic strings, to areas which often seemed impossible for them.

Over the years I have learned that three main prerequisite conditions were necessary in order to get through a new area of growth, with all its challenges and difficulties:

The first condition - This area of growth must stem from personal motivation, and not from a desire to impress or satisfy someone else

In this case one can assume that failures will not cause a breakdown, but rather will create opportunities. There were children working in places which were very difficult for them, and yet their experience held possibilities, not crashes.

One of these, Sigal, ten at the time, insisted on studying English despite great difficulties in language acquisition. When I asked her why she went on, she answered that it was very important for her, because she was interested in video filming and most of the material on the subject was written in English. This answer might seem simple, but it shows a source of motivation for learning. Sigal did not say "It's important to learn English in order to succeed in life", but rather explained the personal importance that learning English held for **her**.

Among younger children, particularly in the earliest grades, the failures and frustrations occur on a daily basis, but these young children quickly learn that failure is not a disgrace, but rather an important part of their growth. The adults surrounding them convey a message that lack of success, like success, is a natural part of the learning process.

The second condition - Power that stems from areas of strength and from a feeling of capability, so that the frustration will not threaten the student's self image and his own faith in his powers

This factor is particularly evident in infants. We see them repeating a particular movement for a long period of time, although it seems to us that they have exhausted the possibilities of that process/game. They are not tired of it, and they repeat it again and again.

Actually, babies are engaged in charging the batteries of "their faith in their own capabilities", by remaining in the area of strength recently acquired. Only after their battery is full do they move on to the next activity, where they are back at square one (a growth area) and they must deal with many frustrations. This "battery" gives them the power to get through this new area of frustration.

Similarly, schoolchildren go from a journey of accumulating energy in their personal areas of strength, to attempts at coping with areas of growth.

One example of this is Yaron, a child who was diagnosed with severe dyslexia. During his years at the school he invested considerable efforts in coping with reading and writing, experiencing many serious slumps. In parallel he invested time in his areas of strength. He excelled in various kinds of sport, was very active in the social sphere, and led his friends in a number of projects, particularly in the area of the school's physical improvement.

In Yaron's many diagnostic evaluations, one can see the recurring comment: "I have never met a child with such great difficulties, who has such a high self-image and has no fear of entering a learning process that includes reading and writing."

The third condition – A central role model

There is great significance in how a child grasps his parents'/ advisors' coping with difficulty. Most of us have learned that not reaching a desired objective is equal to failure and shame. We have internalized this so that most of us criticize ourselves harshly and destructively. When this happens we serve as a model of destructive coping for our children.

We often wonder how our encouragement and

support do not arouse our children/students to the desired learning process. From my experience, the path to success must go through us ourselves. Without a personal change in the parents, in most cases there will not be a change in the children's attitude towards failure.

Since most of us find it hard to see failure as an opportunity for growth, it is best to leave a child alone in his unsuccessful moment (if he hasn't yet adopted our patterns of behavior) and thus to enable him to cope with the difficulty and grow from it. Our child is usually braver than we are, and can take this step. We only have to be there for him, to believe in his ability and in this case to learn from him.

Coping with difficulty is affected considerably by the child's personal situation. If he has experienced an area of strength, one can assume that the difficulty will challenge him, and he won't run looking for another activity the moment he confronts an obstacle. A flowing process includes daily difficulties, and the child seems to accept them naturally. Even when the challenge seems impossible to the outside observer – the child's behavior shows that he is not afraid to try again and again.

Let us return to the spiral of learning. The area of growth and development is always where we see that "little bit more", the real challenge. There we see a flow, and from what I have seen, children are not interested in less. Several years ago, a group of children in the school asked to build a climbing wall twelve meters high. The adults around them explained that this would cause insurmountable difficulties. The Parliament had no budget for such a wall, they would need complicated letters of approval from the municipality and the Ministry of Education, and they would have to find an insurance company that was willing to ensure the climbers. Despite all the explanations, their enthusiasm did not flag for a moment. They called in a safety engineer, raised money through work and contributions, and applied to the municipality and the Ministry of Education. A year later the climbing wall was standing. The children were responsible for the planning process, the obtaining of approval and the performance.

Sometimes, the children's inexperience opens gates that seem locked to many adults, because of their experience. There is no point in trying to protect them from failure which no one knows will occur, or when.

I believe we should support the children even when we think they have poor chances of success, as in the case of the climbing wall. And we should support them even when they do fail, as we saw in many cases at the school. It is our job to shed light on the opportunities that the failure has opened up to us.

Questions and Answers – Life in the Circle of Pluralistic Learning

How can children know how to choose, if they aren't familiar with all the possibilities?
The basic assumption of a regular school is that "if we learn a little bit of everything, when the child reaches high school age he will be able to choose what he wants to study in depth." The democratic school's basic assumptions are somewhat different in this as well:

It is unnecessary and impossible to experience "all the options". The claim to "teach a child a little bit of everything" is inherently false. As we have already mentioned, human knowledge increases at the rate of 40-50% every year. In order to know a little bit about everything we would have to study all our lives, and that still would not be enough. The other option is to assume that adults know in advance what one must know, and therefore the school must rank for the child what is more or less important. The viewpoint embedded in this is that the school has discovered the "magic path" that is most effective, which will lead the child to "success".

In the democratic education outlook, this assertion is arbitrary. There is no universal agreement as to what is considered success, and what the definite ways of achieving it are. Every person must deliberate and choose his own goals and the means of reaching them.

We do not choose out of knowledge, but rather out of a lack of knowledge. When I look at my daily life, another viewpoint regarding this question emerges: Did I, for example, choose my profession after "tasting a little" of every profession? Did I choose my wife after "trying out all of the women"? No one considers reaching the most important decisions of his life in this way. If so, why must a child "taste everything" in order to choose what interests him? The feelings accompanying areas of growth, as I described them in the third chapter – interest, excitement, a feeling of flow, the ability to overcome obstacles – all these serve as measures for the right decision, in both an adult's and a child's life.

We don't know what "the things you can't get along in life without" are. If I knew what things we couldn't get along in life without, I would probably force them on my children. But what are these things? For example, trigonometry is a required subject in all Israeli high schools. Generations of students have invested hours of sweat, and often tears, in understanding it. When I was young I would ask my teachers, "Why is it important for me to know trigonometry?" They would say that I didn't understand, but that when I grew up – I would understand. I have grown up since then, and I still don't know the answer. Would I be wrong in saying that we don't remember about 80% of the subjects that were "important for life" according to our schools? What, in fact, do I remember from my schooling? What is relevant for my life today? The democratic process seeks to release the child from those 80% of subjects apparently important to life (whose?), and to enable students to acquire learning tools, which will help them to obtain any knowledge that is important to them.

"The Basics"

What about "the basics"? Perhaps it's true that trigonometry isn't important to us as adults, but surely the ability to read, to express ourselves in writing, basic arithmetic and English – all these are relevant to almost every adult in today's world. Shouldn't school force at least "the basics" on its students?

In this case as well, the basic assumptions of democratic education regarding children are different from those of conservative education.

Before I touch on the question itself, I must comment that even the expression "the basics" is not to be taken for granted. Would it be right to include in the basic elements of life – breathing, nutrition, love, etc. – reading, writing and arithmetic? I don't know the answer, but it is important to ask the question.

I do agree, however, that everyone should master reading, writing, basic arithmetic and English. The question is, how do we get most students to cope successfully with these subjects? A regular school assumes that enforcement breeds success. It ignores the individual's particular conditions, operating processes of coercion appropriate for the average for that age. Tests of reading comprehension, written expression and mathematical understanding in elementary schools show us the results of these processes of coercion: 20-30% of the students fail in one of these subjects, and therefore are considered as having learning disabilities.

Coercive learning in the basics only damages the natural curiosity of children. When we force a child to learn to read when reading does not interest him, or when he is not yet able to engage in reading, we develop a psychological block in him, which will prevent his mastering reading later when he is interested.

I call the operating principle here "the borscht principle". When I was a child, my mother knew what the healthiest food in the world was ("basic food"). Although there were many kinds of food in the world, I would be a strong, healthy child only if I ate borscht. As I grew up, she kept on trying again and again to get me to eat borscht. The result today is that I feel nausea just at the sight of beets. Even the word "beets" can make me gag. I encountered the borscht phenomenon again when I was a student at university. Among other required subjects I also studied statistics. And here I discovered that many students who were brilliant in various areas of knowledge became terrifically pressured when they had to cope with any field that reminded them of numbers. They told me that in statistics lessons they couldn't think, they were sweating and their pulses raced - just as I felt about beets. When I tried to find out where this started, we almost always arrived at the elementary school teacher, who "wanted to help" and demanded more investment of effort in math, arousing all their anxieties.

Let us return to reading and writing. Observing children, it is easy to see that curiosity is part of their natural approach to the world. Reading and writing are useful tools for all the adults around them, and it seems reasonable that their natural curiosity will lead them to these areas of learning, at the right time for them.

However, the range of age is much broader than generally accepted, and it ranges from three to eleven. Any attempt to find a common factor that will fit all the children, will hurt a certain percentage of them, causing them to operate "the borscht principle". Thus we will find children who are "scared to death" of math, children who steer clear of written material, and adults who have great difficulty in expressing themselves in writing.

What motivates children to approach the basics? I have followed many children who attempted to learn reading and writing, and I discovered that every child is different from the others in a distinct and unique way. My six-year-old son has been mesmerized by books for the past few weeks, imagining what is written in them. He still does not know how to read them, but this seems to be the beginning of his path. Another child I met was interested in cars, and would walk about with a car catalogue, trying to understand what was written in it. Other children were interested in animals and wanted to know what was written about the objects of their interest in encyclopedias about animals. The process has already been described here. The child relates to what fascinates him, and grows from there. In this process of growth he usually needs written words in order to develop. In this situation he will ask for help in reading, and thus the learning will occur in a natural / random way, to be channeled into the main subject that interests him.

Similar things happen with regard to arithmetic. I know children who learned to calculate the change they were to receive at the school store, long before they formally "learned" arithmetic. Others learn from games that require mathematical thinking.

English is more relevant to Israeli students than other subjects, because of their connection to movies and computer games in this language (in other words, there is extrinsic motivation, which is not connected to school or to language learning). The example that can demonstrate the opposite phenomenon is the education system's total failure to turn the Jewish students into people who know Arabic, despite the many compulsory hours invested in teaching this language. The Jewish children of Israel do not feel (unfortunately) that Arabic is relevant to their world. Because of this feeling of irrelevance, coercive studies of Arabic do not achieve their goal; on the contrary, they create resistance and rejection of Arabic language and culture, like the rejection of all other required subjects that are irrelevant to the students' lives.

Whoever is shocked by this example, and still feels

that students should be forced to learn Arabic because of its importance, I suggest substituting for the word "Arabic" the word "physics". How many children have been motivated to learn physics because it was forced on them, and how many have rejected it for life? In my estimation, if physics were an elective subject (not as a high school stream but from an early age), a high percentage of students would experience this subject and learn its wonders. Instead, today most students will never come near it.

I must add that from my experience as a parent, coping with the basics is not simple or clear. I still believe that one must enable the child to arrive at reading (as at every other subject in his life) at his personal time and pace. Still, I am aware of the fact that even a completely free child, whose parents do not pressure him at all, can develop a psychological barrier and low self-esteem as a result of his daily encounter with a world that still expects a clear cut chronological order in these subjects.

I have no unequivocal solution to this problem, except the sensitivity of the adults surrounding the child, and their ability to help him at the appropriate time and place, so that there is an integration of the child's internal pace and his need to integrate into society.

Those with Difficulties
How does the democratic school relate to children who have difficulty arriving "naturally" at learning the basics?

In order to answer this question we can't avoid going back to the usual concept, by which all children must succeed in these tasks – reading, writing and arithmetic – by age 7 or at most 8. Anyone who reaches this finish line without the necessary knowledge is generally defined as "learning disabled". There is no need to say that anyone who is thusly defined will respond to his classification with a low self image and natural feelings of inferiority.

If we addressed in a similar way the beginning of walking or speech, and developed an entire industry (diagnoses, institutes, private tutoring, etc.) for the development of walking and speech skills, the criterion of age would apparently lower (after all, the earlier the better), and as a result, the population of those who have difficulty walking and speaking would be considerably larger than it is now.

Moshe Feldenkrais pointed out that the eldest children of a family have a higher percentage of spinal problems than the general average. He assumed that the young and inexperienced parents "walked" their child before he was ready to walk, and thus caused damage to the development of the child's spine, and to his motor abilities. Later on the parents calm down and learn that children begin walking naturally at the appropriate time for them, without needing "their parents' help".

Similarly, children who live in a literate society, where people read and write, begin to read and write at an appropriate time for them, depending on their cognitive abilities and interest in the subject. There is no point in "walking" them. Thus democratic education rejects the entire set of definitions as to what is a "learning disability", and the age range on which it is founded. I have never met children who didn't want to read. But I did meet children who were exhausted by the attempt to "teach them" through coercion.

Elad arrived at the Democratic School of Hadera when he was at the end of tenth grade. In the introductory conversation with his parents, they told us that in his former schools he had been defined as "having severe learning disabilities" and that he didn't even have minimal ability in basic reading or writing. The parents arrived with diagnoses from psychologists and neurologists, which all explained his lack of ability. Elad sat through the conversation quietly. He was a thin, tall child, lacking in confidence. During his first months at school, I watched him passing like a shadow among the trees, bent over and cautious, as if afraid of being seen by those around him. In my conversations with him, I understood that Elad's fear of being seen stemmed not only from a lack of confidence in new surroundings, but also from the real fear that people would recognize his learning disabilities.

After about two months at school, his mother asked to share with me a problem that they had at home. She said that Elad had stopped talking to his parents, and that he hadn't said a word in months. When they tried to draw him out, he would leave whatever he was doing and lock himself in his room. When I asked her what she tried to talk to him about, she said that she would ask how school was, what he had learned and so forth. At the conclusion of the conversation, I suggested the mother try an experiment: "Don't ask Elad anything about school, just about other things". She agreed.

Some time passed and we met again. The mother began: "For two months we haven't said a word about school – and nothing has changed! He still isn't talking to us!" Before I could reply, Elad stood between his mother and myself and shouted in a voice I'd never heard from him, "You don't talk! But your eyes talk!" After a few moments of silence, both Elad and his mother burst into tears. The mother hugged her son, saying that she understood and that he was right. She had so many fears regarding school, and it was hard for her to accept her son as he was.

Immediately after that conversation, there was a change in Elad's relationship with his parents at home, and a parallel change in him at school. Elad began to show an interest in painting. He drew miniatures in black and white that amazed the art teacher. Towards the end of the year he began painting small pictures in color, and gradually painted pictures of different sizes. Within a few months, he became a star at school in the area of painting. Every day children and graduates came to see what Elad was painting in the art room. At the end of the year Elad organized the scenery for the graduation party. It was a huge creation, 6x6 meters, the likes of which had never been seen in the school. At the same time, I could see that Elad was no longer walking among the trees, but now had the confidence to cross the schoolyard, where everyone could see him. He agreed to be "seen". Even his physical build had changed. He had grown and now stood straight, looking older and more handsome. His mother told me that there was a change at home as well, and that they were like a new family. "All these years I was busy with diagnoses and treatments," she said. "Now, suddenly I can see my child."

Elad was very wary of the approaching summer vacation, fearing the separation from his creative and social anchor in school. But during the vacation he found that his social connections did not weaken but rather deepened, and his independent work in painting continued and bore fruit. In his second year, in eleventh grade, Elad continued to blossom. The art room became "Elad's room" – a center of attraction for many students. Towards the end of that year, his mother asked to discuss with me Elad's possibilities in the army. I thought there might still be a problem, as the IDF does not hurry to accept recruits with problems in basic reading and writing. The mother looked at me in amazement: "Don't you know that Elad has been reading and writing for over half a year?" I was astonished. I felt chills of excitement, and I do now as well, as I retell the story. When I turned to him, excited, and asked, "Is this true?" Elad replied, "Yeah, it's nothing, I don't even know how it happened", and went on to talk about his thoughts on army service. I was not able to find out in school how it had happened.

Elad's teacher-advisors said that they hadn't taught him at all.

Learning reading and writing had apparently been possible for Elad for many years (despite the neurologist's diagnoses), but the psychological barrier of a "disabled child" had kept him from succeeding. It was only after he had discovered his area of strength in art, and been filled with the energies of people who respected and loved him, that he could free himself from this barrier. Later Elad asked to do the matriculation exams, but didn't pass a single one. It wasn't easy, but the crisis was not that serious because he had meanwhile discovered a new area of growth – photography. Elad was captivated by the video camera and the artistic possibilities in it. In this field, too, he became a success in a short time.

Towards graduation Elad asked me if I thought he could get accepted into the IDF video unit. I told him I had no idea what the process was, but I suggested that he find out who the unit commander was and try to talk to him.

Some time after graduation we lost touch. Then one day a friend of mine who was living up north, asked to tell me "an amazing story about a kid from your school". He told me about a boy who had called up the unit commander of the video unit in one of the army corps, requesting a personal meeting before his enlistment, in order to explain why he had to join that unit. The commander was a friend of my friend's and as he said – this was the first time anything like this had ever happened, being approached by a young recruit with no connections or pull.

The boy was Elad, who indeed spent his military service with this unit, and completed it as an outstanding soldier.

I can't finish this story without describing my next meeting with Elad. Several years had passed, and we were looking for a new photography teacher. One of our teachers told me about "an amazing boy who is working with my husband in a film company. He's very successful, and a real people person – something extraordinary." I came to meet him.........and there was Elad. He taught at the school, and later went on to develop further in his field in other places.

Elad's story, and many similar stories that I experienced in my work at the school, led me to think that there really is no place for the term "learning disability", which indicates a "correct" learning process based on measures of content, time and skill.

I would rather speak of **"learning diversity"** – each of us develops a pace and a style of learning in accordance with his uniqueness, characterized by different areas of strength and of growth. This "learning diversity" becomes a disability only in the eyes of educators living in one-dimensional systems, which operate according to a single predetermined track. Unfortunately, these systems fail to see, appreciate and utilize skills which are outside this "track".

About 20-30% of the students, who cannot meet the conditions of the "correct track", are defined as "learning disabled". Life in a track that doesn't suit them, and that prevents them from discovering their "areas of strength", creates a psychological barrier that is very hard to break. Thus, when these students reach the chronological-cognitive stage in which they are able to acquire reading and writing, they still find it very hard to learn. They are hindered by their own low self-esteem, which has developed as a result of their former inability to meet the terms of the track. This self-image is almost impossible to change, determining: "I'm not good at this"; "I can't meet the expectations of those around me". As a result, a child who learns to read and write at age ten will still see himself as a failure, because he did not meet the expectations of the system.

Physiological Learning Deficits

Despite all I have described, about 1-2% of the children will have difficulty acquiring reading and writing skills even after age eleven, and may not succeed in acquiring them at all. These are children whose physiological deficit denies them access to these areas. Can a democratic school cope with these children as well?

The question is, what does "coping with them" mean? Does it mean "to keep trying to get them to read", or to let these students accept their natural difficulty and learn to live with it, as with every difficulty or handicap that one is born with, and then to identify their areas of strength in other places.

The following story from school can clarify the question. Several years ago, a new family arrived at the school with two children. One entered the ninth grade, while the second joined our early grade level. These two children belonged, apparently, to those same few who find it particularly difficult to acquire reading and writing. The elder child had gone through great suffering at his former schools. He was classified by his teachers as "learning disabled" and by his classmates as stupid. After many long years in the regular school system he had a basic knowledge of reading and writing, but he had a deep hatred of anything connected with these areas. At the democratic school he showed preference for the technical field, and he has found himself there ever since.

His younger brother came to us at pre-school age, and he also graduated school in twelfth grade with a low level capability for reading and writing, much like his older brother. However, unlike his brother, he was fascinated by the worlds of reading and writing. It was interesting to see that his areas of strength lay in social activity and the animal compound, which he ran and organized. His time there was considered the peak of interest in the animal compound at school. But the places he was attracted to (his areas of growth) were in the humanist-philosophical field. Today he is completing his Masters degree in history.

Democratic education enables children with true organic learning disabilities to discover that life is complex and rich with possibilities. Therefore, even if they do possess an insurmountable obstacle, they can still engage in their personal fields of interest (areas of growth) by developing ways to circumvent the accepted paths, instead of getting stuck in their barriers. .

Stimulation

Is it our duty to create stimuli that will encourage the children to discover new areas of interest, which they would not arrive at naturally?

We live in a world flooded with stimuli. This is a relatively new situation, which began some thirty years ago. The problem of most of today's children is not a lack of stimuli but rather a surplus of them. About twenty years ago, Israeli television broadcast the series "Little House on the Prairie". Among other things, it portrayed a small mixed-age school where the main characters studied. In their world, in the late 19th century, it was of great importance to expose the children to fields that they never would have arrived at otherwise. The teacher told the children of her small class about places they had never seen with their own eyes, and probably would never see. Could the children of "Little House on the Prairie" be compared to the children of today? An hour of watching TV provides today's children with sights, stimuli and food for thought for many days afterwards. The conservative school still sees itself as the place where children will absorb stimuli and be exposed to more and more pictures of reality. In fact, for the children, it is simply another "TV channel" – and not a very interesting one – which offers them irrelevant options. It is similar to a child drowning in a pool, while the lifeguard (the teacher) runs to put more water into the pool. In my perception, the school should stop dealing with "stimuli" and start dealing with a new field – learning. Not stimulation, not classification, not measurement, but to start teaching in school.

And learning is possible only where there is curiosity. The new role of school is to connect to the curiosity residing in every child and to empower it. The great challenge is how not to put out the fire of curiosity – the process that "stimulating" schools have become experts at through the years.

For democratic education, the important question is, who will decide what is relevant among the huge variety of stimuli that surrounds us – the curriculum that was determined with no specific child in mind ("Today we will learn about wagtails", because that is what was decided four years ago when the curriculum was written), or the child?

I believe that for there to be significant learning, we must choose the second option, and enable the child to engage in subjects that fascinate him. Otherwise, we convey that the areas of the child's curiosity do not interest us, and in fact "extinguish" his natural curiosity.

Mixed-Age Groups

Why is there mixing of ages in a democratic school? Aren't the younger children hurt by the older children's advantage? On the other hand, don't the older children feel bored and held back by their younger classmates?

In the Democratic School of Hadera, the children belong to three broad age groups: the youngest division (age 4-8), the elementary division (age 9-13) and the high school division (age 14-18).

Formal and informal learning enable complete mixing of ages in accordance with the level of interest and ability of the participants. Of course, most of the learning groups are in line with the social division of the three age groups. But alongside them there are lessons and activities that have a broader age range (see examples in Chapter 2).

Mixed-ages did not begin as an ideological statement. They originated from the fact that when we began we had relatively few students, and several age groups were put together. Later we realized that mixed-age grouping held great advantages for the children:

- **It does away with prejudices regarding age.** At a democratic school there is no question like "What grade are you in?" Many children don't know exactly how old their friends are, or know only vaguely. Five-year-olds play with seven-year-olds and with four-year-olds, and in some games they may join even older children. To all parties, younger and older, it is clear that the system is egalitarian, and the older children protect the younger ones.

- **It enables mixed-age gatherings around fields of interest.** Children prefer to learn from older children. One can see this at home, as a younger brother prefers to learn many things from his older sibling rather than his parents. The mixed-age approach enables natural gatherings of children of different ages, providing all parties with fascinating learning possibilities.

- **It teaches tolerance and regard for others**. We often see high school students age fifteen and older spending time in the area of the young division, helping the younger children's advisors to look after them. This encounter is apparently important to all parties, as it is out of choice and not at the request of adults. In the midst of all this, the older children learn to show tolerance, gentleness and a direct approach to the younger children.

One of the problems of mixed-ages is how it can be resolved with the stages of mental development according to Jean Piaget. Piaget divides the qualities of thought into several stages that develop at different ages, stages which would seem to require division by age. But also in accordance with his claim, the stage of formal thinking (for example) occurs at around age 12, with a statistic deviation allowing for a range of 2-3 years in either direction, i.e. between age 10 and age

14. This means that there is not necessarily a difference in thinking between a child in fourth grade and one in tenth grade. The attempt of the conservative system to determine single-year divisions, seemingly based on cognitive skills, has not been supported, as far as I know, by any research information. The claim that cognitive skills grow in one-year spurts, at a uniform pace for all of the same age, is not grounded in any research. In fact, the division into grades is merely a simple organizational tradition. Why aren't the children divided by two-year groups – or half-year groups? There is no real reason.

The statistic data are not relevant to work opposite a particular child. We must see each child as a whole and independent individual.

Just imagine, would you be willing to live in an adult world divided into single age groups, or even five-year age groups? A world in which it has been determined that a particular activity is suitable only for those aged 35-40? Would we be willing to say that because our mental ability decreases after sixty, people over sixty could not hold executive or political positions? Of course not. But what we would refuse to determine for adults – is completely accepted regarding children in the education system.

Measurement of Achievement
Tests and grades are part of our world; doesn't the school cause children to fail by not teaching them to cope with tests?

First I would like to know just what grades show us. When I was a child it was customary to give grades in physical education lessons, in accordance with our achievements in various kinds of sports. I, for example, was born tall and did a good broad jump. As a result I got high grades in sports. What gave me my good grade? The genetic package I was born with. Another child might invest much more effort than I in the broad jump, but in accordance with conservative education methods, because he was born with a different genetic package, he could not receive a high grade. The method is a distortion, because it places high value on the final product (which often depends on genetics) and not on the process. An opposite example comes from my private life, that of English. At school I thought that English was the most important subject, and I put most of my time and effort into it. Still, I always got low grades. Apparently, my internal makeup includes a deficit in language acquisition. Sheerly, my wife, reads, writes and speaks English fluently from a very early age, with no connection to her English lessons at school, most of which she did not attend. In her case also, the blessing (language ability) is a given, and not a result of the "method of education".

It is important to understand that the evaluation process does not only check existing reality, but also creates a reality for the child. In the physical world as well, for example in quantum mechanics research, it is known that there is no such thing as a neutral examination.

The very act of examining causes a change in data and the creation of a new reality. In most regular education systems, the tests and grades become the goal and a main tool for creating "the bigotry of the square" (see Chapter 3).

What reality is created in a child's consciousness when his achievements are examined in tests? Actually, the evaluation process ("how I am in comparison to the average of other children my age") urges the child to compare himself with others and find his "real" place on the normative curve. In the terms I used in the previous chapter, the child is pushed **into "the square"**. Thus it happens that when a child fails in English, he learns that in general (and not only in English) he is a failure compared to other children his age.

Another problem of tests is the attempt to quantify knowledge in numbers. A few years ago I was involved in an attempt to create a new matriculation exam in civics. Unfortunately, I couldn't sneak a hidden camera into the discussion, which would have revealed what goes on behind the scenes in a school evaluation process. Experts and teachers participating in the discussion attempted to answer the question: how many points do we allot for different answers on the exam. For example, what words must appear in a "correct" exam paper, how many points come off if a particular word does not appear, and how many points should be added if the word does appear. Every time we asked the team members to answer questions, and every time – throughout the three years that I accompanied this process – there was a gap of an entire answer among the team members! In other words, there was almost always an answer that received the full number of points from one evaluator and 0 points from another. In the end we would always have to take a vote to decide which of the evaluations we could accept.

My conclusion from the discussions was that if a student wanted a high grade on the test he had to give "the answer according to the book", in as exact a manner as he could, and not complicate issues by giving an opinion, or by writing something in depth, creative or different.

At any rate, this preparation of the civics exam was very serious. The team that thought it up and prepared it worked for several years on its preparation. But we might also ask: How much thought does an average teacher invest in the test he makes up for his class?

Here one should remember two important subjects to be considered when preparing a test: the questions of validity and reliability. **The validity of the test** is the extent to which the test actually examines what it is supposed to examine. **The reliability of the test** is the extent to which tests that are used again will obtain similar results at different times and with different evaluators. The validity of a test in Bible, for example, depends on whether the test actually shows the student's knowledge of Bible, and not his knowledge of written expression, short-term memory capabilities or level of test anxiety. The reliability of the test depends on whether it reflects the student's level of knowledge at different times (not necessarily at the time of the test) and by different assessors who would give him the same grade.

Do teachers examine the validity and reliability of their tests? This question disturbed me, and I tried to examine it with various groups of teachers that I met through the years of my work. Unfortunately, I never met a teacher – not even one – who conducted examinations of validity and reliability of his tests. This fact just shows how seriously the teachers themselves take "the knowledge of the square" in their work.

Tests in schools are a kind of ritual that has no connection to an examination of knowledge. In my estimation, the ritual's purpose is to serve the need to control the students, and to direct them into the prison where the teachers themselves can be found. If we, the adults, are in an intellectual prison, which directs us to busy ourselves with grades that don't really assess knowledge, and convinces us to believe in useless tests – what right do the children have not to be there?

The strange basic assumption of the world of "those who know", and among them the teachers, is that learning is a clear cut and understood cognitive process. This assumption totally ignores psychological knowledge, according to which most learning involves unconscious processes. When we ask the child "What did you learn in school today?", there is no real answer. A large part of the learning occurred at an unconscious level, and will become apparent to the child only in the future. Some will be expressed in behavior changes, and not always in his verbal consciousness.

Assessment in the Democratic School

There are children who wish to receive a written evaluation at the end of the year. For them we created a "verbal report card", which describes the teachers' and advisors' views of what the student had done during the year. The student also wrote down his own evaluation of his activities on this "certificate" and his feelings and thoughts about the teacher and the lesson.

Hadar's story demonstrates the method of assessment in our school. Hadar came to us in the seventh grade. She felt that she was lost, and could not seem to join in on the daily activity. She asked me, as her advisor, to ask her at the beginning of each week what she planned to do, and at the end of the week to ask her what she had in fact accomplished. At our first meetings, Hadar claimed that I wasn't doing my job properly, because I wasn't reacting severely enough when she didn't do what she had taken upon herself to do. She directed me towards the kind of mentoring she needed at the time. Our meetings went on like this for about a half year. At the end of that period, Hadar said she felt that she had the strength to function on her own now. For several years I continued to be her advisor, and we held regular meetings of advisor and student. She often reminded me of our early meetings, which had helped her get into the activities at school.

I believe that at the heart of democratic education is the relationship between the advisor and the student. Through this relationship, the student is supposed to raise doubts about his familiar world, to ask questions, to test his activities and also to gather strength to continue. I want to emphasize that this is a complex relationship (parents, too, are involved – see Chapter 5), whose main tool is dialogue. Through relaxed, non-judgmental conversation, a relationship is formed between the student and his advisor. If we speak only of "assessment", that is an attempt to dissect this entire relationship and attribute significance to only parts of it.

The advisor's goal is to enable the child to examine himself in the light of the goals he has set for himself. What these goals are, where he is on the way to realizing them, and does he still want them. In addition, the advisor should help the child examine his own conduct in school, in light of the school goals: leading an independent lifestyle, free choice and human respect and dignity. The advisor examines, together with the student, on a regular basis and as part of school life, whether he is independent in his choices, how he feels about them, and if he also can see the others around him.

Matriculation Exams

Let's say that a child studying at the Democratic School achieves success in his fields of strength (for example, he builds websites, is a talented musician, etc.). Is that enough? Can he advance, professionally

and socially, in real life without a matriculation certificate?

I will reiterate one of the main goals of democratic education: **to help the student acquire tools for the realization of his goals.**

If the student wants a matriculation certificate, the school will help him acquire the tools he needs to realize this goal.

But how will students pass matriculation exams if they have never been tested in school?

When students who reach high school age express interest in taking matriculation exams, we help them to learn how to pass exams effectively. For example, we have a history course for anyone who is interested in learning history, and there is a separate course, preparing students to take the matriculation test in history. This is not an in-depth history lesson, but rather a course on "how to take a history matriculation exam". We have established an entire track of courses on how to study for tests. In these courses the kids take many tests, but without the pressure of a "real" exam, only to acquire test taking skills. This is another tool that the student acquires to help him realize his goals – like all the other tools he acquires in school.

Regarding the matriculation exams, like with other subjects, the Democratic School of Hadera went through an interesting and complex process from its early days till now. In our first years, all our high school students came to us from the regular education system, and despite all levels of freedom that we had created – the main subject interesting the high school students was the matriculation. The students divided into two groups – for and against the exams. But their common frame of reference revolved around what they had known from their former school systems – in other words, the exams.

During the years, there were more and more students entering high school who had grown up in our school. Thus there came about a change in the status of the matriculation exams. They lost their centrality in the lives of the students. Many of them developed amazing worlds of growth and areas of strength that were expressed in most impressive personal projects.

Still, many of them choose to take the exams at the end of their studies, but they prepare for them in a short time, as students do in external schools.

Others do not take the test at all. They make this choice out of a feeling of achievement, not from anxiety or fear of failure. One graduate recently told me: "I took two matriculation exams, and discovered that it was no "big deal". I can do the others when I want. Why should I waste my school time on that kind of activity?" This statement gains in power in parallel to the feeling that the creative powers of our graduates, in and out of school, are constantly growing. Another boy, who was about to graduate, told me about the matriculation: "I don't understand why I have to take the test. Everyone thinks it will help me 'later', but I'm already living my 'later'." This student, whose areas of strength are acting and writing, is already, at seventeen, working in fields that fascinate him – making a living as an actor in theater, TV dramas and commercials, and he is about to publish his first book with a well-known publisher. From his point of view, his process of growth and his discovery of areas of strength have led him to the outside world, and he proves himself on its terms. Thus it is clear that for him, the matriculation exams would be a step backward, not forward.

It is important to explain that this attraction to the matriculation exams, in the school's first years, did not stem only from fear or from conformism to social systems. It was also motivated by every graduate's wish, at some point, to find out "just what I'm worth in the real world". For them, the matriculation exists in order to see if they are "worthy" in the outside world as well, not just in the community that knows and loves them. Adolescents at school assume that their parents, and also their advisors and teachers, are not objective with regard to them. As a result they are looking for "an indifferent opinion", which in the early years they obtained through the matriculation exams.

Various subjects of interest among the school's adolescents have created the need to call on people who are not teachers, people from the "real world" who come for shorter periods of time to meet with the students. Thus we had a photography teacher who was working at the same time as a filmographer, active artists who gave master classes, a veterinarian who had students working in his clinic, and more. I noticed that the older students were quite attracted to these "outside" people, and through them tried to discover their own worth in the outside world.

This presence of professionals in the school lessened somewhat the adolescents' need to "do the matriculation". Some of them reached a point where they had jobs in some fascinating work places, a year of two before the exam in that particular area.

It seems to me that some of the graduates of the Democratic School do not really need a matriculation certificate, even as a tool for the realization of their goals. The students are busy fulfilling their present goals, and they are not afraid to postpone their acquisition of matriculation to a time when they find it relevant to them.

The Question of Boundaries
What is democratic education's view of boundaries?

Let's say I take a group of people up onto a roof of a tall building with no railing. There will be balls, creativity corners, desks and other possibilities for activity. And then I will tell them that they can do as they please.

Will they take advantage of the freedom, of the possibility for creativity? Probably not. They will probably crowd together in the center of the roof and focus on its lack of a railing. Every so often a few of them might approach the edge, to check out the height and estimate their chances of falling off. Now let's think of the same people, on the roof but with a high, safe fence around them. They won't waste any time thinking about the railing; instead, they will move about freely and act as they please.

The boundaries that we spend so much time discussing, concerned about their existence, are like that railing. When they are not there, it is impossible to act. When they are there, clear and agreed upon, we don't have to think about them or attach importance to them.

In 1995 I set up a program for the Ministry of Education entitled "Schools Experience Democracy". In a survey we conducted while planning the program, we checked out the boundaries in schools throughout Israel. We asked principals, teachers, students and parents to give their opinion of the school's credo, to try and define the substance of various central institutions of the school, and to state ten clear boundaries of the school.

The results were frightening. In all 30 schools we surveyed, the range of perceptions as to the school's credo was very broad, and there didn't seem to be any basic agreement among members of the administration.

Among the four layers of the schools' population we could not find a framework, or a single formal position, with some agreement as to its purpose. The average rate of agreed on rules was two out of ten that they had been asked to mention.

In parallel surveys which we conducted in democratic schools, the results were quite the opposite and unequivocal – a broad knowledge of the rules and boundaries (even if some of those surveyed stated that they did not agree with them).

Two of the basic principles underlying the democratic school are clarity (knowing the required process for changing rules in the school) and transparency (knowing about the present activity in the democratic frameworks). Without these, it is impossible to have involvement and partnership in the daily life of the school's community.

The ambiguity of the boundaries in a conservative school is designed, in my estimation, to serve the "elite" (usually, the principal and the main teachers). This is because, in a place where the rules are not clear, the "strong ones" determine everything. Many principals do without the need to reach complex agreements and build clear boundaries, which will in many ways require them to behave in a "transparent" fashion.

My main claim is that there must be clear boundaries in a school.

But let us make no mistake. Boundaries are the framework, not the goal. In other words, as long as they don't exist, they are the main business of the school (mostly because of discipline problems and unpleasant relationships among different parts of the school community). As soon as the boundaries are clearly defined, they should stop being a main issue in the school and make way for other subjects regarding the students' development.

Individualism as opposed to Social Responsibility
Does the democratic school guide students towards becoming individuals who are responsible only

for themselves and busy with their own goals, or is there some thought given to social or community responsibility, and to the relationships among different individuals in the school?

I believe that the future development of democratic education is concerned with the balance between social thinking and individual thinking, as, alongside individual goals, we see more social or community-oriented goals. This is a process that is already taking place. At the Democratic School of Hadera, and in other schools, there are active human rights clubs, as well as other kinds of organizations within the surrounding community. I believe this will continue to broaden.

In addition, the community in the democratic school is a significant part of the daily functioning for adults and children. Decisions are made together (in the parliament) and carried out together (in committees). Students, teachers, and also members of the administration may have to do things against their will, because of a decision of the community. There is always tension in the school between individual and community decisions, and every person in the school must cope with both poles.

When a student wants to succeed in assignments he has set for himself, he often finds that it is difficult for him to operate alone, and it would be better to put together a team or group to accomplish the mission cooperatively. Teams like this get together naturally, both among teachers and among students.

We assume that our students are naturally moral and

that there is no need to force "moral" activities on them (like the personal commitment projects in the regular school system). Moral people reach a stage themselves at which they wish to act for the good of the community, without it being forced on them. We have seen this throughout the years at the school.

In the sixth chapter I will expand on the subject of democratic education and society.

Graduates
How do graduates of the school lead their lives, and are they different from the lives of other school graduates?

This question is also often asked by parents and children entering the democratic education system. I don't know if our graduates have uniform characteristics. After all, we are all the graduates of our own personal histories, which include genetic, familial and social systems. School is only one part of the big picture. And yet, I assume that there is a high correlation between a family that sends its child to a democratic school, and life within the school. For this reason, despite the diversity, one can find some common characteristics in our graduates (students who have spent at least three years in a democratic education framework). I will try to describe a few:

One characteristic is the ability of our graduates to initiate processes of growth and to make changes in their lives, without getting stuck in a "safety zone" (staying in places which are no longer interesting only out of a need for security).

Graduates I met after they had completed their studies told me of journeys to areas that fascinated them, discovery of new areas within themselves, and the possibility to go on to new things without fear.

For example, Danny was a student at the school who chose to learn cooking. After completing his studies abroad and becoming a licensed chef, he began taking an interest in sociology. The subject fascinated him, and he began to leave his occupation in cooking and deepen his knowledge of this new field. While studying sociology he began to take particular interest in the Bedouins of the Negev, and decided to work with Bedouin tribes and deal with their concepts of human rights. He is presently completing his doctoral dissertation in the subject. The important point here is, in my opinion, not the university degree, but his courage to leave what he already knew and to plunge into the unknown, because of the interest it held for him.

Another example is Tali, who studied law in London, and was quite successful, but found herself drawn more and more to work in education. She decided to leave the world of law and study Montessori education. Today she works as a pre-school teacher using this method.

Another common characteristic of our graduates is their high rate of participation in groups who work for human rights in Israel. I believe that the constant contact with issues dealing with human dignity, has led many of our graduates to continue dealing with these areas after they complete their studies.

Another prominent characteristic of our students is that they do not fear authority. In the army base where I do my reserve duty as a psychologist, I met a soldier from a training course who was a graduate of a democratic school. His name was Idan. One day it got out that they were going to throw Idan out of the prestigious course because of a mistake he had made. His commander, who knew me, told me that Idan had been an excellent trainee, but that the mistake he had made meant removal from the course, no questions asked. At the end of the day I again ran into the commander, who told me that Idan was still in the course, in spite of everything. It turned out that while Idan was completing the process of leaving the course, he met the commander on the way to the mess hall. Idan saluted as required, but also told the commander that he urgently needed to speak with him. This was in total violation of accepted military procedure, but the commander took him for a conversation. He was impressed with Idan's sincerity, with his in-depth analysis of the situation and clear presentation of the background of his mistake, and decided to keep him on in the course. When I met Idan later, he didn't see anything special in what he had done.

I often hear similar stories when I speak with graduates of the school. It is easy for them to create normal relationships with adults around them. Even students who spent some time at the Democratic School of Hadera and then moved on to regular schools are able to develop special relationships with their teachers. This lack of fear of authority and ease at forming relationships with adults, are probably the most prominent characteristics of our graduates.

During the years, I discovered that actions I had attributed to "the area of courage" come to our graduates out of independent and authentic thinking and occur naturally. Life does not frighten these young people, and thus they can find out what is fitting for them and move on with ease. The world, for them, is a broad and open platform of opportunities.

Chapter Five

From Teachers to Learners – The World of Adults in the Democratic School

Until the industrial revolution, one of the most important roles of the adults in human society was to pass on their past experiences to the younger generations, in order to prepare them for the future. For thousands of years, people knew exactly what their children would do when they grew up; there was a fixed order to the world, and a child born into a particular professional and social status was expected to have the same occupation as the one all the previous generations of the family had had. This fact gave considerable importance and value to the knowledge and experience of adults.

The appearance of printing, in the seventeenth century, created a revolutionary change. For the first time, knowledge could be found in writing, and not only from the mouths of elders. Of course, it took an additional two centuries till this knowledge became significant for most of the population, but for the last 150 years we have been able to speak of the access of widespread populations to knowledge acquired through reading. This is even truer since the advent of free mandatory education in many countries of the world.

The revolution of "the law of mandatory education" brought about the first significant change in the status of adults with regard to children because, unlike usual until that time, children were exposed in school to knowledge that had not been accessible to their parents.

The mechanism which replaced the ancient traditions was based on a new definition of what was perceived as "important knowledge", or knowledge worthy of propagation, as opposed to "unimportant knowledge". Now the nature of "important knowledge" was determined by an intellectual elite (scientists and people of academic politics), which had access to stores of knowledge and the ability to propagate this knowledge through its ambassadors – the teachers of the education systems. Thus, eventually, despite the revolution of printing and of mandatory education, the children received "filtered education", which had the approval of the intellectual elite and the relevant political and governmental factors. As a result, the youth's dependence on "adult experts" was perpetuated.

Adults and Children in a Changing World

The information revolution that has been going on in the past twenty years has fundamentally changed the old patterns of propagation. The Internet enables every individual, regardless of age or social standing, to spread information. Knowledge of the electronic medium, and understanding of how to navigate it, also offer access to worlds of knowledge formerly accessible only to experts (such as medical knowledge, judiciary knowledge, commercial knowledge, etc.).

The meaning of this is the loss of the advantage the adults or their "messengers" have as propagators of information, and as decision makers with regard to the filtering of the information to be passed on to youth. The younger generation's mastery of the secrets of the computer and the Internet gives them a significant advantage over their parents and teachers. Youth now encounter uncensored contents and are creating their own new culture. In many conversations I have heard parents expressing concern over their inability to communicate with the world of youth. They feel their children have developed a new "language" that they don't understand, and that the old familiar educational tools no longer work.

Naturally, the change in the relationship between children and adults is also evident in the education system. But this system is imprisoned in its fixated patterns of thinking, and is having difficulty adjusting to the change.

The international press is full of articles describing the phenomenon of a loss of control in education systems. The Japanese press describes a situation in which 40% of the teachers are experiencing "broken classrooms" – classrooms in which the teachers have lost control; the students ignore them, don't listen to them, and exercise violence and vandalism.

The Japanese teacher's dilemma is not unlike the Israeli's, or other teachers in democratic countries, or even in countries going through processes of democratization.

An article that appeared in the Israeli newspaper "Haaretz", under the headline "You Wanted a War – You've Got It!", shows a similar picture, as it describes the relationships between high school seniors just before their graduation and the teachers and principals of their schools throughout the country. The article surveys a long list of violent events organized by graduating students – throwing garbage in classrooms, spraying slogans and even uprooting trees. The principals said that these were excellent students, active in youth movements, candidates for active combat duty in the army – the cream of the crop. This definition of theirs made the question only more acute – what had happened to them?

One of the principals, from a school in Tel Aviv, stated: "The affluent population has lost its respect for the system. This unruly conduct stems from boredom, from emptiness, from a need to provoke the system and test its boundaries." And the Director General of the Ministry of Education claimed: "I am shocked by the cruelty and wickedness of these children. The best advice I can give is to put this subject on the public agenda and to call the police when necessary."

Could it be that those who had been defined as good students and involved in social and community action were the very ones who felt "the need to test the system", the ones who were "cruel and wicked"?

Education systems all over the world have begun to lose control because the tools that worked well in the past, that gave the adults their status and authority over the youngsters, can no longer work in a world trying to adopt a democratic culture.

I have already mentioned, in the context of "conservative schools", the book "Change" (Watzlawick, Weakland and Fisch), with its description of three basic ways to fail in solving problems. These can also be identified in the way the education system is coping with its present crisis:

1. Denial that the problem exists – "We don't have any violence".
2. Attempts to do more of what has failed – "We must return the distance between teachers and students".
3. Escape into peripheral matters which do not address the problem itself: "We must raise the flag every morning at school".

Parallel processes are taking place within the family. Many parents feel they have lost their "natural" authority over their children as the ones with knowledge and experience. Some are trying to return to the "good old tools" to rehabilitate their authority. Like the education system, they are trying to do "more of the same that failed", hoping to change their children's attitude towards them. They are using the same processes of coercion and discipline which caused the problem to begin with.

Other parents are channeling their difficulties into other places - waging war against the conservative schools. They take a defensive stand towards their children, standing behind them against the authoritative system. These parents see themselves in the role of "liberators", and thus create a double standard system in which their children find it hard to function. Is the student allowed to disrespect the teacher or principal, because this is what he hears at home? What is the significance of the child's failure to prepare his lessons, and how should he cope with punishment? And most important – what alternative is being offered to this negative view of school?

Some of these parents, at one stage or other, arrive at a search for an alternative to the non-functioning system. Thus, out of a negative viewpoint, they come to the democratic school.

Till now I have described the "ground being pulled out from under the feet" of parents and teachers in our time. In the rest of this chapter I would like to suggest a different view of the place of adults in human society. This approach, which I call "from teachers to learners", describes a completely different place, where the adult can once again feel stable ground under his feet, where he can walk with the child – not against him or ahead of him – while he restores his self-worth and his worth in the eyes of the child.

The Liberal Parent Trap

When parents send their children to a democratic school out of anger and frustration at the regular school, and not out of acquaintance with and acceptance of the ideas of democratic education, they can be expected to fall into a dangerous trap – "the liberal parent's trap". The parent, who in the regular school played the role of "the liberator", finds himself now, at the democratic school, in the role of "the limiter".

Parents who arrive at a democratic school without deeply examining the ideas of democratic education, believe that "there, in an open, free space, better things will happen to my child". Some of them are impressed with the outward appearance, with the atmosphere of freedom between children and adults, and with the feeling that the children are "doing what is good for them". Many of them are impressed simply by the fact that "this doesn't look like the way we were raised as kids". These parents tend to believe that their own education as children was not successful, and they are trying to help their kids escape a similar fate.

Out of these internal expectations, the parents create a picture of all "the good things" that they want for their children. One parent believes that his child, so talented in music, can at last have the time to concentrate on it; another believes that his intelligent child can complete his matriculation earlier, and then "be free" to do what really interests him; and so on. There are as many different expectations as there are parents.

Unfortunately, these expectations clash with the message that democratic education conveys to the child, a message that calls out to him to choose his life and do what is right for him – not for his parents.

As long as the child's choices are compatible with his parents' expectations, no problem arises. But when the child turns to other directions, and particularly when he falls into places of not-knowing and goes through periods of frustration, confusion and even fear (as you remember, this is part of the learning process, on the way to growth!) –the parents fall with him.

This process of frustration, integral to learning, causes the parents to doubt their earlier considerations. Oddly, they are finding themselves returning to their old beliefs, those they were escaping when they sent their children to the democratic school.

Actually, most of the parents are showing natural concern for their children's welfare, and want their child to be satisfied and take interest in his fields of study. And yet, the crises of learning arouse in them a deep internal anxiety, perhaps because they identify their own fears as adults from situations of not-knowing in their lives.

Their fears lead to anger and frustration; they have sent their children to a place where "it would be good", and here – the democratic school has let them down. Because of this anxiety, the parents may demand their child to attend certain lessons (at least the important lessons...). In other words, they find themselves in the position they had not intended to be in – "the limiting position" towards their children. Other parents enter into a struggle with the child's advisor, or with the democratic system. Sometimes these become power struggles, as they skip the use of the school's democratic tools (Parliament, committees), in order to change the democratic entity of the school and suit it to the familiar pattern they remember from childhood.

More than once I have faced parents who were angry, frustrated and disappointed. In these meetings I tried to explain that this frustration need not lead to struggle, and that one can see it as an opportunity for learning together. Their discomfort can lead them to a deep personal learning process, in a true attempt to understand the philosophy of democratic education. I refused to take the place of "the expert", and for the most part I did not use theoretical knowledge, but rather tried to help parents create cooperative learning, through their own personal world. I filled the role of a learner participating in this process.

Parents who agreed to enter the cooperative learning process usually embarked on a journey of pluralistic learning, in which they raised basic questions about their goals in life and about the courage to face not-knowing in their personal lives. The journey led some of them to areas of strength and growth, and enabled them to increase greatly the level of freedom and trust that they granted their children.

Many philosophers of democratic education, such as A.S. Neill and Danny Greenberg, see the school as a world which must be protected from parental interference. In this world a child can act freely, grow and also fall – without pressure from parents. He must face the consequences of his actions without parental protection.

Two main thoughts underlie this idea. One is to prevent parents from directing the children towards what is "right" for them and to allow for a "parental interference-free environment", where the child can encounter his own choices and beliefs and examine them for himself. The second is that parents, out of their own natural instincts, may prevent their child from failure (out of sincere concern) and thus arrest his development within the cycle of pluralistic learning. Thus they prevent the child from coping with the experience of frustration that accompanies learning.

At the Democratic School of Hadera, we believed that cutting off parents from the school would make them reduce the amount of freedom they gave their children. In other words, we thought that if we did not create a program that could reduce the parents' fears, they would develop hidden "strings" with which to direct their children. Thus the parents at our school are a part of the school system in every way – from partnership in our daily school life, in committees and in the Parliament, through idea and educational partnership using cooperative learning. We felt that if the parents were to experience a partnership in the democratic process, and in creating the school, at some stage they would feel the need to examine the ideas of democratic education in depth, through learning processes accompanied by personal experience.

Only when the adults have a deep understanding of the ideas of democratic education, can they "liberate" the child to choose his own life. This understanding was achieved by changing the status of the adults (parents and teachers) in the school community, from teachers to learners.

Today, after years of experience in a number of schools, I find it difficult to decide between our approach and that of Summerhill/ "Sudbury Valley".

The issue of the relationship between parents and the school has yet to be resolved.

Tension between Parents and Advisors

It is natural for the parents to feel anxiety when their child is caught in periods of uncertainty and not-knowing, periods which are part of the learning process. This anxiety sometimes pushes them to level harsh criticism at the adults at the school (advisors and teachers).

Yoram came to us in fourth grade. Till he reached sixth grade, everything seemed fine. He entered all the "right lessons", and his parents were proud to tell others of how well he was using his time in the world of freedom. However, when Yoram grew a bit the problems began. His parents thought he hadn't acquired enough knowledge in math and English. The child, who had been defined as a "mathematical genius", found those lessons difficult, and eventually refused to take part in them. The parents thought the problem was rooted in the level of the math and English teachers in the school. Later on whirlpools of unresolved angers and complaints were created. The parents rejected the efforts at cooperative learning with the staff and called them "nonsense". Why learn if they already had the solutions? They "knew" what had to be done and demanded the school "carry it out".

Attempts to rethink ideas, while examining those they had raised, were blocked by them entirely. We felt a high wall had gone up between us, and that their only wish now was to turn our school into a "good" school, like "all the schools".

At the same time, Yoram was withering. The clashes between home and school weighed on him heavily, causing him to isolate himself from the adults and later from the children as well. After our attempts to find a cooperative solution failed, I suggested the parents move him to a place that was more compatible with their outlook. But the parents were hurt by this suggestion, and saw in it an ignoring of their problem. "It's our school, not yours", they said, "and we will decide what to do".

Yoram completed twelfth grade at the Democratic School of Hadera in the same condition of a personal and ideological rift between himself and most of the staff. His and his parents' feelings were that the school had not lived up to their expectations.

This situation, of Yoram's parents and of others (though

to a lesser degree), stems from the linear learning on which we all were raised. We believe that when a process is not familiar, it is probably wrong. One of the gloomy outcomes of this outlook is that many parents "supervise" the advisors, and try to give them specific directions regarding the child's daily schedule. In such a situation, just when a positive relationship is formed between the advisor and the student, the parent feels left out. The idea that a stranger, whom he doesn't trust, is in a position of influence over his child, frightens him, and therefore he begins to convey negative messages about the advisor to the child.

There is also an opposite possibility to the example I have given. Some parents interpret the conception of democratic education as an invitation to total non-involvement in what goes on with the child at school. They assume that, in order to let the child "go with the flow", they must "drop out", take no interest, ask no questions and not visit the school. When the parents drop out of the advisor-student-parent triangle, they absolve themselves of all responsibility for the process the child is undergoing. As a result, in times of crisis, the distinct and clear guilty party is the advisor.

It should be remembered that many of the advisors, too, have arrived at democratic education from a world of linear learning, and they, too, must go through a long process of change in their thinking patterns. But as the staff is constantly in processes of learning, they feel that they understand more and more the terminology of the democratic world. And yet, when the advisors face the angry parent from the standpoint of "those who know", as opposed to the "ignorant" parents, this causes the final disconnection of the parents. Thus, instead of learning together and advancing mutual interests, the advisors and parents find themselves on the familiar opposite sides. The main injured parties in this type of situation are, of course, the children.

All of us, as adults, arrive in the world of democratic education with the heavy load of our own limited education. We are (as in the Bible expression) the generation of the desert, and we are addicted to the "Golden Calf" – whether it is our need to receive outside affirmation that we are "the ones who know better", or the need to prove we have the right answer. This is true both for the advisors and for the parents. And thus, when we ask to make a real change, and not just "more of the same", we must learn together. Together we must get to know the winding paths on this new way, where we have chosen to walk with the children.

The Road to Advisorship

The suitable person to work in a democratic school is one to whom values of this education are dear, who sees human dignity and the independence of the learner as basic values. It is important for me to clarify that an adult who is suitable for this work is not necessarily the one who defines himself as "loving to work with children", but rather someone who defines himself as loving to work with people, and can create an encounter at eye level with anyone.

Too often, people who come to work in education systems believe that "love of children" is the main condition for this work, and are proud of their "excellent relationships with young people". The problem is that in some cases, they arrive at the educational encounter out of disappointment or failure in the adult world, and bring their feelings of anxiety and inferiority with them to their work. These advisors may convey to the children all their prejudices towards other adults (the message may be "I alone understand you, and other adults won't be able to"), and in addition – when they encounter parents – there will be clashes and a mutual feeling of misunderstanding.

An advisor in a democratic school is required to support family learning, whose purpose is to expand the space of freedom given to the child and to support him. As a necessary condition, this must be a person who has experienced the encounter with his own areas of strength and growth, and has arrived at the educational arena out of curiosity and interest and as part of his personal process of growth, and not out of a sense of having no choice, or as a convenient way to make a living.

There were also people in the school who had ambitions of being artists, scientists or high-tech workers, and had not fulfilled these ambitions. They arrived at education by default. In most cases this was a serious mistake, both for them and for the children. These adults with "broken dreams" found it very difficult to support a student in his journey towards the areas of strength and growth. Their personal message, a product of their life experience, was "life is harsh and cruel, and you must compromise".

On the other hand, a teacher who had experienced fields that fascinated him, and had come to the school to find another place for him to grow and thus help others – this kind of teacher could convey the message: "Life is a wonderful field of new experiences and opportunities". This kind of teacher will enjoy supporting young people in their struggle to reach their areas of strength and growth, and will see in their growth the opportunity to strengthen himself in his personal journeys.

Two stories can clarify the differences between these different motivations for work at the school. The first is the story of a teacher who came to us after having experienced repeated failures in her field of expertise. During her work we could see that she was advancing average and weaker children, devoting many hours to them, but running into power struggles with the most talented students. It seemed she felt threatened by anyone who had reached a high level in her field. The best students complained that they had no one to work with, and the subject reached the care of the Teachers' Committee. At the first stage it was decided to put her in a different position, and after the same difficulties appeared, she was fired. I still believe today that her work in the school did significant damage to many students.

On the other hand, a teacher came who had been a successful painter, had had exhibits, and was considered a significant figure in her field. Her encounter with the students produced a large group of active artists, many of them still active in this field, years after finishing school. This teacher knew her areas of strength, had experienced failures but knew how to move on, and this helped her give true freedom of action and support to the children around her.

I must clarify that when I speak of a teacher who has encountered his areas of strength, I am not necessarily saying that he has conquered the world; but rather someone who has identified opportunities for growth in his life, someone who knows his own strengths and sees the school as part of his own personal process of growth. Some people may only work for a few years in the school, others – for longer. But they all must recognize the stage at which they must change their place in the school, or leave, in order to continue their own process of learning and growth.

Difficulties of Advisors and Teachers

When a new teacher is accepted at a democratic school, he may experience "freedom shock" similar to that of the children. Teachers come from different places, with different past experiences, but most of them are graduates of the regular conservative school system.

As a result, this freedom shock they feel stems from an undermining of the beliefs and concepts they have held in many subjects.

Loss of Confidence and Lack of Responsibility

Teachers and advisors at the democratic school are asked to take part in the processes the children are going through, without guiding or directing them, and this causes some of them to lose confidence in their authority as adults opposite young children. Prosaic expressions of this regard, for example, the external appearance of some of the advisors. The men stop shaving; the women are careless about their appearance. They interpret freedom as the right to look neglected. This is also true for the physical appearance of the school.

There are worse instances where children do dangerous things and the adults do not stop them, out of confusion regarding their role. One time I stood in the schoolyard, and I saw children putting a young child into an open barrel and then rolling it down the hill towards the road. Two serious adults from the staff were standing there near them, having a conversation. To my astonishment, they didn't stop the barrel-rolling, but continued with their conversation, despite the obvious danger. I quickly ran and stopped the barrel. In my inquiry with them, they claimed they had deliberated whether or not to stop the children's game. This was a dangerous situation, in which the adults' confusion and lack of confidence was endangering the children.

Luckily, throughout my years at the school there were only a few such mistakes.

Formal Demands or Containment

Another area which creates difficulties for the adults is related to the issue of discipline. On the one hand, the advisor is faced with the formal demands of the school framework and of the education system, and on the other hand, the expectation that the advisor can contain the difficulties of a student in distress. For example, what is the right thing to do when a child leaves the school premises without telling anyone, and then the advisor discovers that the child has left because he had a quarrel with another child and left in great distress? Many advisors would think that in such a situation it would not be the right thing to go to the Discipline Committee, but rather to take a stand of containment and acceptance. I believe this is a mistake. The clear boundaries set in school on various subjects, through the Parliament or committees, were not meant to lessen the dialogue and personal discretion. On the contrary! A breach of school rules is an opportunity for the advisor to support the child opposite the formal authorities. His role, for example in the situation I have just described, is to refer the child to the Discipline Committee, and at the same time represent him before it. He should mention the extenuating circumstances, listen and stand by the child in any decision made by the committee.

An advisor should never show his devotion to a student by ignoring an infraction. It is very important that no one break the law, and whoever does - adult or youngster – must face the results of his deeds.

However – and this however is significant - following the determined rules does not contradict the advisor's obligation to listen to the student, to contain his difficulties and to stand by him throughout the process. The application to the Discipline Committee, right as it is, is not enough. This is an opportunity for the child to learn that there is no contradiction between preservation of the laws of the school and the direct, warm relationship between him and his advisor. This is an opportunity not to be missed.

Asking for Help

The difficulties advisors experience in school often stem from the thought that they must be able to solve all the problems of the children in their care. This is one of the subjects we discussed often at our advisorship meetings: when does an advisor admit – to himself and also to the parents and the student himself – that he cannot solve a problem? We spoke about the importance of passing on certain subjects to the care of other staff members, such as the school psychologist, the social worker or welfare departments of the municipality. Part of the learning process of every advisor is the understanding that his strengths sometimes give out. He must know when, how and from whom he can receive help. Of course he must understand that asking for help helps him become a better advisor.

Tensions within the Staff

Teachers and advisors in a democratic school are not in an easy psychological situation. They must be "chosen" anew at every moment and constantly put to a "popularity test". The children choose the lessons they want to learn; they choose the adults with whom they want a relationship and the teachers who fascinate them. Sometimes, this situation arouses an implicit competition between staff members: into whose classes do the most children go? Who is more popular? How do staff members "promote" themselves?

And this raises the question of charisma. Is a good teacher at the school necessarily a charismatic teacher? Will a quiet person, whose positive qualities are not immediately prominent, succeed in the school?

This implicit contest sometimes creates "blockage" of initiatives, to stop the popularity of one of the teachers, or – on the contrary – "competing initiatives", as teachers suggest "alleged initiatives" not because of real needs, but because of the atmosphere of competition.

Staff conversations revolve around this subject often. From my experience, when the teachers learn that the principal of pluralism regards the respect for the other and recognition of the importance of the different, and when they understand that this recognition can contribute considerably to their effectiveness in school, they give up the competition. They begin to take much greater interest in teamwork and in the building together of something new. As their ability to see and appreciate the other, the staff around them, grows, so their ability grows to see and appreciate themselves. When that happens, their personal activity (in addition to their work) improves greatly. The need for competition, in order to establish their self worth and their worth within their surroundings, almost disappears.

Advisorship as an Aid to Growth

Certificates and years of formal learning did not interest us when we looked for a new teacher for the school. We looked for a teacher who would teach what was alive inside him; a teacher who could "get into the flow" of the area in which he taught. This ability is the true present that he can pass on to his students, young or old. At the Democratic School we preferred that our students meet with learning adults, rather than knowing adults. This was so that they themselves could join in fascinating learning processes.

My own personal experiences as a teacher in the school are also associated with areas of growth. For example, towards the end of my role at school I found myself very attracted to the area of high-tech enterprises. Children and youth who were likewise interested gathered around me, and together we founded a start-up company. Since I had no prior knowledge of this field, we sat together for an entire year to learn subjects related to enterprise. Some of us focused on computerization, others on marketing and business strategy, other children found material about good management. As the group progressed, more adults and children who were interested in what we were doing joined us. The product we wished to market failed, but many of the participants in this group later came to high-tech enterprise companies, equipped with all the experience we had accumulated together.

The story of the failed start-up company once again demonstrates that in teaching, there is no critical significance to success or failure, but rather to the personal and group journey. A school that operates on the principles of pluralistic learning is not only a greenhouse for the growth of the students, but also – and no less so – one for the growth of adults, the staff. In this context, when a person is at his best, the connection to teaching helps one's personal growth considerably, for teaching others is often a tool for self-learning.

Ronald Mehan, an English educational researcher, shows in his studies that the most effective way to learn is through teaching. At the Democratic School of Hadera, the teaching was left not only in the hands of adults, but also in the hands of children. A nine-year-old boy, for example, taught his friends a climbing course for over half a year. A sixteen-year-old taught a large group of teachers and students cooking. There are many more examples of unique lessons that were given by children over the years. Some were multi-disciplinary and provided the participants with opportunities to teach or share their fields of interest with the group. They had names like "Mischief" or "This Interests Me". Some focused on various kinds of expertise, such as computers, video, musical instruments or immunology.

In many ways, one could say that children teach each other every time they play together. But some of the lessons that the children asked to add to the curriculum, in order to teach by themselves or together with a teacher, were frontal lessons.

An additional phenomenon, which is interesting in this context, was that teachers in a process of growth did not remain for long in the same area, but rather went on to teach other lessons, sometimes in new subjects they had not known before. For example, one of the teachers arrived at the school to teach chemistry and biology. During the coming years he gave nature lessons, was an advisor in the junior high school, and set up a carpentry shop at the school. Another teacher came as an advisor for the youngest division, and gradually discovered the subject of mediation, then in its earliest stages in the country. He brought mediation into the school, as another alternative for solving problems between community members, and eventually left the school and established a company that deals with mediation.

Other teachers decided to join in and invented lessons with new titles, in accordance with subjects that interested them during that time. One of the best examples of this kind of cooperation was a "searching lesson", which included a variety of combinations of teachers over the years.

Children Facing Growing Adults

The description of the adult (advisor and teacher) who is growing and developing in the school, raises the question whether we have gone too far - have we put the adult's growth in the center, ignoring, at least partly, the needs of the children? Is this "flowing" adult, concentrating on himself and the processes he is undergoing, able to see the children around him, to make room for them, to enable them to go through growth processes of their own? And what about the possibility of manipulation – a charismatic adult's ability to influence the subjects that the children choose?

At the "Sudbury Valley" school, learning initiatives are left up to the students only. The adults' duty is to accompany the youngsters in their learning processes. Danny Greenberg writes that he is interested in enabling children to remain in the area of not-knowing as long as necessary, without giving them anchors and ropes in the form of adults who make suggestions for learning, invent lessons and lead the way.[14]

My belief is that an adult, who has a deep interest in what he does, can create a very fruitful encounter for the children. Usually, the children do not exactly "stick" to the adult's precise field, but rather recognize the powers of growth, and adhere to the belief that dreams can be realized.

At a certain period of time, I was very interested in the psychology of Alice Miller (author of "The Drama of the Gifted Child"[15]), and I swept along with me a group of students who were studying philosophy and psychology. The years passed and the students I was teaching had long since finished school. I don't think that any of them has gone on to work in the field of psychology, or with Alice Miller's teachings – but whenever I meet them they always mention how the experience of meeting with an adult, who is in a process of discovery and enthusiasm, gave them the ability to go through similar experiences themselves later on.

I do not believe there is one unequivocal answer to this very question. There are surely children at "Sudbury Valley" who would have gone through more significant processes, had the adults there filled a more active role in their lives. On the other hand, there are certainly students at the Hadera School for whom the presence of an adult lessened their internal growth. When faced with this dilemma, one can only act on one's belief and not be afraid to try new ways. I have no doubt that, beyond the specific field that fascinates the teacher (art, communications, animals etc.), he must be able to support the growth of the young students in fields that fascinate them.

The Advisor as a Helper in Learning

The answer to the question how to support the student's journey towards growth, is found, I believe, in the knowledge of the advisor, in his awareness of his role and himself, and in his ability to conduct meaningful dialogue with the student. I would attribute less importance to the tools the advisor uses or the way he chooses.

Knowledge

The advisor is supposed to be curious about democratic education. He should learn and examine constantly the theoretical models underlying it, such as the one described in Chapter 3 and other models which are published from time to time, as this education spreads throughout the world. From the learning process, the advisor should ask questions and examine issues which need clarification.

Along the journey to learning, it is important not to forget the main goals of democratic education: independence – helping the student in creating and acquiring tools which will enable him to realize his goals – and human dignity. The relationship between the advisor and the student should be built in light of these goals.

Even when this connection is stable, and certainly in its initial stages, the advisor should remember that the picture he sees is limited and lacking. Only prolonged dialogue, and clarification of the different pictures seen by the advisor and his partner in dialogue, the student, can lead to a focus of this dialogue. The goals of the student and the tools at his disposal should be identified, and it should be examined to what extent he can see and respect the other.

Self-Awareness

The meaning of self awareness is in the deep knowledge of the teacher of the idea of "not-knowing", and his ability to distinguish between the terms "I know", "I believe" and "I think". The awareness of these three components strengthens tolerance, and enables the advisor to create a climate of freedom to grow beside him. The "not-knowing" serves as a necessary platform for the acquisition of the three skills required for the encounter with the "other":

The ability to trust;

The ability to enable the freedom to make mistakes and learn;

The ability to appreciate the other's deeds and to believe in him.

There is a concept according to which a young child needs a clear and well-known world, and his exposure to the "existential not-knowing" will upset him. Many say this is true of adults as well, and therefore they believe in a constant supply of "opium for the masses", i.e. answers that hide the questions. Unfortunately, a large part of the world goes by this perception, and thus it is so important for adults to give the right answer, and there is far too much readiness to fight against those who have given the wrong answer.

In order to create a generation that learns and is curious, and a world that stops struggling and starts learning, we must deal with the not-knowing in spiral fashion. In this way, the more I learn and know, the more the not-knowing grows.

The Ability to Be There and Conduct Dialogue

The educator is not "transparent". He exists, not as an example of what he is "supposed" to be. He must be able to conduct an egalitarian dialogue with the student: not a condescending one, or a "proper" one, but rather a dialogue which succeeds in living the unique existence that evolves at the present time and in the present space, while respecting the uniqueness of each of the participants in the discourse.

Many students in democratic education have told me of their difficulty in connecting to adults who constantly praise them. They say "Oh, how beautiful!" about every picture, are impressed with every deed. Students stop believing these adults. Most students are looking for the adult who is not afraid to express his true thoughts, as long as this is done in the framework of "this is what I think or believe. Take that into consideration, because I could be wrong".

A Learning Community

Finally, there are objective difficulties for all the adults in democratic education, difficulties arising from our own education – in the world of linear learning, in the world of the normative curve, within the square (see Chapter 3). None of us, teachers or parents, grew up in democratic education. Being open to this world requires changes in the way we look into ourselves – without any connection to the kids: Do I, as an individual, know my areas of strength? Am I, as an adult, ready to embark on a learning adventure to new areas of growth? Do I have the strength to withstand the falls into the abyss of not-knowing within the spiral of pluralistic learning? Am I ready to erase the statements that "know" that "this is life", to make way for fascinating yet frightening visits to new worlds?

For this reason, when adults – parents or teachers – enter the world of democratic education, it is necessary for them to enter a process of personal learning. The more the adults learn about life in the world of the school, the greater chance there will be of positive feelings from the children, and for the growth of their options and choices.

I have no recipes for success, and after dozens of meetings it is clear to me that every case is separate and personal and unpredictable. Still, I believe that a process of cooperative learning, between advisors and parents and with the participation of the students who choose it, will enable the adults as well to empower their strengths and arrive at their personal areas of strength and growth. When I speak of "cooperative learning" I do not mean didactic learning, where there are those who know and are "right" and others who are supposed to receive knowledge. In pluralistic, dialogue-based learning, there is no need to decide on the better viewpoints, but rather to recognize different viewpoints and arrive through them at personal insights.

We did an interesting experiment at the school called "open Friday". On this day, parents and teachers could be active partners as students and teachers at the school. Friday became a true celebration. I remember multi-age drama and movement lessons (age 4 to 80). My lessons, which were about democratic education, also drew many students of various ages.

Through the years, there were attempts to create a variety of parents' groups engaged in learning (parents teaching parents, senior parents with newcomers, etc.). Likewise, groups of students were formed to learn about the principles of democratic education. Still, it is clear to me that we are only at the beginning of the fascinating process of creating a learning community, which I believe **must exist in every democratic school.**

At this point I will attempt to describe one of the possibilities for the practical structure of a learning community:

a. A monthly learning meeting for all members of the community (parents, teachers and children). This meeting will include theoretical material (lecture/ film) and an experiential workshop.

b. A personal advisor for the school's families – to accompany families who are not satisfied with only the support of the child's advisor. This advisor will counsel families in learning about democratic education and in coping with difficulties.

c. A "greenhouse" – a framework that will provide accompanying for adults – parents and teachers – in their personal journey to the discovery of their areas of strength and growth (a similar model is presented in Chapter 6, in the greenhouse for educational and social initiatives).

The learning community, with all its three components, can be accompanied with an Internet site. The site can include various virtual courses in the field of democratic education, a forum for questions and answers, and links to relevant sites.

Development of additional models of a learning community is a necessary part of the reality of a democratic school.

The Role of the Principal

If I try to define the official role of the principal of a democratic school, there is one anchor that does not change. The person filling this role must find the areas of strength and growth that are unique to him, and define his own role and the way he will fill it through them. All this must be done with the best interest of the organization, its goals and its continued existence, in mind. Beyond this, every principal must find the unique job descriptions that fit the particular school, its philosophy and the community that makes it up.

In Hadera, there was no clear separation between

those filling administrative roles and others. True, on accordance with the requirements of the Ministry of Education, we had formally defined roles (Dorit Gutman – the Administrative Principal, Rani Abramowitz – Assistant Principal and in charge of curriculum, and myself – Pedagogic Principal). However, in fact, many teachers, and even students and parents, filled significant roles in the general daily management of the school. They led committees that dealt with significant areas of the school: accepting new teachers, building the budget and managing it, responsibility for the school buildings and more (see Chapter 2).

A special atmosphere was created and a feeling that the school belongs to everyone, that anyone could lead in areas of importance to him. A large group of community members took administrative responsibilities on themselves, and this enabled the fulfillment of many goals that could not have been attained by the limited administrative staff. Still, the model we used in Hadera cannot serve as the exclusive model for running a democratic school. As with all the ideas raised in this book, this model does not serve as a uniform formula. In fact, there is no such formula. Today, if I were to return to an administrative role, I would add an additional system that would function similar to a government. It would be made up of the chairpersons of the various executive committees in the school, representatives of the general Parents' Committee, and the chairperson of the Parliament. Its function would be to coordinate all the activities going on in the school and to follow up on the carrying out of the decisions of Parliament. In other words, I would also change the model that we have been following. And yet, I will try to describe the way I worked, a way that represents my conception of this role.

My daily schedule was constructed in accordance with this conception:

Morning hours (8:00-13:00) were generally open, without "set" plans determined in advance. During these hours I would spend time in the schoolyard, living all that was happening. Most of the morning I was free for conversation and play with the children.

Afternoon hours (13:00-16:00) were devoted mainly to personal conversations with teachers and advisors.

Afternoon hours were free for meetings with parents and outside people, and for administrative work.

Evening hours were devoted to meetings of work teams, parent groups, lectures in and out of school, etc. Fortunately, at the time the school was established, and for the first five years of its existence, I was not yet a parent. During our fifth year Sheerly and I had our first son, Yaniv, and life became quite intense.

My work focused on three main areas:

A. Preservation of the Democratic Idea

My central role was to see that the democratic idea found real expression. Since a school principal has a legally defined status, and is responsible, according to the Ministry of Education, for all that goes on in a school, he can use his legal authority and turn the democratic education system into a kind of game. Just as happens in a corrupt democratic government, the institutions of the law can become devoid of all content when a representative of the country acts upon them with no transparency, allegedly because of security or for other reasons.

Because of this, I would repeat over and over in discussions of Parliament that whenever anyone claimed, concerning an initiative, that "we have no money" or that "our insurance doesn't cover it" or "what you want is contradictory to the instructions of the Ministry of Education", the participants in Parliament should remember that these arguments may be attempts to block democratic processes in the school. The role of Parliament is to determine the best decisions that are right for the school, and only after that to discuss questions of money, insurance or negotiations with the Ministry of Education.

Today, too, I believe that most administrative limitations are an attempt to strangle initiatives in the making, not out of badness but merely out of a limited vision. We often have difficulty recognizing the possibility of changing reality so that it will serve the decisions of Parliament. It was my duty to see to it that democratic processes were not hindered by outside factors. Disrespect of procedures and skipping them could eventually cause corrosion of the school's principles, and even perhaps abandonment of them.

I shall give an example that demonstrates the need

to be on one's guard in such subjects. For a long time, the Building Committee worked hard to obtain a budget for paths in the schoolyard from the Municipality of Hadera. At some point I was informed that within a day the Municipality would be sending us a contractor who was temporarily available. I deliberated long whether to bring the contractor, while skipping the prolonged democratic procedure that might cause us to miss the opportunity. At last I decided to give the Municipality a positive response, and to use the map the Building Committee had drawn for the paths, which had not yet obtained the approval of Parliament.

Later I understood that this had been a wrong decision, which rightly caused agitation at the school. The paths were less important than proper procedures for decision making. This mistake clearly demonstrated how important democratic vision was to my role as principal of the school.

B. Raising Resources

I often had to deal with finances, not a favorite subject of mine. It was clear that in order to operate a school like ours properly, and to provide the children with many choices, I must deal with raising resources - particularly because I objected to increasing the parents' tuition payments (actually I had hoped to stop charging tuition entirely. We did not reach this goal, but over the years the parents' payments have been gradually reduced).

Our innovative character attracted many people

who wished to become partners. Almost every year we started a special project in the school, and every such project was accompanied by supporters who helped us finance it. Many times, I had arguments with members of the school community, who claimed we should keep a low profile and go about our daily business. No projects, no people from outside, no exposure to the media, and no constant flow of visitors. We should be content with what we have and concentrate on our own internal activity. I could understand this approach, but I believed that our giving the school its place as a leading educational institution in the country would give us both protection from pedagogic/ political interference from outside and economic resources. As years went by, we built the "Jimmy Jolley grounds" - a playground with wooden facilities that kept the whole community busy (see Chapter 2). We established an international network of democratic education (see Chapter 6); we were the first school to receive an Internet line from the Ministry of Education; and we took part in a number of experimental programs while adjusting them to suit our outlook.

The important point is that not only did we manage to survive economically, even in hard times, but we could also realize dreams in the school that various people had considered impossible, and could persevere with enterprising, groundbreaking initiatives.

C. **Advising the Advisors**
The main and central part of my role as principal was

supporting the advisors and staff members at school. I took upon myself the role of advisor to the advisors, and I attempted to create a model of advisorship work through our relationship.

Work at school is difficult, and not financially rewarding. Therefore, I felt I had to try to create a group of adults in the school that would feel like researchers in an educational laboratory, so that they would have a sense of inner reward in their roles. Just as a cancer researcher does not receive high financial compensation, yet he is devoted to his task out of a sense of challenge and a need to discover new worlds.

The question that engaged me was how to empower another person. I thought that if I could discover the right path for work with the advisors, it would help us all to arrive at the right path with the students.

One of our important decisions was not to force anyone in the staff to teach something that didn't interest him, and to let each teacher decide what he would teach and how. This decision involved considerable administrative difficulties. For example, we took on someone to teach history for matriculation, and after a year of two he informed us that he was no longer interested in teaching for matriculation, and that he felt a strong need to work with the children in the youngest division. In cases like this, I would show the staff all the data and conduct a discussion of how to solve the problem – the teacher's true wish as opposed to our circumstances of budget and personnel.

The rule was always to enable a teacher to teach in his "areas of growth". We understood that if we wanted to have learning adults in our school, as opposed to "knowing" adults, who have been entrenched for years in familiar areas in which they have no more interest, we must enable staff members to keep changing their role and their place in the school.

At the heart of the staff's work was the general teachers' meeting, which took place once a week after school hours. Before each meeting, we would organize a meal together, rotating responsibility for it among the staff members. As time went on, we saw that the quality of this meal was an indicator of how the staff was doing at the time. Responsibility for conducting the meeting was also rotated. Our meetings had several main goals:

1. To present to the staff members leading ideas in the field of democratic education in the world.
2. To acquaint the staff with leading personalities in relevant fields from the education system and from Israeli society.
3. To try to find new solutions to old problems.
4. To create critical thinking about what existed and belief in the possibility of change.

In these meetings and in their contents, I saw the heart that would create life (and change) in the school. In addition to the general teachers' meeting there were advisors' meetings, working in small teams of four or five people with the school psychologist. Their goal was to support the advisors in their personal work handling specific problems with their students. In addition, I met each advisor for a regular periodic personal conversation, and as necessary for unplanned meetings, if for example they were in distress, or if a need had arisen in their work.

As part of the support system for the advisors, about 20% of the daily budget of school (not including salaries) was invested in in-service training. This enabled every teacher to choose courses that he wanted, in and out of school. Once every six years we enabled each teacher to go for a training course abroad, at the expense of the school. Actually, that time range was shortened, and a constant flow of trips and exchange of delegations was created. Thus we created a team of staff members who were engaged in areas that fascinated them, and who felt that they were at the front of research in the field of democratic education, in Israel and in the world.

In addition, teachers at the school supported the establishment of new democratic schools, and gave courses to teachers of other educational frameworks on subjects of democratic education: courses in advisorship, pluralistic learning, committees and so on. The ability to teach the profession you are engaged in is, in my opinion, the central tool in professional development and in the development of professional pride.

This is a partial description of the support system for

advisors, which was intended to create for them an arena of activity, where personal processes of growth could take place. The broad range of possibilities did not make all of the staff happy. There were some (happily few) who claimed that they had "come to teach and not to waste time". But most of them entered the process gladly. As I have already mentioned, the personal development of the staff encouraged some of the teachers to discover areas of personal growth outside of school. An educator who helps his students to fulfill their dreams begins to ask himself what his areas of strength and growth are, and whether he feels truly connected to them. Many parents at the school reported similar processes. They "envied" the processes of growth that their children were experiencing, and set our on parallel searches, which sometimes were expressed in changes in their professional field, or in changes in life styles. I was very happy to hear the stories of these parents and advisors, because they contain within them one of the critical conditions for the existence of democratic education – having the adults learning and growing alongside the children, and thus enabling the children, too, to experience pluralistic learning with all its complexity and difficulty.

I am like them, too. After ten years of being principal, during which I underwent many changes in the framework of my role in the school system, I found myself taking great interest in areas outside the school world. I understood that the time had come for me to leave this place, which had been, till then, almost my entire world, and to embark on a journey to discover new areas of growth.

Chapter Six

From a School to a Social-Educational Movement

I have been asked many times, what motivates and drives me to promote the activities of the Institute for Democratic Education to be described in this chapter. I have no answer. At least, there is no unequivocal answer to the process that began with founding a school on a small hill in Hadera, and that today takes me on journeys throughout the country and the world.

All I can say is that I don't know. By this I mean the sense of unknowing that always accompanies me. This is not a sense of confusion or losing one's way; on the contrary, it is a feeling of sharpened senses that causes me to doubt, to look for other ways, not to take what has been done thus far for granted. Sometimes people around me accuse me of inconsistency and feel frustrated when yesterday's truth disintegrates before their eyes. I will risk this sounding like a cliché, but these are not easy moments for me either. Sometimes I would rather rest on "safe ground", to feel like "the winner" who has discovered the truth, to stop searching. But on the other hand, the sense of "unknowing" recharges me every time, burns in me like a fire that joins the fire of my incendiary comrades. Together we created the bonfire of the Institute for Democratic Education. A bonfire that reveals to us again, that the main condition for the existence of a world committed to human dignity is the search itself. Asking questions, making mistakes, learning to do, and once again, discovering that ...we were mistaken.

In this chapter, I will present the stories of various places where we worked throughout the years. Some are not considered classic stories of success, looking back, but this is exactly why they should be told. The stories of the experiments mentioned in this chapter have formed the basis for our present and future work.

Part One
From One Inspiring School to a Network of Schools

The Need – to Escape the Trap of Isolation

Already during the first year of founding the school in Hadera, a year considered difficult and intensive by all, I found myself involved in supporting the founding of two additional schools: one in Jaffa (Tel Aviv) and the second in the Tefen Industrial Park (in the Western Galilee).

People around me thought this strange. We had just founded the school in Hadera – was it worth our while, under the pressures of the first year schedule, to support the founding of additional schools? I saw it as a necessary process.

In 1987, after a long dying period, the Open School of Rishon Letzion closed. Its closing was a sign to me of the difficulty of sustaining an unusual school within the regular system. In fact, all the experimental/open schools that were established during the 70's in Israel were unable to go on for long; some were actually physically closed, while others changed ideologically. This disturbed me and I tried to understand what had happened. I saw that every school which tried to be different was under heavy pressure from two main directions. One – external pressure from the educational establishment, which was expert at taking the "different" and changing it to "similar"; and the other – internal pressure within the schools themselves: adults, parents, teachers and students, who were afraid to remain in an isolated position, radically different from the accepted one, and were leading processes of change towards the "middle", towards being "like everyone else" (see Chapter 5).

Erich Fromm describes in detail this process of a pendulum swinging between uniqueness and conformism in his book "Escape from Freedom".[16]

When we founded the school in Hadera, it was clear that as an isolated school we would not be able to withstand the pressure we'd be subject to. We assumed that we would have to establish a wide-ranging educational movement in Israel, in order to compel the educational establishment to confront an entire movement rather than a solitary school. We also assumed that this kind of move would give parents and teachers an inner feeling that they were not alone in their positions, but rather backed by a comprehensive movement.

Today, over twenty years since we began our journey, the Democratic Education Movement of Israel has some 25 schools in which about 7000 students study, representing a wide range of publics from all of Israel's population. We have founded the "Entrepreneuring Incubator", an academic course in the Kibbutzim College of Education, Israel's largest teachers training college. In this course, over 200 students study democratic education in a four-year program. We have developed a new educational framework, a "Democratic Education City" for cities and towns wishing to create an all-inclusive municipal framework that implements the ideas of democratic education. We initiated the founding of IDEC, an international conference to unite all those working in the democratic education field around the world, and today representatives from more than thirty countries throughout the world participate in it. At the heart of all these initiatives is the Institute for Democratic Education, a fascinating organization whose array of activities I will attempt to present in this chapter.

It is important for me to say, that despite the fact that the vision and the image of the future which I hoped to reach were clear to me already at the first stages of my journey, they became reality after a number of years, and then were replaced by new dreams and new images of the future; and they, too, were limited to short-term vision. As I look today at the variety of activities at the Institute, it is clear to me that at the beginning of the journey, I had no idea, intention or capability to predict the image of reality in which we are today, not to mention the visions of the future I look towards.

Creating a Unique Community

The founding of the school in Hadera resonated throughout the country, creating waves of interest in our doings. In the mid-90's the school had a waiting list of over 3000 students all over the country: from the Golan Heights in the North, the Jordan Valley in the East and till Eilat in the South. Their acceptance seemed impossible in the light of our decision not to expand the school to more than 350 students. Thus we initiated meetings with parents from different areas of the country who wished to register their children at our school. We explained that the only chance they had to find their children in a democratic school would be to found one themselves.

Advisors and teachers from the staff of the school in Hadera helped me support groups which were slowly emerging in different parts of the country. In 1996 we founded the Institute for Democratic Education, which undertook the propagation of the ideas of democratic education, and among other things accompanied groups in a process of establishment.

Most groups of parents who took interest in what we were doing wished to establish a school using an identical model to ours in Hadera. On our part, however, the **first rule** of work with such a group was that every group **had to invent the school that suited it**, and not to copy what already existed. The product of every group's conception had to be different, in accordance with the surrounding conditions and the people involved. What was suitable for a group in the Galilee is different from what would suit a group operating in a large city like Tel Aviv, with a completely different population. Today, 20 years after we set out, we can say that among all the existing democratic schools, there are no two that are completely identical in their ways.

The **second rule** was that **the support would be provided at no cost**. The process of founding a group, forming its ideas and working with the educational establishment – all these are done without pay, and it is only when the training of the staff begins that we, as supporters, receive wages. In the Democratic School of Hadera, this created some opposition. It was asked: why are we using the money from parents to spread the democratic idea to other places? I held a serious discussion on this subject in order to clarify my position, according to which the existence of more groups in the country would strengthen us (in Hadera). This discussion enabled the staff and parents to understand the many opportunities hidden in founding a widespread educational movement, for the strengthening of our school.

The **third rule** was that the group being supported had **no obligation of any kind to the Democratic School of Hadera** (and later, nor to the Institute for Democratic Education). The group being supported was not required to be called a "Democratic School", it was not obligated to participate in in-service training or staff training at the institute, and was not even obligated to conduct any relationships with the other schools in the movement. The intention was to create autonomous groups, who would in the future operate freely, without any dependence on the Democratic School of Hadera or any other central body. I believed that it was this kind of thinking that would encourage cooperation among the various schools. This came from the understanding that different people have different opinions and ideas about implementing human rights in a school framework. Cooperation would be generated by curiosity and the desire for mutual support and inspiration, rather than by dependence and authority.

Along with the principle of respect for the other, from which these rules derive, there was a common fundamental concept, which we saw as necessary, to all the groups that we supported throughout the years, from the very first year. According to this concept, the group is trying to establish a school whose main goal is education towards human dignity. I estimate that almost every school in the world would define human dignity as an important goal, and will declare that within its walls "the children are educated to awareness of human dignity". The relevant question from our point of view is whether human dignity is the first and most important goal of the school, and whether the school invests its main pedagogic and economic efforts in advancing this goal. In other words, during training, in-service guidance or curriculum building (for example, in mathematics) – are all efforts directed towards mathematics itself, or in thinking how to teach mathematics in a way that will serve education for human dignity. When we examine the teacher's or the student's achievements as well, the relevant question deals with the school's achievements in the area of human values, as opposed to its achievements in other areas.

The concept of human dignity is of course open to broader interpretation. We have chosen to identify with the UN Bill of Human Rights, and to see the protection of its principles as a necessary foundation for the existence of a democratic school.

The Path to Establishing a Democratic School
The Institute for Democratic Education, which first operated in the framework of the Democratic School of Hadera, and in 1999 became an independent NPO and moved to the Kibbutzim College of Education in Tel Aviv, has accompanied to date (2007) the founding of some 30 schools. About 25 of them define themselves as democratic schools, and are in constant contact with us. The others preferred other definitions, and are in contact

with organizations that have other outlooks. However, they, too, see their main goal as the value of human dignity and its development.

We decided, already in the first stage, that democratic schools should be part of the public sector – because mandatory, free education was also a part of human rights principles.

We saw ourselves as a part of the population of the State of Israel, who had the right to educate their children according to their educational concepts, like all citizens of the country and with the full economic support of the country. Of course, we did not fill in applications and wait for permits that would never have come; rather, as in most "educational initiatives", we established the school with the financial help of parents or donors and then began the struggle for our right to become part of the public sector. Today, almost all the schools we founded have obtained the partial or full support of the government.

I am often asked how we succeeded in founding so many alternative schools, despite the well-known obstacles of the establishment and the Ministry of Education bureaucracy. The answer is that we understood quite early on that the "Ministry of Education" is a creature with many heads and faces. In other words, there are different people there, many of whom accept the ideas of democratic education. We sought out these people, and not others in the abstract entity called "the Ministry of Education" who opposed the idea.

For example, Dr. Eliezer Marcus, who initiated the

Organization of Experimental Schools in Israel, gave me personal consultation towards the establishment of the Democratic School of Hadera. Later he was appointed Chairperson of the Pedagogic Secretariat in the Ministry of Education, one of the most important positions in the Ministry. His entry into that position opened up direct channels for us for discourse with the Ministry.

Dr. Marcus formed the Department of Experiments and Initiatives, which was in charge of experimental schools from within the Ministry itself, and put at its head Ganit Weinstein, who had, till then, been principal of the Golda Meir Open School in Bat Yam (an innovative groundbreaking model of a unique school, which was a place of pilgrimage for all those engaged in innovative education in Israel). This deepened our connections with the Ministry. Actually, the Department of Experiments and Initiatives was a source of support and strength for innovative educational experiments of all kinds. A very important step for us was taken in 1998, when the Democratic School of Hadera was recognized as "a model worthy of being publicized". This was a kind of government stamp for the activity of the Institute for Democratic Education in forwarding the ideas of democratic education.

In 2003, a committee formed by the Minister of Education, Limor Livnat, headed by Ganit Weinstein and Prof. Rina Shapira, determined for the first time in Israel a legal and clear track for the establishment of unique and democratic schools. The peak of this process came in 2006, when the Minister of Education Yuli Tamir set as one of the main goals of the Ministry of Education "the integration of all democratic schools into the framework of public education". **This trend, towards turning the democratic schools into an accepted stream within the public education system, is growing and strengthening with time.**

Processes of Democratization in Public Schools

In parallel to the establishment of democratic schools, a new and fascinating branch of activity has been growing – democratization of the existing school systems.

The story of this process began in 1993, when Doron Shohet, then the director of the Unit for Education towards Democracy and Co-existence in the Ministry of Education, adopted the Democratic School of Hadera. Doron turned the school in Hadera into a "demonstrating school", and sent large groups of educators from throughout Israel and from abroad to visit us. Thus he changed the status of the school in the eyes of the establishment, from a school on the fringe to the "right cursor" of the entire system.

After this change, the school in Hadera had visits from ministers of education, Knesset members from all parties, senior figures in the Ministry and the State Comptroller. The Democratic School of Hadera became the representative of a new educational trend. In 1994 we received the National Education Prize. In parallel we received the title of "Knight of Quality Government."

During that same year (1994), Doron Shohet asked me to establish in Hadera a national center for the application of processes of democratization in the established schools. In retrospect this became the second main activity of the Institute for Democratic Education (the first was the accompaniment of founding new schools). We decided to try and cope with the challenge before us, and during the first year of our work we formed a theoretical plan for democratization in regular schools. Unfortunately, only one school turned to us for implementation of such a plan ("Oranim" School in Neveh Monson).

A significant change in the extent of applications to us occurred after the assassination of the Prime Minister, Mr. Yitzhak Rabin, on November 4th, 1995. A week later I was called to an urgent meeting in the Ministry of Education, headed by the Minister of Education Amnon Rubinstein, who asked to give an educational response to the harsh implications of the assassination. In the discussions we held during that period, Rubinstein asked us to build a wide-reaching program of democratization, of a scope similar to that of the program for computerization in schools. Thanks to Doron Shohet's initiative, we already had a plan prepared, including theoretical foundations and an operational team. The program was called "school experiences democracy" – democratization for the entire education system, and Amnon Rubinstein gave us the go-ahead for action. During the first stage, more than 100 schools from all the different sectors joined the program.

Democratization and the Israeli Democracy

The assassination of Rabin was a staggering experience for all of Israeli society, and within it, for us – as people engaged in democratic education. We were required to reexamine our original assumptions, the group in which we were operating and our personal and educational path.

A few months before the assassination, an event which demonstrated how fixated our thinking had been took place. A group of teachers from the settlement of Tekoa in Samaria arrived, their visit initiated by Rabbi Menahem Fruman. They told us about the difficult conditions of the settlers, in light of what then seemed to be the final steps of the peace process with the Palestinians. They described the alienation of the Left from them, and asked to create an ongoing dialogue with us. They claimed that a change as great as that which Rabin and his government were proposing, required internal dialogue among Israelis, not only external dialogue with the Palestinians. They suggested creating a series of weekly meetings, alternately in Hadera and in Tekoa.

We held a meeting of our Parliament regarding the meetings with the people from Tekoa, and at its end it was decided not to respond to this initiative. The declared reason was the opposition of many of us to "crossing the Green Line". The people of Tekoa suggested holding all the meetings in Hadera, so as not to lose the initiative. At that very same time we had a visit from Yossi Sarid, then the minister for environment quality from the Meretz party (a leftwing-green party in Israel). We asked him for his opinion, and he said, "First let's finish with the peace process, and then we'll have time for the internal discourse". The Parliament was persuaded, and the meetings were put off.

I remembered this incident as we faced the ramifications of Rabin's assassination on the Israeli society and on us. We renewed the contact with the people of Tekoa and conducted a fruitful and fascinating dialogue. Today I fear it was too late. I recall how our "feeling of imminent victory" disrupted our beliefs in the importance of dialogue with the other.

In May 1996, the government in the State of Israel changed (a rightwing government replaced the existing one). The late Zevulun Hammer, who had replaced Rubinstein as Minister of Education, decided to establish the Administration of Education for Values, in an attempt to connect between the democratic vision and the values of Judaism. Now we faced a new challenge. We were required to cooperate with religious people, with different opinions and a different set of values and agenda.

The "democratic group" included mainly people on the Left, while the group representing Jewish values included mainly people on the Right, of the modern Orthodox stream. At the beginning of our common journey there were harsh feelings on both sides, discussions exploded in shouting, and the basic experience was one of mistrust. In this pressure cooker we confronted our own prejudices. We thought that religion meant closed-mindedness; we believed that democratic values "belonged" to us, while "they" were out to hinder democracy; actually, we had taken for ourselves the ownership over democratic thinking, without realizing how undemocratic that was.

Slowly and gradually trust was created within the leading group, and we learned to truly respect each other. We learned that democracy did not belong to us the "secular", nor did Judaism belong to the "religious". In days that were magical and not simple, of a fascinating attempt at rapprochement, I learned that the encounter with the other was perhaps the best way to learn about myself, about pluralism, democracy, Judaism, and being Israeli.

The process we underwent created in us openness for introducing processes of democratization, not only in the urban schools of the center of the country or in the kibbutzim, but also in religious schools, Arab sector schools and development towns. The circle of those who applied to us broadened. Our discourse opened doors to new areas where we had not operated before, and this is significant today as well in the dialogue the Institute conducts with people of different ideas in various sectors throughout the country. In 1999, Yossi Sarid, then Minister of Education, declared that this process of democratization was part of the Ministry of Education's official policy ("in the Direction of Democracy").

How Democratization Takes Place in the School

The Institute for Democratic Education has been operating during the last ten years in dozens of regular schools throughout the country, in all its sectors: in peripheral settlements (Be'er Sheva, Mitzpe Ramon, the Southern Arava, Ofakim, Migdal Ha'emek, Upper Galilee, Mevo'ot Hermon), in neighborhoods defined as "weak" (Jesse Cohen in Holon, in South Tel Aviv, in Givat Olga and more), in Arab schools (Kfar Kara'a and Ar'ara), in religious schools (the Yeshurun Ulpana in Petah Tikva, Nov in the Golan Heights and the Torani school in Mitzpe Ramon), in rural areas (Pardes Hana and Gedera) and also in special education schools (Ziv-Kishorit) and in other cities and settlements throughout the country.

> **The process of democratization is defined as a process of conceptual and organizational change, which creates dialogue within the school's community on the subject of democratic values. The process leads to change in organizational and pedagogic frameworks, in accordance with the needs of the school and the existence of democratic life within its framework.**

The change is organizational and the proposed contents are democratic.

Our entrance into a school takes place in five stages:

1. Mapping – whose goal is to understand the school's situation and its background at the time of our entrance.
2. Forming a common vision – the entire school's community takes part in this stage.
3. Drawing up a strategic plan – a description of the practical stages of the school's transition from its present state to the realization of the declared vision.
4. Operating the plan – the Institute's instructors conduct in-service sessions and training for the school's staff, towards the operation of democratic education programs in the framework of the school community.
5. Evaluation – all four former stages are accompanied by evaluation of the changes in the viewpoints of the community about what is going on.

This is in fact a cyclical process. The five stages return in varying aspects throughout the school's life, as an organizational learning process similar to that of the pluralistic learning circle.

These tools exist in processes of organizational change in general; however, at the Institute we have altered the usual tools to fit democratic ways of work. For example, the stage of mapping has been modified from the accepted "doctor's model", in which an external organizational consultant draws up the map. In the work of the Institute this is an impossible model (we are not interested in conducting "examinations" of schools), and therefore we teach the school's staff to conduct their own mapping, chiefly of their personal and organizational strengths, which form the foundation of our work. On the subject of the vision as well, what is generally regarded is the vision of the head of the organization, or of its leading staff, while in our work we have developed tools to address the entire community, in order to formulate a shared vision. Also, we do not see the vision as a single, finite statement, but rather as a developing process to be reviewed and recreated by the entire community, at least once a year. This enables every member of the community to feel that he is participating in the creation of the school, rather than operating in a predetermined framework.

The Rogozin School of South Tel Aviv

The Rogozin School is one of the most interesting examples of work processes in introducing democratization to a school. Because of its location, in South Tel Aviv, it serves a public living in difficult socio-economic conditions, sociologically defined as a "weak population". This was our first experience with a population so defined.

Till the late 1980's, Rogozin was a large school in the South of the city, with about 1200 students, and it was considered the pride of the neighborhood. With the opening of areas of registration in Tel Aviv, and the opportunity to register students at any school they chose in the city, the students who were considered as having "potential for success" left the school in favor of schools in the North of the city. When we came to work at Rogozin, in 1998, there were only about 198 students! The school's population was made up of children of foreign workers, new immigrants from the CIS, Arabs and a minority of veterans who had not transferred to schools in the North of town.

The school teachers were mostly older, some of them waiting for their pension to come and others who were ready to give up.

They turned to us when the school seemed on the edge of closing. For ten years there had been constant turnover in curricula and in principals, and nothing had changed. More and more students simply left. Yossi Argaman, the principal, and Gila Calderon, the head of the Municipal Department of Education, defined their application to us as a last attempt to save the school from closing. Both tried to clarify with me what we planned to do. I explained that any expression of democratic education depended on the community operating it, and therefore I had no idea what the outcome would be. Gila said that this was the first time she had ever paid a body that could not define the expected outcome of its activity. The staff felt the same.

According to the mapping done, we understood that the situation was indeed a harsh reality. In the past ten years, six different educational programs had been tried in the school; each worked for a year or two and then was discontinued. The obvious danger was that we would be this year's project, and that was how we were seen by the staff and parents.

We approached the creation of a shared vision with some trepidation, but we were actually met with enthusiasm for the new process by the school's community – parents, students and teachers. For the first time they didn't have an "appropriate program" dumped on them, but rather were asked to formulate a program that would be uniquely theirs.

But despite their enthusiasm, the principal and teachers expressed concern regarding a vision that might change the place into a school for music or football. They wanted us to give the parents and students a list of options to choose from. I explained that we saw no problem with a school that focused on football or music, and that the main question regarding the program we offered was, according to which norms the school would operate, and what ways of learning there would be for the students.

For almost half a year, groups of parents, teachers and students met during after-school hours, investing thought in the question of the school's nature. Slowly and gradually they came to realize that the power of determination was being transferred to them, and that with the help of the Institute they could create a framework that would suit their viewpoints. To help free their thinking, we included work with music and art. The homogeneous groups (all teachers, all parents, etc.) were mixed and vision papers were passed on among the groups. In about the middle of the year we held a vision day, in which we discussed various proposals and voted on them. Then came a special evening on which the entire community met to decide together on the definition of the school vision.

The change was visible. Many of the members of the community, people with a passive self-perception, felt new energy for action and a sense that they had the power to create change. At the end of the stage of preparing the vision, a five-year strategic plan was drawn up together with the Institute. The plan determined the operative stages in the school's journey from its existing condition till the full realization of the vision.

In 2004, the goals which had been determined six years previously, and which had then seemed almost impossible, were attained. Moreover, the school attained achievements we had not even dreamed of. I will attempt to examine the organizational learning process that enabled the place to undergo such a significant change in six years:

In 2004 the school had some 400 students, three times as many as four years previously. The school laws were determined by the Parliament, and arbitration committees examined and responded to incidents of violation of the laws. The studies were conducted in the form of personal study programs, in which each student had a personal advisor. The learning program included mandatory subjects (in which the child could choose his way of learning) and elective subjects (in which both the subjects and the ways of learning them were chosen), as in other democratic schools.

The unique processes that developed there included

very strong ties between the school and its surrounding community, as it became a sort of regional community center. Thus, for example, the third floor of the school, which had previously been empty, was rented out to local artists in return for their commitment to work with the students. The school building, which was grey and prison-like, was covered with the artwork of students and local artists. The large hall on the ground floor, which was not in use, was rented out to a local circus group, in return for which they undertook to instruct students. A room at the school was put at the disposal of the Florentine neighborhood newspaper, and the students took part in its publishing. A TV company set up a local broadcasting studio in the building, in which the students were partners. And in the gallery at the school, group exhibits were presented by students and adult artists – and gained widespread press coverage.

In fact, the school became a neighborhood center, and the children studying there could choose fascinating fields of interest connected to their natural surroundings. Instead of their former embarrassment at belonging to the South of the city, they began to feel local pride.

Two main phenomena accompanied this change. First, the violence that had characterized the school initially vanished almost completely. The school principal told us that during the first stage, when only the Parliament and the committees began their work, there was a decrease in violence but it did not disappear completely. But as the other changes were implemented – pluralistic learning, freedom to choose subjects and the personal advisors – the violence disappeared.

The second phenomenon was also connected to the freedom to choose learning subjects. The more freedom there was, the more subjects appeared in school that hadn't been dealt with before: social involvement, struggles for human rights and addressing the local surroundings as an arena for social activity.

In one of my visits to the school, one of the students told me: "For the first time in my life I enjoy studying. In my other school I knew I was a weak student, and today I instruct children in fields where I'm strong". The students enjoyed the fact that study had turned from a difficulty, an experience of constant failure, into a positive and rewarding experience, a feeling that matters were in their hands.

This process also succeeded according to external criteria. For example, the number of students who successfully complete their matriculation rose. Matriculation is not a main criterion in the view of democratic education, but the students of Rogozin and their parents saw the matriculation as an important challenge and a ticket to the adult world. Thus there was still a deep significance to success in this area. After all, when a student achieves the goals he has set for himself, one of the central goals of the idea of democratic education is thus realized.

Finally, the school became a home. It did not belong

only to the parents and to the administration, but to the entire community. The building was open almost 16 hours a day. The teachers and students had their own keys, and would come to workshops at all hours and see themselves as responsible for all that went on there.

Organizational Pluralistic Learning

When we examine the reasons for the success of the process at Rogozin School, a place where so many other experiments had failed, we find a very significant point: the ability of the school (and the entire organization) to get through crises of uncertainty (see Chapter 3) and begin to grow anew.

An individual's learning process includes a crisis which represents the separation from old perceptions of the world, and the growth of new perceptions. This crisis takes place in the area I have defined as "the area of uncertainty". It is characterized as an experience of chaos, loss of confidence and a feeling that the way is lost. Similarly, significant organizational change involves a separation from old working patterns and from the familiar world outlook. In addition, a change takes place in the defined positions formerly filled by each individual in the organization. Here, too, the crisis leads to the area of "unknowing", but because the organization is made up of people, there may be a frequent situation in which some of the people feel they are losing their grip, and "drowning" within the process of change, while others feel that the change is right (those who have already entered the "area of growth"). The "drowning" one feels means that his old position has been gravely harmed, and that he may have to leave the place because he "does not fit in".

In this sense, the organizational learning is different from individual learning. Not all the people feel they are leading the process, and some of them experience being "thrown into the pool of unknowing" with no control. Not all the participants can undergo the stages of learning at the same pace, and this fact is one of the reasons for the massive opposition to an organizational change like the one we wished to lead at Rogozin.

And indeed, after a period of euphoria, during which the mapping was conducted and a shared vision formulated, a period during which the entire community and staff felt they were going through an important change – the crises began. As I examine schools and organizations which did not succeed in internalizing significant processes of change, I recognize a pattern in which, after the euphoria of the beginning, the crisis that signals the end of the process appears. In most cases the program is discontinued, and the organization tries out a new program that "might be better".

This had been happening at Rogozin for ten years. The teachers and staff members expected our program to last two or three years as well, and then to be changed. And indeed, at the beginning of our journey there were huge crises that seemed to have no solution. The first significant crisis stemmed from the teachers' firm opposition to decision making in the Parliament. Heavy pressure was applied towards having initial discussion in the teachers' room, and only then passing the decision on to the Parliament. In addition, there were demands for a raise in pay. There were claims that "what's good for a school in the North won't suit the South", and "how can we decide on our own learning program and still go by the instructions of the Ministry of Education". Later, when artists and other adults were integrated into the school, some of the teachers saw it as harming their status. The equality of teachers and students in the arbitration committees was also perceived as a hindrance to their status.

At certain moments it seemed that the arguments in the teachers' room would cause the entire program to disintegrate. At times, the struggle in the teachers' room turned into verbal and almost physical violence. The crises of the beginning generated sad thoughts: the principal thought he might have to replace the staff, and asked for "more powerful advisors" from the Institute to help him manage the crisis.

There had been expectations that the change would be pleasant, because it was right. And indeed, during the stages of mapping and forming the vision, the positive experiences gave the community and the staff power and a sense of cooperation. But the first crisis frightened them. They wanted to return to calm, and thought that salvation might come in the form of replacing teachers.

How do we get through crises? As in personal learning, in organizational change, too, the path to the area of growth goes through a crisis. Skipping the crisis means skipping the change.

First condition for success: helping the staff members to get through the crisis and reach areas of growth

The general idea is that one should develop the staff, rather than replace them. Just as one does not expel a child from school because of a crisis, so one should also give teachers room for crisis. The teachers' oppositions expressed for us their integration into a significant learning process. There is often animosity between older schemas of "school teaching" and newer perceptions led by the democratic change. This kind of internal struggle can be difficult and painful, but it is necessary for true learning. In parallel, and for similar reasons, we made it clear that we had no intention of replacing the Institute's counselors because of the appearance of a crisis.

Yossi Argaman, the school principal, accepted this approach. The message conveyed to the teachers was that there would be no forced change, and that it was legitimate to raise reservations and ideas. The way had not been predetermined and there was room for their influence. This calmed them down. It was decided that there would not be a majority vote regarding pedagogic and personal issues of each teacher, and that any teacher who wished could work in his "older ways" in his own class.

As we went on we saw a variety of processes in the teachers, different in their forms and pace. Some, even those who had seriously opposed the change, accepted it with time and even supported it enthusiastically and led some of the work. Other teachers could not find their place and voluntarily left. And yet, after a few years there was a waiting list of teachers who had heard the rumor about the "revolution" at Rogozin, and applied to teach there.

Second condition for success: development of a leading school staff

Much has been said about the importance of the principal's role in the organization. A charismatic and successful principal can lead change in situations of growth. Yet, in my opinion, lasting crisis situations will gradually weaken even such a principal, until he finds himself exhausted and perhaps out of the organization.

In Rogozin, a leading staff was formed of eight people, to lead the change as a solid group. Each of them was in charge of teams that operated the changes at the school. When crises arose within one of the teams, the "leader" in charge would get strong backing from the administrative team.

Third condition for success: passage through areas of strength

As mentioned before, passage through areas of strength and accumulation of experiences of success are meant to supply positive energy, which will help the individual in his personal journey of growth. It is the same with an organization. When we began the project at Rogozin, the place had most negative stigmas. It was tagged as problematic, there was little local pride, and people wished to leave the school because they did not see themselves growing within its framework.

Just as for an individual, for a school as well, recognition of its capability is important to identify its areas of strength. At Rogozin, particular importance was given to extrinsic recognition of the positive processes that the change had brought on. For example, a visit from the Minister of Education in the school's Parliament, the election of the Parliament's chairperson as spokesman for the municipal youth council, recognition of the school as an experimental school (out of 200 applications for this matter, four were recognized, one of them Rogozin). A survey, published in 2001 in "The City" newspaper, mentioned Rogozin as the school that was best loved by its students in the Tel Aviv area; in addition, it was chosen the "Dream School" of the Israeli education system by the Ministry of Education.

All these influenced the entire system – students and staff – and attracted more and more people into the circle of the program. It is important to emphasize that the focus was on developing the internal program and not on attempts to win appreciation – but the external recognition brought in new strength that facilitated an easier undergoing of the crises.

The last crisis in the school, around the opposition to the change from homeroom classes to personal advisorship, had already passed and posed no threat to the organization's existence. And indeed, at the end of the year the teachers and students reported that the advisorship system was the most significant thing that had happened to them since the program had been initiated.

Fourth condition for success: staff counseling

An important factor that influenced the success of this change relates to the accompaniment of a team of counselors from the Institute. The team included two to four counselors. Its makeup varied in accordance with the circumstances, and always included people from the field of organizational counseling and others with experience in new initiatives and in working with the democratic education approach.

Many times when I guided organizational counselors, I discerned that the first stage of the counselor's work brought on an organizational arousal (the spectrum between not-knowing and knowing). With the appearance of the first difficulties and with them again opposition, many counselors have difficulty supporting the organization and the program fails (the underlying spectrum from knowing to not-knowing). In addition, as I sense it, counselors who come only from the field of consultation often feel helpless at the actual stage of operation of the program, and therefore they delay it. I estimate that many programs like this fail only because of the counselor's difficulties. In the mixed staff that we built (people from different areas), a new kind of suspense was created that enabled operation. As a result, the people of Rogozin felt that these were people who were coming to them "from the field", people who could understand the difficulties of the teachers and the crises they were undergoing. The team of counselors knew how to support situations of crisis, and succeeded in containing the angers and working with the school in hard times as well.

In particularly difficult cases we had to "hand over the torch" from counselor to counselor, to prevent burnout. On the work front, facing a crisis, there should always be counselors who can be out in the field and contain the difficulties. We realized that in places where a single person might collapse, a group of counselors could take on the shared burden.

Fifth condition for success: full backing of the Municipality and the Ministry of Education, not only in times of success but mainly in crises
This backing enabled us to focus on pedagogy, and not on politics. This condition brought us to the idea that it would be best to initiate processes of democratization under city/regional auspices, giving broader pedagogic freedom to the schools.

At Rogozin these five conditions were fulfilled, and the program succeeded in surviving the change through the first year. There, for the first time, we succeeded in passing on principles of pluralistic learning from the personal to the organizational level.

In 2006, seven years after the initiation of the process in Rogozin, the principal Yossi Argaman retired. A new principal came to the school, one with different educational viewpoints. She discontinued relations between the school and the Institute for Democratic Education without even a conversation with us, and despite the opposition of the school's community. Representatives of the municipality defended the principal's right to lead the school towards a different pedagogic direction which she believed in. The artists were asked to leave and the workshops were closed. The school went through a process of change from the democratic approach to other directions, which the principal thought were more right for it.

Despite this disappointing ending, the story of the democratization process in the Rogozin School in South Tel Aviv is an important episode in our learning on leading change, and a foundation for all the processes I will describe later on.

Part Two
The Institute for Democratic Education

A Journey from "the Democratics" to Innovation in the Heart of the Education System

Since 1996, there began to be a need in the organization to give a response to the five main needs that appeared in the field of democratic education:

- The founding of new democratic schools.
- Processes of democratization in public schools.
- Academic training of educators in areas of democratic education.
- Research and development of new models of democratic education.
- Creating an international network for learning experiences, and developing multinational and multicultural initiatives.

Around these five central missions the Institute for Democratic Education was built – at first in the framework of the Democratic School of Hadera, and later in its new home at the Kibbutzim College of Education in Tel Aviv.

The Institute serves today as one of the world leaders of democratic education. It operates in unique democratic ways and creates a platform that encourages initiatives in fields connecting education, society, environment and economics.

The Institute is growing most rapidly and today has over 100 staff members, initiators and developers of innovations in the field of education and society.

Democratic Education in Frameworks of Higher Education – "The Educational-Social Entrepreneuring Incubator"

One of the main problems in the world of education (particularly in Israel) is the quality of those who seek a career in education. Today, most students (87%) who choose to study education do not do so because of a desire for personal growth or educational ideology, but because it is their only option. This is due to the low acceptance threshold, or because of the convenience of teaching as a second job in the household (convenient working hours and vacations). A general change in education systems requires that we see that those entering the system do so for reasons of personal growth. Only educators working from these motives can help their students to continue their own personal growth. Therefore, when we thought of a comprehensive change in the system, we had two options: one – an experiment such as the one carried out at Rogozin, of activating "sleeping engines". In other words, to arouse in the existing teachers the vision and will to create a revolution, as part of the mission of their lives. The second option – fostering new personnel who wish to carry on the revolution in the education system.

In order to realize the second option, we initiated a program called "**the Educational-Social Entrepreneuring Incubator**", in the framework of the Kibbutzim College of Education. This program grants a Bachelor's Degree and a Teacher's Certificate in the

Humanities and in Life Sciences with an environmental emphasis.

This initiative began with a request I received from Dr. Yossi Assaf, head of the Kibbutzim College of Education. He proposed to conduct an ongoing dialogue to check various options for cooperation between the Institute for Democratic Education and the college. This dialogue did indeed create a fascinating window of opportunities. It was joined by Efrat Ben Tzvi and Gilad Babchuk of the Institute, while joining us from the college were Dr. Tzipi Libman, the Dean, Dr. Shula Keshet, head of the School of Education, and heads of various departments in the Humanities. After several months of development, they executed this rather complicated initiative by establishing a new academic course, recognized and supported by the Department of Experiments and Initiativse in the Ministry of Education. After four years of experimental operation, the course has been defined as a success. A summative book entitled "Democracy in Action", edited by Amnon Yuval, was published, and direction of the program was placed in the hands of Eyal Ram of the Institute and Dr. Esther Yogev who had become Head of the School of Education in the college.

This fruitful collaboration between the Institute for Democratic Education, which operates as a non-profit organization in the third sector, and the Kibbutzim College of Education, a public academic college, became the key factor in the success of the program and the mutual learning of both bodies.

The Incubator is meant for people who wish to advance the vision of democratic education in all its varieties, in "regular" or democratic schools and other educational frameworks, and for people who wish to work in the future in existing frameworks or in initiating new educational projects. Its main goal is to help each student express his own uniqueness as an educator.

During the years of the program, each student gets his own advisor and joins the "Incubator group" of about 10 students, who accompany him in a process of development and creation of his professional identity, and of locating, learning and producing an educational venture that can express his uniqueness. Each student in the Incubator makes a commitment to put five weekly hours, beyond his studies at the college, into projects he has chosen for himself, in accordance with the year's process.

The course goes on for four years. **In the first year the main topic is "search":** Every week, a half day is given to be engaged in things beyond the usual daily schedule. This day is devoted to searching for areas that fascinate the learner, for exploration and for internal examination. This journey is an attempt to track down the line that leads to areas of growth and to map the learning methods of each student.

A weekly workshop is devoted to a shared examination by the participants of their "search" projects. The members of the group examine the process that each student undergoes, as well as the process undergone by the group. During his participation in the Incubator, each student receives feedback on his activity on three planes: between the student and himself, between the student and his advisor, and between the student and the group. Beyond this feedback, the students receive different tools related to the process and the structuring of the group.

The goal is that each participant chooses at the end of the first year that area in which he wishes to deepen his knowledge. There is of course the possibility that the choice will not be in the area of education, and then the person may feel he should leave the program.

The second year is the "year of deepening" in the chosen area: During this year the students at the Incubator deepen their studies in the areas they have chosen during their "search" (in the first year). Each student builds himself a personal learning program in the SML method – Self Managed Learning. This method comprises five stages: 1. an examination of the students' personal histories; 2. their situation today in areas they chose during their first year; 3. the goals they wish to fulfill during the year of deepening; 4. the way in which they would like to learn in order to fulfill the goals they have set for themselves; 5. the criteria they set for themselves as signs of success of the program they have chosen.[17] Among other tools, the students receive enrichment lessons on various ways of study and on how to accompany them.

The third year is the year of production: During this year the students formulate the educational venture which they would like to carry out, by studying the principles of social-educational initiative. The learning program during this year deals with three main subjects: the first – how to turn the educational idea into an educational-strategic program; the second – educational-entrepreneurial economics and how to build a business plan for their venture; and the third – how to maintain cooperations with private and public establishments and with non-profit organizations from the third sector. Beyond processing the idea and receiving tools for its production, each student is required to operate a "pilot" of the production, i.e. to put part of it into actual operation and to evaluate its activity.

The fourth year is the year of application: In the fourth year the application of the programs is carried out with accompaniment, in one of the schools or in other places.

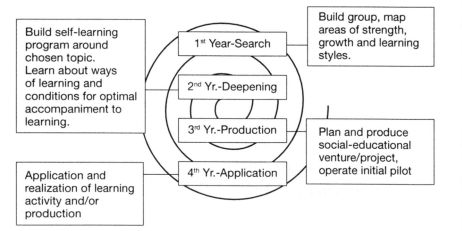

Build self-learning program around chosen topic. Learn about ways of learning and conditions for optimal accompaniment to learning.

1st Year-Search

2nd Yr.-Deepening

3rd Yr.-Production

4th Yr.-Application

Build group, map areas of strength, growth and learning styles.

Plan and produce social-educational venture/project, operate initial pilot

Application and realization of learning activity and/or production

At the personal level, we have discovered over the years that the students simply go through their own personal stories as soon as they are enabled to do so, and from their narrative into production of initiative. A student who had had cancer in her youth, and therefore had given up dancing, went back to dancing during her time in the Incubator, deepened her interest in dance although she was studying sciences, and eventually taught dancing at the oncology ward at a children's hospital. During that time she also helped the children complete studies in biology, as she explained their various illnesses to them.

A student with a learning difficulty that had greatly affected her life discovered her areas of strength in the Incubator; and when she became a teacher she opened a center for LD students in her school. A student, who had grown up in a home with a secular mother and a religious father, founded a mixed Scouts group. Another student who entered the world of hi-tech started a company for the development of educational software, and a student who is a D.J. at parties now also teaches history using music relevant to the messages he wishes to convey.

Part of the Incubator process is accompanied by participation in a center for pedagogic initiative and development, which gives the student tools for developing initiative and gets students and alumni together for cooperative educational creation and initiative. A student who had deepened her study of pre-school children met with a student who had established a non-profit organization, and together they founded a democratic kindergarten which went on to become an entire network. During the Students' Strike of 2007, the Kibbutzim College had no representatives in the Student Union to lead the struggle. In the Entrepreneuring Incubator, a group from the central forum got together and decided to have a study day about the strike. Over half of the students attended the study day, while their friends were spending a day at the beach, and they quickly set up work teams and discussion circles that created great cooperation of students in processes of decision making regarding the strike, and the lack of agreement to leave everything in the hands of Student Union representatives. Different students cooperated in this endeavor, and following this experiment the "Center for Participatory Democracy", which activates students in a variety of schools, was founded.

The intention of the Incubator is to develop capabilities of independent learning, curiosity, creativity and the courage to grow as an initiator and an educator. The Incubator facilitates human interaction, which accompanies these processes of personal and educational growth and development of the students. The basic assumption is that an educator, who has gone through this kind of learning process, can help his own students through it as well.

The idea of the Incubator is an essential innovation as opposed to parallel academic courses, particularly in two ways:

- Unlike programs dealing with the study of innovation using the old tools (lectures, exams, etc.), which lead to traditional learning experiences for students of teaching, this program enables three years of practical experience in pluralistic learning.
- Unlike the usual training course, which trains the student to be "an apprentice teacher in a school of veteran teachers", this program trains the student to be an ambassador of change and of promoting new initiatives in the world of education.

Regular studies for the B.Ed. are conducted parallel to the work of the Incubator. Their contents were determined by the Council for Higher Education, and cannot be changed, but the teaching methods are suited to the approach of pluralistic learning and there is a social emphasis on the contents themselves.

Recently, we began operating the idea of the Incubator as a program for personal development, with no connection to the academic field – democratic education as a lifelong journey. To our satisfaction, adults report experiences similar to those undergone by students of democratic schools on their personal journeys to discovery of their areas of strength and growth.

The students' community of this course met our expectations and more. The course drew educators and social and environmental activists from all sectors of society, from various youth movements, hostels, boarding schools and more. 65% of the learners are men, average age 27. Beyond the division into Incubators, all of the students, throughout the three years of study, are partners in bi-weekly community meetings in the framework of the studies. At these community meetings the students offer a variety of workshops on subjects that interest them – areas regarding their own worlds, local current events or subjects connected with their study experience. Some ten workshops are offered simultaneously, and students from all years of study choose what is relevant for them. These community meetings create a connection between students from different years of study around shared interests. The connections are created initially for study, and later – for cooperative initiatives.

One of the first initiatives created by the students of the Incubator and its graduates was the "Pioneer Program" in Givat Olga, with the Democratic School at its center.

"Givol" – The Democratic School in Givat Olga

Nineteen years after the establishment of the Democratic School of Hadera, I found myself returning to work in my home town, where I still lived. During the end-of-year party in the Democratic School, the mayor of Hadera, Haim Avitan, suggested I "stop saving the world and come back to Hadera". I said immediately that if I were to come back to Hadera, it would be for the purpose of establishing a new school in Givat Olga. We shook hands – and got started. Givat Olga is the western neighborhood of Hadera, located on the seashore. It has 11,000 residents, 60% of whom are immigrants from Ethiopia and the Caucasus Mountains, and it is socio-economically the weakest neighborhood in the area. I was born in Givat Olga, and so for me it was a "return home" to an exciting challenge.

A group of students and graduates of the Incubator were "turned on" by the idea. We began thinking together what the school in Givat Olga would look like.

Today (2008), the school in Givat Olga has been active for three years.

The Democratic School in Givat Olga signals a new and exciting direction. This is because the last twenty years have been leading up to it, twenty years in which democratic education in Israel was born and developed. (See the third clause of this chapter on democratic education and social thinking). Several central changes enabled this:

1. The change from socio-economically strong groups who could afford democratic education – to free democratic education for all.
2. From a democratic school with a uniform and a determined ideology, which says "either you accept the ideas or you look for a different educational framework", to a democratic school which can contain many educational ideologies. A democratic school which can absorb all families and all individuals.

3. From a school with one central goal – to put "the student at the center", to a school with two central goals – one personal: the self-realization of each student; the second social: development and advancement of the community and environment in which the school works.

In the Democratic School in Givat Olga, for the first time, the studies cost no more than the fee to the Ministry of Education (some 300 NIS a year).

A school day goes on till 4:00 PM and includes lunch.

Every student has a personal learning program built by himself, his personal advisor and his parents (who also determine the amount of choice given to their child). There are families who decide that all school subjects will be elective, while others choose that all will be mandatory, and still others let the child choose some of his subjects while others are mandatory.

At the heart of the educational idea is pluralism. The students learn that different families have different outlooks and that they can respect and accept the differences.

In any case, the creation of a personal learning program obligates the parents to get off "automatic pilot" and create their own educational credo for their child. The advisor, by definition, is not neutral. He should try to influence the learning program so that it will develop through the student's areas of strength and growth.

At the community level, the school is managed by

democratic educational frameworks as in every other democratic school.

The school is part of a broader program, the "Pioneer Program" in Givat Olga.

The "Pioneer Program"

In the Israeli narrative, pioneering is related to the Pioneers of the time before the establishment of the State – groups of young people that settled in undeveloped areas, motivated by a vision. Great obstacles, natural and man-made, were put before them, but they were undeterred, and by such heroic acts as "drying the swamps" and "conquering the wilderness", which today are metaphors synonymous with fulfilling dreams, not only dried the swamps but created a new culture. For example, the "Hadera Commune" operated in Hadera in 1909, and formed the pioneer group which founded Degania, the first Kibbutz.

We would like to see the "Pioneer Program" as a continuation of the way of those first pioneers. The "swamps of the 21st century" are the areas of poverty and distress in the State of Israel. A group of some twenty "Pioneers", graduates and students of the Entrepreneuring Incubator in the Kibbutzim College, went to live in Givat Olga. The goal is that the neighborhood should become the "Degania" of the 2000's, developing a "new Israeli culture" in whose center are education systems, culture, occupation and environmental development, operating on the principles of democratic education.

I see a "new Israeli culture" as a culture based on developing cooperation and mutual guarantees, to advance:

1. Personal and professional development of all residents of the town.
2. Development of the quality of life in the town, including its social, environmental and economic life. This development utilizes the areas of strength unique to the region.
3. A view of Israeli culture as growing from a variety of roots (various cultures), recognition of the importance of this variety of roots and fostering roots that are weaker. An attempt to unite the different roots into a single uniform root, strong as it may be, will not hold up the tree in times of "strong winds".

As a result of this outlook, the group of pioneers does not operate only in the framework of the Democratic School, but also in frameworks of informal educational, welfare and employment in Givat Olga. For example:

- The "Circle Program" – a neighborhood time bank. Children help children according to the principle that every student is both a teacher and a student (Yael's project in the "Incubator").

- Development of community gardens involving all residents of the neighborhood and encouraging them to take responsibility for their close surroundings (Assaf's project in the "Incubator")

- Conducting a program of study and events emphasizing Ethiopian or Caucasian culture, to which many of the school's children belong

- The "Stories of Olga" – a program initiated by the "Key Stories" organization, which works with the community near the school, collecting stories from the different communities in Givat Olga and publishing them in books.

- Developing a neighborhood employment center, whose goal is to create new places of employment, through education for business initiatives for the residents and through encouraging various business factors to work within the neighborhood.

- Developing a library, computer center, circus, technical center for repairing bicycles, music center and other centers that are open in the morning to the school and in the afternoon to the general public of the community.

The essential change we are aiming for is that at least half of the "educational pioneers", who moved to Givat Olga and are working as educators at the school, will continue and become principals in the general education system, so that every year ten "pioneers" will become school principals in various parts of the country. In other words, the school is not only an educational framework focused on the community in which it operates, but also an incubator for future educational leadership (and perhaps political and public leadership as well) of Israel (think about it – in ten years some 100 educators from the school will be school principals throughout the country).

The school in Givat Olga and the Pioneer Program as a whole aroused considerable interest in the Israeli media. Immediately upon its establishment, dozens of intellectuals, media people and economists hurried to make contact. Some had decided to teach as volunteers in the school, and some donated their time and money. Professor Yuli Tamir, the Minister of Education, decided to adopt this educational model and even to give it a full budget from the Ministry of Education, and in addition, to examine the possibilities of trying it out in other weaker neighborhoods throughout the country. The feeling was that the school was on the map of educational events at a time when Israeli society was ready to adopt it.

From a Single School to an Entire Town

In the summer of 1999 I was invited by a group of parents from Mitzpe Ramon for consultation on the subject of establishing a democratic school in the town. I took my whole family down for a weekend in the desert. Parents from Mitzpe Ramon toured the town with me and on Saturday night I had a conversation with the residents. I was surprised to see that some 200 people came to this meeting – parents, school principals, the head of the council and others. They expected to hear reasons to found a democratic school there. To their surprise, after two days in the town, I had arrived at a different conclusion – in Mitzpe Ramon it would be better to work with the community as a whole rather than focusing on one school.

This conclusion stemmed from the impression I received of the town that weekend. Mitzpe Ramon has some 5700 residents. It is isolated and distant from other settlements, and unusually heterogeneous: its population is comprised of veterans who immigrated from North Africa in the 1950's, most of them religious and traditional; of a large group of new immigrants from the CIS, who immigrated in the 1990's; of a group of career army officers, some of whom see the place as their temporary home; of people from fields of nature and ecology, who came to work in their fields in the area of the Big Crater; of "urban refugees", most of them artists and alternative therapists, who were searching for a better quality of life and the chance to create a new kind of community; of religious students of the high school and college-level Yeshiva in town, whose lives revolved around their religious studies; of "Hebrews" – an Afro-American community within the town; and of Bedouins of the area, who also use the schools of Mitzpe Ramon.

I thought that if every community within the small town were to establish its own school, their alienation and the lack of communication among them would only deepen. On the other hand, here was an opportunity to create a multicultural Israeli community. If we could find common ground and create this kind of community, it could shed light on other possible solutions for the crises tearing apart Israeli society as a whole today.

I shared my thoughts with the people there, fearful that the meeting would end there, and that perhaps they would even be angry with me for failing to keep my promise to advise them on establishing a new democratic school. However, at the end of the evening the head of the council, Dror Dvash, told me I had given him food for thought, and asked me to come for an urgent meeting with him. In parallel to this, the parents who had invited me were enthusiastic about the new idea of including the entire community in the change, and said they were ready to make great efforts to promote it.

A week later I met with the head of the council, and he asked for more details of the program. As always, I explained that I had no program. I suggested convening a first meeting of core figures who would discuss the educational plan for Mitzpe Ramon, which would gradually be conveyed to the entire community. It was decided that the first core would be the school principals of the town. At that time there were six educational institutions: the "Ramon" Elementary School, the "Shalom" High School, a boarding school of the arts, a religious democratic elementary school, an environmental high school Yeshiva, and a state-run religious elementary school.

At the first meeting, the principals strongly opposed what they called "another program being foisted on us". They attacked the head of the council, who was proposing still another program in addition to those the Ministry of Education had "dumped" on them. I said that for the first time, they had an opportunity to create a program for the community of Mitzpe Ramon that would be suited to the place as they saw fit, rather than importing an existing program.

During our discussion, I could feel a change taking place within me – I had intended to send guides from the Institute to work in the town, and now I found myself promising the principals that if they joined the process, I would join them myself. The idea of the democratic community in Mitzpe Ramon aroused great interest and enthusiasm in me (using the terminology of Chapter 3, I had entered a new circle of learning), and indeed, I began to visit Mitzpe Ramon for a day or two every week, to work with the principals and other members of the community.

A Town-wide Learning Community

The year 2002 was the third year of my activity in Mitzpe Ramon. During the two previous years, I worked with various factors in the town: the head of the council, directors of various departments in the local authority, school principals, teachers, parents and many other residents. Gradually we created a fascinating educational program, directed towards the town's unique needs and utilizing the special resources that are there in the area, offered to its guests.

Although our activity in Mitzpe Ramon concluded,

due to reasons which will be detailed later, I decided to tell about it. This is the fascinating story of a town taking responsibility for determining its life style, while implementing principles of democratic education.

The story begins with many of the locals defining Mitzpe Ramon as a "train station" – a place people pass through, not one where they stay. I interviewed some of those leaving, and was surprised to discover that most of them still loved the town and felt they belonged there. The education system took second place in their reasons for leaving, right after employment.

Since the population of the town is so varied, it contains a great variety of educational philosophies. This situation creates a "structured dissatisfaction" within the different populations in the town, in some cases leading to the dissatisfied family's leaving. "Structured dissatisfaction" means that because it is a small town, the number of formal education systems is limited, and have difficulty meeting such a variety of needs.

After a long period of meetings between different communities in the town, a vision for the town's education system was set:

- Creating an innovative education system which sees Mitzpe Ramon as a town-wide learning community.
- Giving a response to all the different populations in the community.
- Utilizing and expanding the existing learning resources in town.

- Creating a model, on a national level, of a groundbreaking education system in the field of working with towns in the periphery, to make them a magnet for new residents.

The first challenge in this work was establishing a system which would enable every student to excel in his chosen area, by creating a personal learning program, focused on the areas of growth and of strength of each student. After some time, we realized that we would never succeed in this mission if we addressed only the frameworks of schools existing in the town. It was clear that the schools could not offer a response to all the unique needs of each and every student.

Thus, the idea emerged of harnessing all the town's resources for the purpose of expanding the school systems. At the time, Mitzpe Ramon had 44 artists' workshops, an astronomy observatory, the "Hai Ramon" zoological garden, laboratories for the study of the desert that belonged to Ben-Gurion University, and many other regional learning resources. It was decided to create, in ordered fashion, learning programs to be operated in town-wide learning centers.

Every student in the Mitzpe Ramon school system would have a school-based program (mandatory – in accordance with the core program of the Ministry of Education) and a personal learning program (elective). In the framework of the "personal program", the student could use the external systems existing in the town.

The goal of the personal learning program was, as always – to strengthen the student's capability for learning through engagement in his personal areas of strength and growth. In order to support the "town centers", it was decided to establish a branch of one of the academic teachers' colleges in the town, with around 100 students who would assist in the initial operation of the centers. At this stage we could no longer avoid the question of funds. Students' learning in the artists' workshops, or in the other learning centers to be set up, would cost the local authorities money. How could it be done? How could the budget be enlarged?

At this point we understood that the educational program had to be expanded and become a comprehensive economic plan, with a completely new angle. This was the idea:

In Mitzpe Ramon there is an average of 1000 overnight lodgers per night, and there is a great potential to turn it into "the national capital of desert tourism" and perhaps even into an international center for this field. However, this potential has not been realized: there are few jobs, mostly because the tourists may stay over in the town but they operate in the desert.

We hoped to make a change, so that the travelers would stay in the town and use the "learning centers" as a part of their vacation. Each center would provide subsidized services for the education system, and in return they would receive marketing services from the community, which would refer tourists to them.

For example, an "open kitchen", which would be a "learning center" for the residents of Mitzpe Ramon (students and adults), would also be an authentic restaurant for the travelers in the desert.

I call this mode of action "**mixing colors**". When one paints in red, the color remains red, even if one changes the painting technique (a change of more of the same). In order to create something new, one must mix different colors. Focusing only on education will leave the system in similar conditions as it is at present, or, at best, will cause a limited change. Similarly, focusing on employment alone will yield solutions that are similar to the existing conditions. "Mixing colors" means seeing the town as a single organic unit, and thus reaching "groundbreaking" solutions, which would be impossible to obtain with "one color" alone. Making the connections between education and all the other factors working in the town, such as employment, urban planning and building, welfare, etc., created a new and colorful picture.

In 2004, the work of the Institute in Mitzpe Ramon was discontinued. The head of the council who had led the process was not re-elected (because of controversy which had nothing to do with the educational process), and the new one, who saw us as being under the previous head's auspices, discontinued the process.

To our surprise, the vision began to show independence. Educators in the town continued on their own to promote the ideas we had begun to develop in the program. We could say that we discovered that the vision can be greater than the sum of all its parts.

The Future Center

The "mixing of colors" in Mitzpe Ramon occurred almost intuitively, as a result of the development of out relations with the place. During our last year of work there an idea began to form, to establish an organization whose role would be to create an ongoing, planned "mixing of colors", i.e. a body which would see this approach as a central motif and not as chance. We called this body a "**Future Center**" – a physical, organizational, community space at the disposal of all the residents (from all ages and groups) and organizations operating in the town, to create a town-wide vision operating according to principles of a "sustainable community". In other words, the plans would not focus on shortsighted politics of limited interest, but would stem from long term considerations to advance the area. In addition to the vision, the goal of the center was to create a civil system of decision making, connected to the local council's process of decision making. The residents are the ones who formulate the center and are responsible for its contents. At the end of the process, in Mitzpe Ramon they gave up on the establishment of the center (perhaps because in a small community, one can uphold the principles of the Future Center without actually establishing a physical center).

Following our work in Mitzpe Ramon, several towns

turned to us asking to develop town-wide programs with them. One of them was Be'er Sheva, the largest city in the South of Israel, the "capital of the Negev", with a population of 200,000 residents. There, for the first time, a Future Center was implemented.

We were asked to create a groundbreaking citywide program for the entire education system (40,000 students). In fact, the part of the program which actually was carried out was the Future Center. It was established in the "Settlement Teachers' Center", one of the central buildings in town, which turned from a teacher training building to a Future Center.

Yael Schwartzberg (director of the Institute for Democratic Education) and Ron Dvir, who were enthusiastic about the Future Center, began to study the idea in various areas of innovation throughout the world, and in parallel to develop a unique model in Israel which, as mentioned, was first founded in the center for developing teaching staffs in Be'er Sheva, by the director Haya Avni.

The components of the center include:

1. A place for discourse of "mixing colors" – an opportunity for encounters that don't usually take place, among people from different fields. For example, in a discussion on science education in the South of Israel, there were educators, industrialists and researchers, discussing different ways to study sciences. This encounter between different

disciplines created a different process of decision making.

2. A "future museum" – where one can see future images of the contents that the Future Center deals with, presented visually and from a multidisciplinary angle, with relation to "assets of the region".

3. An "innovation laboratory" – a lab to accelerate innovation and initiative, through creative thinking, fruitful sharing of ideas among various factors in the town and outside it, developing and fostering of ideas, using pictures of the future as a source of inspiration, and "matchmaking" between ideas and resources.

4. A "learning center" for the development of training programs for teachers, in keeping with the picture of the future created by the center.

Today, the center serves as a central tool for developing and implementing educational innovation in all the education systems in the south of the country.

The Bat Yam Personal Education Model

During my work in Be'er Sheva I met a very special person – Albert Assaf, the former Deputy Mayor of Dimona and today a representative of the Sakta-Rashi Foundation.

In the fall of 2003, Albert asked me to come with him to Bat Yam. "There's a mayor there that you should meet. I think he is the mayor you're looking for", he said.

Albert was right. At the first meeting in Shlomi Lahiani's office, I saw a completely different picture than what I had known before. From my experience in meetings with mayors, the participants would quickly "close ranks" with whatever the mayor said, applaud and nod enthusiastically. In Lahiani's office I saw young, energetic people (directors and assistant directors), disagreeing and even arguing with him. And Shlomi, with most charismatic leadership, navigated and created visions out of the many ideas emerging from completely open discussions.

I sat there impressed and then he turned to me and asked me to tell them about myself, and about democratic education. When I had finished speaking, he said that he, too, believed that every child was bringing something unique to the world, and that it was the duty of the education system to give this uniqueness expression. Shlomi Lahiani asked me a question that no mayor had ever asked me: Could an education system be created in which success at surfing would be a legitimate achievement?

I replied that this was exactly our work at the Institute for Democratic Education. At that same meeting we decided to set out on our way together.

Bat Yam has 170,000 residents and about 20,000 students in its education system. We decided to work on an educational vision with the leading staff of the city. After several meetings devoted to vision – I realized that Bat Yam had set very high aspirations. At that time I read the articles coming out on "the small schools" revolution in the USA.

And thus, within a short time, there we were – Shlomi Lahiani, Esther Firon (the head of the Education Department), Nurit Ramati (the secondary schools Inspector), Sigal Peretz (Assistant Director of Community Affairs), Erez Podamsky (Assistant Director of Development), Albert Assaf and myself – on a plane to the USA, for a tour arranged for us by Prof. Michael and Susan Klonsky. The visit included the "MET" School in Providence, a meeting with Deborah Myer and David French at the "Pilot" schools in Boston, and a comprehensive tour of the small schools in Chicago.

We saw various models of schools. Some worked well, others less so. Meanwhile, we got to know each other very well and became a real team. In the discourse that went on among us during the tour, we gradually shaped the basic principles of the picture of the future we wanted for the city of Bat Yam.

The MET school and the meetings with Dennis Littky impressed us the most. When we arrived there on Monday morning, we were invited into a morning meeting of a small homeroom class. The group's teacher-advisor for the past six years, who was accompanying us, turned to every student and also to us, to ask how our weekend had been. It was heartwarming to see the group dynamics and the support they gave each other. This was especially impressive for us, remembering our selves as children in the regular school system, who enter their school on Sunday and go to one of the regular classes, math, English, etc., without anyone being interested or asking about their weekend.

Later on we discovered that twice a week, the students study in the framework of professional specialization in one of the public or private institutions in the area of the school. Each student chooses an area of interest and contacts an appropriate organization or business, and reaches an agreement with them that he would intern there for two days a week, and would be guided by one of the workers there. During the three days he was at school (a campus of 600 students, divided into six groups of 100), each student has a personal learning program that reinforces him in his chosen area of specialization.

The results for the MET school graduates are amazing. It operates in a community in which some 5% of the students continue on to higher education, and yet more than 90% of the MET students go on to college.

When we returned to Bat Yam, we did not intend to translate the programs we had seen into Hebrew. We wanted to gain inspiration from them, and to create a citywide program that would be appropriate for Israel and for Bat Yam – and thus we developed the Bat Yam Personal Education Model of, one of the only citywide programs I know which are actually in operation and not just written down. The model was designed with the participation of all the educational staff of the city, including all the Ministry of Education inspectors, headed by Tzila Sheffer, all the school principals, the municipal education staff and representatives of the Sakta-Rashi Foundation.

The program is designed so that each class (in junior and senior high school) is divided into two homeroom groups of 15-18 students.

Every group/class in town (elementary schools included) meets during the first hour of the morning for a "morning session". Each group has an educator (someone in the field of education), who receives for this activity expanded hours (about a third of a position in junior and senior high school and extra hours in elementary school). In this way we created a new balance of working hours for the teacher (who previously focused only on his particular discipline), with the possibility to talk to and get to know the students there before him. We returned education to the field of teaching.

The personal education program in Bat Yam realizes the perception that each student is a person with unique talents and needs. The goal of the program is to give a personal-familial response for every student in the town, to enable him to realize the unique potential within him.

In the "morning session" each student builds his own personal learning program, in whose framework he sets himself goals in the learning, family and social areas, and in the field of excellence – a particular area in which the student has chosen to excel.

This personal learning program sees the student as a part of the family and social surroundings in which he lives. For this there must be cooperative work between the education systems (formal and informal) and the welfare systems. The goal of this cooperation is to create a store of resources among all the services given to the student and his family by the city. In this way a circle of new solutions is created, to be presented continuously for every specific problem or subject that emerges during the work.

An example of these solutions are the learning centers which support personal learning contracts, which began to operate in schools during the school day and continue after it, centers in which students can receive help in various areas mentioned in their personal contracts.

Another example is the "Stars" program, created during our second year of activity, in which 100 students were located in the city who needed more intensive personal mentoring and aid in finding their areas of personal strength. These students were provided with personal advisors, besides the educators of the homeroom groups.

Today, about three years after the beginning of our work, one can say that the program is fulfilling our expectations. Academic achievements have risen, mostly because the students' motivation has increased.

Violence in school has decreased by more than 70%. We learned that even the boys and girls, described as most violent, created strong ties with the educator, discovered their areas of strength and gave it expression in the framework of school activity. Their violent behavior disappeared.

And what especially makes us happy, is that local pride has grown immeasurably. When we began, some two thirds of the students reported that they did not reveal in public where they live. Today 97% of the students report that they are proud to say they are from Bat Yam. At the beginning of 2008, the program "Bat Yam Model for Personal Education" won the National Education Prize, and the Minister of Education, Professor Yuli Tamir, adopted the model as part of her comprehensive educational reform "New Horizon" in junior high schools.

The main question facing us today is whether the success in Bat Yam can be duplicated. Can these ideas of democratic education be carried out on a national level? I hope that in a few years I will be able to write a book answering this question.

As to the question of how Bat Yam, Be'er Sheva, Mitzpe Ramon or Givat Olga will look in the future, my answer is clear and unequivocal – I don't know. Every education system or other public system – whatever the ideas that guide it are – depends chiefly on people, on their ability to lead others in change, to adjust to change or oppose it. The people who are leaders in those places in the future (see the case of Rogozin) will decide the fate of the processes of change (and sometimes the decision is to return to the conservative-traditional model of schooling). Therefore, what is presented here is limited by the time and space in which I write it. And yet, the stories of these places mark for me the possible directions to take in creating democratic culture in the communities in which we live.

Part Three
Thoughts on Social Aspects of Democratic Education

On Elitism and Democratic Education

When we began, there was no channel within the establishment for founding unique schools in Israel, and every group had to clear its own path. Only religious or ultra-religious groups received permits to establish unique schools. As for secular groups, the assumption of the Ministry of Education was that they were all alike, and therefore the educational response was already existent within the state-run education system. In recent years, groups of secular citizens throughout the country are requesting recognition of their right to be different. Their claim is that the secular, just like the religious, are not a homogeneous group. In our meetings with government representatives, we attempted to make our conditions equal to those of the religious citizens of Israel, so that we too could express our different philosophies of life within the education system.

Parents that set out on this struggle were attacked

severely by the establishment, who made harsh claims against the way of democratic education:

1. These are wealthy parents who are thinking only of their own children and want an elitist education system, which ignores trends towards integration and is creating an infrastructure for private schools in Israel.

2. These parents are abandoning accepted Israeli values and life styles, for the spirit of globalization. Children in alternative schools will never be a part of Israeli culture, because they will not be required to learn its components, such as literature and history.

3. Democratic education breeds individualists who will never take the surrounding society into consideration: "Why should Israeli society invest in people who will never contribute to it?"

4. Democratic education is a small and insignificant stream, and therefore need not be taken into consideration.

As the Chinese saying goes, even a journey of 1000 miles begins with one small step. I also read an interesting saying in Tom Peters's website: "Every great idea began with a single believer."[18]

I would like to add that that same single believer, who took the first step, was probably considered an elitist, separated from those around him.

Almost all large-scale social revolutions began with

groups that we would today call elitist (such as those who fought to advance democracy, socialism, human rights, women's rights, environmental quality, etc.). A similar phenomenon can be seen in the development of democratic education. The first democratic schools had to take money from parents, as the state did not support them at all. Today, democratic education is active in weaker neighborhoods and in development towns, and has considerable effect on the entire education system.

The interesting point is that the expansion of democratic education towards weaker or more varied populations is already contained in its ideological core. This expansion, which I will discuss later, is no accident and certainly does not stem from "pressure from the establishment" or from any desire to be in their good graces. On the contrary, the idea of education directed towards pluralistic values, rather than towards competition over uniform achievements, is one that includes broad and varied publics. In complete opposition to conservative education, **we believe that we are able to give expression to the ability found in every child, in every human being, from any social stratum or area of the country, to reach his areas of strength and to fulfill his personal goals.**

In complete opposition to elitist or interest-related approaches, the people who led the first groups of democratic education acted from mainly social motives. Their goal was to create a change within the education system in Israel, by changing it into a pluralistic system recognizing human diversity. Such a system opposes the social stratification present in schools – groups of the strong (mostly from higher socio-economic levels), medium and weak students. Most of those pioneers, who went to establish various models of democratic education, were fed up with trying to change the system from within. Some of them were stopped even before they began to try, with the argument that they were not part of the system (parents or people not employed by the Ministry of Education), and some (people within the system) began to make changes and were blocked with the argument that they "had crossed the line". They were stopped at a considerable distance from implementing their beliefs, because of the way the system was supposed to work.

The only way left to these pioneers was independent action and creation of a living model of a school in the spirit of their belief. They certainly did not take these steps out of economic motives, but only out of the desire to create an education system that would suit their perception: the existence of a pioneer education system in Israel, that would form the basis for a society which upholds democratic culture and devotes considerable emphasis to empowering Israeli society, by giving place to personal and social diversity within it.

Those, who continue the way of the pioneers today, refuse to send their children automatically to the school in the neighborhood. They thoroughly investigate the kind of education that suits them and eventually choose schools that have dropped out of the blind race for matriculation and "living on a tightrope above the abyss" (see Chapter 3). This in-depth investigation involves a renewed journey in search of values, and entrance into a process of learning that poses great social question marks. During their search, many discover the social issue and form their world perception around it. Another interesting phenomenon in this area is the participation of veteran social activists, who once opposed democratic education because they feared it was not in keeping with their outlook. They joined after they had examined the idea and found that it held special possibilities for advancement of social issues.

There are also parents who exploit the founding of democratic schools as an attempt to create strong socio-economic groups and islands of parental control. First, they are exploiting the situation created by the Ministry of Education, which forces some of the democratic schools to take tuition from parents (by not giving those schools the allocations which every child in Israel has the right to receive). **It is important to clarify that a democratic school seeks to obtain free education for all, as an integral part of the implementation of human rights.**

Second, those parents generally drop out of the democratic education system later on, because this system empowers the Parliament (in which everyone has the right to vote), rather than just those who are economically strong. These groups of parents generally struggle to change the democratic "rules of the game" into the usual rules which have given them an advantage over weaker groups. In such situations, the school enters a period of discussions and disputes, in which the more social-democratic side usually wins. Such a process usually strengthens the school.

There are people, particularly within the political-educational system, who seek to block the "single believer" before he takes his first step. This is because of the feeling that he is threatening them. I believe it is this feeling of threat that underlies all the kinds of opposition to the idea of democratic education.

The threat is that we may actually be right about the idea we are struggling for. Perhaps an education system can be created in which violence decreases drastically, one in which every child finds his areas of strength and growth, and later comes to see them in others. And if we are right – perhaps they have been wrong all along, and after all, we have been taught at school that a mistake is something bad, that should be hidden.

The education system does not look favorably on the process of privatizing schools by economically strong parents, through the creation of unique schools. The system sees this as a central factor in creating social gaps in Israel. A second cause of these gaps, they perceive, is money that is supposed to go to weak students and "miraculously" ends up going to strong students from well-off levels of society.

The claim that unique schools are working to privatize the system is a bit odd, as the State of Israel – the only democratic country which does not enable private education – is the leader of the Western world in social gaps and parallel gaps in academic achievement. If we look at a social state such as Denmark, we see that it encourages founding unique schools by parents, and sees it as a factor that strengthens its education system. How is it that democratic education groups all over the world are perceived as groups of social reform, while in Israel, democratic education is perceived as a privatizing, gap-creating force?

My answer to this is that Israel is still suffering from the childhood ills of over-centralization by the establishment. Any distribution of power, that is considered legitimate in the Western world, is perceived here as crossing all the lines, particularly those of the ones in power today. They have created the sad reality we see, and use us as a scapegoat – the democratic education (25 schools) is responsible for the sorry condition of the education system...

And as for the issue of funds meant for weak populations being allocated to the stronger ones: a quick glance at the schools in weaker areas shows us that in those very schools which are measured chiefly by the numbers of matriculants among their students, funds meant for the weakest students are, as a matter of course, shifted to those with the greatest chances for success at matriculation.

One must therefore ask why the democratic schools, whose main goal is not a certificate of matriculation but rather the human dignity and independence of every child, are considered an elitist group.

Social Education Requires Leaving the "Stratifying Square"

If, when mentioning pluralistic learning, I spoke of the immense damage to students living in "the square", what I have said is even truer for students from a low socio-economic stratum. For affluent families can assure that their children will be on "the better part" of a normal curve.

I know wonderful people doing sacred educational work, who do not accept my ideas. They believe that increasing public resources and proper educational work will lead the students of weak socio-economic strata to high "square" achievements. But the main question I must ask is "what purpose will these achievements serve?", particularly in comparison with the achievements of more affluent sectors.

The present situation is that the combination of a public budget and the budget of an affluent family will always be better than that of a socio-economically weaker family (even with considerable affirmative action). To clarify, I will put this more radically – Even if all the schools in North Tel Aviv are closed, their students will still achieve higher scores in matriculation than their counterparts in development towns. This is because the whole idea of matriculation was created to serve the ideas of social stratification. The "Northern" student will always have at his disposal (from his parents) a greater sum of money than what will come from the government and the third sector to a student in a development town.

Matriculation can be compared to a short blanket (ideologically) that will never cover all of your body; when one's head is covered his feet stick out and when his feet are covered his head is not. Thus I find it strange that people wonder: How is it that the (socio-economically) stronger ones are always covered?!

Have they forgotten that this is precisely why they created the blanket? The role of the matriculation itself is to create an alleged academic threshold, which stratifies us at age eighteen, deciding who the 50% of the population are who are unworthy of an academic course of life.

And to the observer from outside it looks like this: As soon as the average matriculation scores rises, the threshold of entrance to university will also be raised. While funds are allocated to raise matriculation scores in Yeruham, and the grades rise, funds will be discontinued in Ofakim and the grades will fall (in North Tel Aviv this will have no impact), and on the day when everyone passes his matriculation, the "stratifying elites" will see to it that a matriculation certificate does not count, thus knitting a new short blanket.

And I must cry out: the emperor wears no clothes

– focusing on matriculation will never close the social gaps, but will only perpetuate them.

Democratic education refuses to take part in this race. It is a lost race, its outcome clear from the outset. We are offering a completely different perspective. Even the ninth child in a disadvantaged family, in a remote development town, has a unique talent, an unusual capability, something new to contribute to the world. It is hers alone and no one else's. Imagine her parents and teachers believing that. Imagine the State of Israel believing that, and turning over funds allocated for preparation for the matriculation, to the fulfillment of that belief.

Does "Education in the Square" Create a More Egalitarian Society?

Some claim that uniform state-run education (in the square) creates equal opportunities for the entire population and helps reduce gaps and stimulate social mobility. But it is difficult to find any research whose findings support this. In his book "The Limits and Possibilities of Schooling", Christopher J. Hurn writes:

The most disappointing thing, is that there is almost no proof that the increase in possibilities for education has helped to reduce the more obvious inequality among groups in terms of wages and access to more desired occupations.....there is almost no testimony that the chances for upward mobility of children from low economic status have increased in this century (the 20th century – Y. H.). For the lower and working classes there are now more chances to send their children to college, but this rise in educational options was not accompanied by a parallel rise in occupational status.[19]

Here we should again mention what Goleman stated in his book "Emotional Intelligence" – that there is no connection between academic success at the high school level, and any kind of future success in life (see Chapter 3).

In recent years, there have been some very significant changes in the education system, and there are almost no students whose entrance into secondary school education is prevented by economic difficulties or reasons of community, culture, gender or other. Yet these changes did not yield the expected outcomes. Children's social background and socio-economic status still determine their future. They fail (in generalization of course) in the social, educational and occupational competition as opposed to their friends. The main question is, can the schools create equal opportunities, or does their very role preserve the inequality among classes and communities?

The narrow "educational channel", which accompanies our children in their early years of life, is meant to create a filter through which the socio-economically strong will always have a great advantage in the uniform race marked by the education system. This is the "channel" created by the strong for the strong.

Democratic education, on the other hand, strives

to end the regime of capital. It offers to stop trying to develop gimmicks to push one's way into that same filtered channel, and to ask what is it for and where does it lead, and if the existence of one single channel is an unchangeable condition of education.

Democratic education offers to base education on many and varied channels, those which can be personally adapted for finding areas of personal strength and growth for every child. These channels will end the monopoly of the uniform channel, in order to cancel the preservation of power in the hands of the socio-economically strong.

If the goal of success in standard exams (like the Meitzav elementary school standard exam and matriculation exams) – which in recent years have become the main activity of the education system – is replaced by a central attempt to find the areas of excellence for each child, there could be a social-education system which would see this excellence as the basis for the intellectual and professional development of the citizens of the future in a democratic egalitarian society (see Dewey in Chapter 3). Such a system would see its goal as the development of curiosity, and not as proving one's short-term memory capabilities. Such a system is taking its first steps in Bat Yam, in Givat Olga and in other places.

The Israeli education system, which is supposedly aware of the dangers in the social gaps existing in the country and has inscribed on its banner the idea of reducing these gaps, has over time succeeded in perpetuating and even worsening the situation. This is because of the central fallacy, according to which one must do more of the same (invest more in the capabilities of competition within the square). An inaccurate analysis of the factors causing the gap brings on a renewed version of the same system with the same mistakes – a system in which the student sees his peers, throughout his formal education, as rivals competing with him for the same limited resources. We suggest, on the other hand, new rules of the game, which see as the main goal the support for finding each participant's uniqueness.

The Social Vision

Democratic education has a social vision. Many believe that this vision is an unattainable utopia, but I believe that the possibilities of its realization are much closer than we think. It is a vision of a democratic country which adopts the goals of democratic education; a country which will be a pioneer among democratic countries.

I will try to articulate some groundbreaking goals for the realization of this vision:

1. To educate each person to be a lover of humankind.
2. To give equal opportunities to each child, to allow them to develop in their own way and to create an atmosphere that encourages and supports the other.
3. To develop an attitude of respect for human rights, for basic liberties, for democratic values, for upholding of the law and for the culture and views of the other,

and to educate for the striving towards peace and tolerance in relations among individuals and among nations.

4. To develop the personality of each child, their creations and various talents, to broaden their cultural horizons and to expose them to artistic experiences, all in the interest of their reaching their full potential as people living lives of quality and meaning.

5. To reinforce the students' powers of judgment and critical thinking, to foster intellectual curiosity, independent thinking and initiative and to develop awareness and alertness to changes and innovations.

6. To foster social involvement, contribution to the community, volunteering and striving for social justice.

For anyone who did not recognize the above, these are some of the goals of the Israeli education system (6 out of the 11 original goals) – the six educational goals of the Law of Education - the "goals of how". The missing goals are the "content goals" – the "goals of what" – (which democratic education also accepts, as long as they are carried out while upholding the other six).

Are you surprised?

All that is left to do is to try and implement the goals of education as they are put forth in the Law of Education. If we do that, we will turn the education system in Israel into a democratic education system at its best, and in my opinion – we will become the first society in the world to apply ideas of democratic culture in education.

History tells us that in great changes, words precede deeds. In Israel, the words directing us towards goals of democratic education are already there within the public education system. The deeds, too, have begun to be realized, and not only in schools which use terms of democratic education.

But like in every process of change that requires a separation from the old and familiar, this change is slow and painful. I believe that the Israeli uniqueness should be expressed in the creation of an education system different from the international education system, one that gives expression to the uniqueness of Israel. Yet, if we raise the banner of human dignity as a central and main goal of the education system in Israel, this uniqueness will serve as a light for the entire world.

To my surprise, during my visits in other countries around the world, I discovered similar situations in which there are progressive laws of education that are not being implemented in practice.

All that is left to do is to try and implement the goals of education as they are formulated in the laws of education.

I feel that the entire world is waiting for the country that will take the plunge first.

An education system that gives expression to its own cultural uniqueness and, at the same time, raises the banner of human dignity as its main and central goal, can lead the country that develops it to social and economic prosperity that will mark the appearance of the democratic culture in action.

Chapter Seven

The International Journey

The International Network of Democratic Education

My personal journey through the world of democratic education began, as has been told here, with an exciting encounter with A.S. Neill's book "Summerhill", about the Summerhill School in the UK. For a long time before the establishment of the school in Hadera, this book was the most prominent source for the ideas I formed. After establishing the school I met Danny and Hanna Greenberg, from the Sudbury Valley School in Framingham, near Boston. As I have already mentioned here, this was a chance meeting, which led to changes and new insights in all of our educational endeavors in Hadera. Our connections with Sudbury Valley developed and included exchanges of student and staff delegations. We developed some common thinking about the ideas fundamental to democratic education, through a view of the common and the different features of our ways.

In my work at the Democratic School of Hadera (I was 29 when it opened) I sometimes felt that I was alone in the world, taking hundreds of families with me down an unfamiliar path. It was a frightening feeling, but the encounter with the people from Sudbury Valley cheered me up considerably in this respect. I understood that there were other people in the world who had feelings similar to mine regarding what was going on in the conservative education system. Of course I had had this feeling before as well, but the daily life of running the school in Hadera took up most of my time. I was too busy to seek out partners on my path. The meeting with Danny and Hanna Greenberg and with Mimsy Sadofsky (founders of the Sudbury Valley School) lifted my spirits – I was not alone. Here are people who, for dozens of years, have been asking and investigating how to educate children who live in a democratic society.

At the same time (the early 1990's), many changes were taking place in the world: the Berlin Wall came down, Communism collapsed, US President Bill Clinton led new trends of thought, the Internet began to blossom and in Israel, it looked as if there might be a successful peace process. I believe it is no chance that during this very time, an opportunity came up that I later understood was what had led us to a fundamental change in the development of connections among people involved in democratic education throughout the world, and consequently led to the first international conference of democratic schools. This was a meeting which initially connected between schools that think differently and seek out freer ways of education, as an alternative to the existing educational conservativism. Later, the use of the terms "Democratic

School" and "Democratic Education" came into use outside of Israel as well, and the conference became a catalyst in the creation of the International Movement for Democratic Education.

The beginning of the process was when I was approached (almost by chance) by the Israeli Ministry of Education. I was asked if there were schools similar to the Hadera School elsewhere in the world. When I replied in the affirmative, I was asked to recommend central figures in the world of alternative education (in those days, the term "Democratic School" was not in use), in order to invite them to lecture at a large international congress to be conducted in Jerusalem in 1993, the initiative of the "Adam Institute". The congress's title was "MultiCulturalism in a Democratic Society". Here was an opportunity for me to organize all the familiar forces from that period into an international conference on the subject of democratic education. All the acquaintances I had made during that time responded to the invitation and arrived at the congress: Danny Greenberg, of Sudbury Valley; David Gribble, founder of the Sands School in the UK; Lotte Kreizler of Vienna, a teacher in an alternative school and a human rights activist; Jerry Mintz, director of AERO, an international information center for alternative education; and Fred Bay, head of the Bay Foundation which supported alternative education around the world. After the Jerusalem congress we moved on to a secondary conference at the Democratic School of Hadera. To this conference I invited staff members from Hadera, students and Israeli educators who were interested in the field. For three days we sat together and discussed subjects that occupied us all – the conditions in schools like ours around the world, the role of international relations among the schools, and also internal issues such as the connection between boundaries and freedom and the place of parents in the school. This brief meeting created a dire need for more such meetings. A clear sense of how they could strengthen us all was created, and by the end of the Hadera conference we had decided on a second conference at the Sands School in the UK one year later.

Since 1994 there have been two separate international conferences a year, dealing with democratic education: one is the annual conference which presents different and varied perceptions of democratic education in the world. This conference continues the tradition we began in 1993 in Hadera, and initially was called The International Conference of Democratic Schools, or the Hadera Conference. Following it, David Gribble began to publish a newsletter three times a year which kept all the conference participants updated. Later, in 1997, at the fifth conference, held at the Sands School, two students, who were among the organizers, proposed changing its name to IDEC – the International Democratic Education Conference. Their proposal was accepted, and this has been the name of the conference until today. The second conference is held every few years at the Sudbury Valley

School, and it brings together all the schools that operate according to this approach.

At the first four IDEC conferences (in Israel, The UK, Austria and Israel again) no fees were collected from the participants (except for their flight tickets, some of whose costs were defrayed by donations). The effort at organizing the conference was great, and fell on the shoulders of the hosting organization; however, since the fifth conference the participants pay a participation fee (as low as possible).

The number of IDEC participants has grown from year to year, from some 40 participants in the first year to about 1600 in the ninth conference, held in Japan in 2000. Today, representatives of some 30 countries and about 500 schools participate in IDEC.

IDEC today is one of the main conferences in the world for alternative education. It is conducted every year in a democratic school or other democratic organization throughout the world (as we give equal turns to all continents), which also determines the character of each conference. Till today the conference has taken place, among other places, in Israel, The UK, Austria, the Ukraine, Japan, New Zealand, the USA, India, Germany, Australia, Brazil and Canada.

Over the years, the conference developed characteristic patterns: it is a place for the meeting of staff members, students and parents of democratic schools with academics and policy makers in the field of democratic education and educational innovation from around the world. In addition, the conference combines discussions and lectures on democratic thought with the experience of life on an international campus, maintaining a framework of democratic life. Actually, the conference is usually divided into two parts – one is open to the general public and the other is for members of the democratic education community throughout the world – staff members, parents and students, who conduct an international campus where theoretical and practical activities go on in the framework of a democratic school.

I was very moved when Zoë, headmistress of Summerhill and the daughter of A.S. Neill, decided to host IDEC in 1999. She did this as part of Summerhill's struggle against the British Ministry of Education's decision to close down the school. The conference mobilized people from all over the world to support this struggle, and at last, after a long fight, the Supreme Court of England overturned the Ministry of Education's decision and pronounced Summerhill one of the leading schools of the British education system. For me this was coming full circle – to see how IDEC became, at Summerhill of all places, an international movement which could help its members all over the world.

Following these conferences and their publication in the world, many schools changed their definition. Schools which had formerly defined themselves as "open" or "alternative" changed their names, adopting the democratic viewpoint. Changing their names was significant, because language can determine new content and ways of thinking. The use of the concept "Democratic Education" enabled a clearer framework of thinking about the structure and management of a school, as opposed to the educational discourse which had had the ambiguous "free" or "open" at its center. "Democratic" is a discussed and researched concept in various fields, and points out the significance of an individual person as part of the community and surroundings where he lives, indicating a fixed structure of cooperative life.

The Central Question of Democratic Education Is: What Is the Right Education for an Individual in a Democratic Society?

This question takes us to a new and broad field, one in which we are not the only players (it includes educators, sociologists, economists, environmentalists and more). And in the festival of this interdisciplinary meeting we can contribute and benefit.

Of course, when we say democratic education, we do not only mean maintaining democratic procedures in a school, but first and foremost the democratic essence which is expressed in the safeguarding of human rights. The main profit from changing the name is the changing of the discourse from the field of alternative, relatively remote, to the main crossroads at which education meets social issues, economics, culture and other components of the society where we live. There, at those intersections, democratic education is gradually becoming an important and influential player. It indicates the need to conduct democratic culture in the framework of existing democratic countries, a need which forces us to think about education anew, from a democratic point of view.

Beyond changing the name, we see how the international conferences of democratic education have over the years created an encounter among people, ideas and initiatives, which have come from beyond the boundaries of free alternative education.

The IDEC conferences continue to travel the world, gradually drawing in more and more alternative education frameworks and regular public schools, which are discovering the world of democratic education. In addition, as a consequence of the international conferences, regional conferences have begun to be organized in order to encourage exposure to these ideas. In the summer of 2008, the first European Democratic Education Conference (EUDEC) was held. In parallel, regional meetings are taking place in Asia and in the Pacific. Additional schools around the world, who have not gotten to international conferences, are implementing these same ideas to one extent or another, and I hope we will be able to connect with them in the future.

To the outside observer, the common line connecting the various schools coming to IDEC is not always clear. An American educator, a woman whom I greatly respect, told me that she would not come to a conference because many of its participants do not think as she does. I replied that it was precisely this reason that brings me back to the conference each year. Most of the year I work and operate with people who think like me, trapped in the formulas we have created. IDEC grants me an opportunity to meet other opinions, and to rethink all that I had been taking for granted. There, I learned what my greatest mistakes had been. In my opinion, what all the people coming to IDEC have in common is the attempt to implement human rights in various frameworks, by using democratic tools.

Although the ways of implementing democratic education are many and varied, I shall attempt to present an updated picture of what is going on in the world.

In Asia
Japan
The first Asian country to host IDEC was Japan, in 2000. It is not by chance that Japan was the first – Japan has a long tradition of sending students to study in the West, particularly English and Western culture. Many students came from Japan over the years to study at Summerhill, and thus, gradually, ideas of democratic-free education made their way to Japan.

In the 1960's and 70's there began to spring up frameworks of free education in Japan. At first these frameworks were few and far between, but during the early 1990's the democratic education system began growing rapidly, and there are now some 40 schools there. The democratic education system in Japan focuses chiefly on those children who are defined as "school-refusing children", children who were expelled from high schools and are not meant to go on to university. As far as the regular education system is concerned, such an academic failure is considered a failure in life, and it can mean students' suicide out of shame to the family. By establishing a large network of democratic schools, the democratic education system offers these students the possibility of achievement in non-academic fields, and recently a democratic university was established (Shura), which is a significant milestone in democratic education's journey into the academic world. The university is headed by Kageki Asakura, a warm and courageous person, and it is part of the Shura Democratic School Network, led by Keiko Okuchi. In the Japanese model, each student chooses to specialize in a field that interests him, with the accompaniment of a volunteer mentor (a high-level expert in that area). At the end of the learning process, the mentor gives the student a letter of recommendation with which he can begin working either in existing frameworks in that area or in a venture the student himself has developed.

At the same time, at Shura University there are various activities which require a variety of skills. Take, for example, an annual project of building a solar-powered car, involving an interdisciplinary team of students. One is an expert mechanic, another, an expert in design, and another in marketing. Each student connects to the project through his field of expertise. Presently, the first Shura graduates are going out into the world, and the university has begun to think of creating a model of a community that will connect among all the alumni and present students, giving them support. As we said, the IDEC conference in Japan was considered the largest ever held. In its framework, most of those involved in democratic education in the West were first exposed to the surprising extent of democratic education activity in Asia in general and in Japan in particular.

Korea

In Korea, a large network of over 100 alternative schools have been formed, half of which operate with a democratic approach. Some are for students who have dropped out of regular schools, while others are regular schools which have created alternative tracks to success. Their great response stems from the fact that the conventional course of study in Korea is highly intensive and competitive. The 2009 IDEC conference will be held in Korea.

India

In India, the IDEC conference was held in 2004. It was run by Amukta Mahapatra, headmistress of "Abacus", a Montessori school. Ms. Mahapatra founded an organization called Concern for Working Children (CWC) and as a consequence began to take interest in democratic education. At the conference, we (the Western participants) discovered active social-democratic education, growing rapidly all over India, a widespread phenomenon unlike anything we have seen in other countries. The approach characterizing most of the initiatives presented at that conference was the use of pluralistic leaning tools and processes of democratic management.

The central question occupying the educators of India is how to develop an educational system that would be active and relevant to street children and working children (they claim that India has over 100,000,000 such children), who do not come to existing schools at all, most of which operate with a conservative British structure. The educators came to the conclusion that in order to be relevant for these children, a school must deal with subjects connected to their survival, such as commerce, economics and various trades, rather than teaching Latin. Therefore, democratic educators in India began to operate frameworks that would enable the children to choose from subjects that were close to them. Recently, they have noticed that the young children prefer to learn from older children. They speak about teacher-advisors aged 16-17 who work with younger children, where the subjects are determined together. Several models were presented at the conference, in which the children are involved in decision making and in protection of the rights of children who work in their areas. In the framework of one of these model ("Butterfly"), the children run a "street bank" whose purpose is to help the working children save and protect their money.

Thailand

(Nao) Saowanee Sangkara and Jim Connor have founded in Thailand one of the most fascinating centers of democratic education in the world – "Whispering Seed". This is an orphanage which runs on principles of democratic education and sustainability. In addition, the place is a center for in-service training for democratic education and environmental thinking, meant for students and teachers from all over the world.

On our visits to the various IDEC conferences we learned that several democratic schools have also been established in Nepal, Hong Kong, Taiwan and additional countries in Asia.

In the Pacific
New Zealand

IDEC 2002 was held in Christchurch, the largest city on the southern island of New Zealand. This conference was a real celebration, and served as a great boost for the democratic approach in Australia and New Zealand. Most of the free schools in New Zealand, which had been founded in the 1960's, had closed. The two last schools remaining were Tamariki in Christchurch and Motueka Mountain Valley School in Motueka.

Tamariki is today the main democratic school in New Zealand. It is considered an integrative public school, subsidized mostly by the State. For 32 years, till 2004, the headmistress was Ms. Pat Edwards, a pioneer of democratic education on the island. She and representatives from her school have visited schools throughout the world, and are among the leading pioneers in spreading the message of democratic education.

In 2004 I had the privilege of helping a groundbreaking group establish the Institute for Democratic Education Aotearoa (IDEA) ("Aotearoa" is New Zealand in Maori). Today they take part in opening innovative schools throughout the island. At the head of this process of educational innovation is Vicki Buck, the former mayor of Christchurch, an innovator and developer by nature. She has initiated the founding of two schools in Christchurch, the Discovery 1 elementary school and the Unlimited Penga Tawhiti (UPT) high school.

Vicki sees these as only the beginning of educational innovation in New Zealand, and from there in the entire world. These schools do not call themselves democratic, but in my opinion they implement most of the principles of democratic education, such as individual learning programs and the use of the city and its many institutions as a major learning resource. Teachers from these schools occasionally come to IDEC.

Australia

In 2006, Australia hosted IDEC. Most of the alternative schools there have been in operation since the 1960's.

AAPAE, a network of 14 schools, is the main organization working in alternative education on the continent, and at its head stands Cecelia Bradley, a courageous and impressive woman who has led this movement for many years. At present, many other groups are taking an interest in the implementation of principles of democratic education and innovative schools are being established throughout Australia.

In Europe

The number of democratic schools established in the early 1990's was small, but in recent years one can see a great awakening. As mentioned, in 2008 the first EUDEC (European Democratic Education Conference) was held in Leipzig, Germany, designated for European countries only.

We see this new awakening chiefly in Eastern Europe, where the political change brought about interesting searches in the area of education:

Eastern Europe
Russia

The collapse of the Soviet Union in 1991 was a key point in the appearance of groundbreaking "new schools". Innovative educators in Russia saw in the early 1990's a huge window of opportunity opening up to them, and many hitherto suppressed dreams began to come true. This is mainly because the revolutionary change in the political scene left a temporary organizational vacuum, which created a platform for the development of new educational ideas. Today, with the reorganization of the Russian system, the options are limited. However, the revolutionary foundation created in the early 90's still serves as a basis for established innovation developing today within the public schools. A large part of these innovative schools has been dealing in recent years with the question of the nature of the citizen in a democratic country and with ways of educating for democracy. One of these schools is the Self-Directed School in Moscow, founded by the innovative educator Alexander Tovalsky, with some 1200 students. This is a fascinating model combining Russian culture and democratic education. In a conversation we had before his death in 2006, Alexander Tovalsky told me about a network of democratic schools developing throughout Russia.

An additional interesting school is the International School of Film, where groups of students and teachers choose various projects around the world each year, study the subjects, raise money and go to spend about a month in the relevant place. Each project is filmed as a documentary. For example, one of the groups did a film on a person who is involved in reconstructing the native culture of the Canadian Indians. Another group went to China and documented research on methods of treating the hyperactive. By 2008, groups from the school had visited in 15 countries around the world. In addition, every year the school organizes an annual international conference, where representatives from film schools all over the world and creators in various fields can meet. In this school, I discovered a magical world of close teacher-student relationships, and great powers of creativity, fueled by proven experience and by the belief that one could lead processes in the world, even those that seem impossible in light of the meager resources at the disposal of the school.

Recently in Russia, a network of future schools was established. It shows great interest in promoting the ideas of democratic education and of a "learning city". Its students experience active involvement and partnership in leading democratic processes within the public systems.

In almost all the countries of Eastern Europe, we are witnessing great interest in promoting the concept of democratic education and in founding study groups. Here we should mention IDEC 1998, which was held in Kiev in the Ukraine, as well as the fascinating conference on democratic education which took place in Lodz, Poland, in 2007. Although the number of schools actually involved is still small, interest in Eastern Europe is constantly increasing, and we keep hearing, with great excitement, of new groups emerging.

Western Europe

In Western Europe, the most prominent country is **Holland**, where some 20 democratic schools of various kinds were established recently. These schools are recognized as public schools.

In the countries of Scandinavia as well, we are witnessing the appearance of democratic schools with partial or total government funding. It should be mentioned that many regular schools in Scandinavia are also undergoing processes of democratization.

Germany

IDEC 2005 was held in Germany, hosted by Krätzä, the children's rights organization of the Spiel/ Kultur Network, operating in Berlin and throughout Germany. There are some 50 open schools there (an open school is by nature a small, private school), some of them working with "free approaches" as survivors of the great wave of free schools operating in Germany in the 60's and 70's. At the same time, interest in democratic education is being expressed by groups of young activists and social initiators interested in founding democratic schools in Berlin (Krätzä), Leipzig and other places.

Arno Lange is working in the city of Jena in East Germany and operating a surprising center for alternative education (in a city of 100,000 residents, there are five alternative schools). Arno has formed connections with AWO, an organization for workers' rights, and together they founded the first democratic school there and plan to expand and establish a network of democratic schools and a national teacher training program (in cooperation with the Institute for Democratic Education in Israel).

Profound public discussion is developing in Germany regarding its hierarchical and segregated education system, in whose framework a child must choose a defined learning track (academic, vocational, etc.) at a very early age, depriving him of opportunities for growth and change already in early childhood. All the signs indicate an ongoing revolution in the making and serve as a great opportunity for democratic educators.

Similar conditions exist in Austria, which hosted the third IDEC conference.

Spain

Alongside several alternative schools which were founded in the 20th century, there is today the beginning of interest in the area of Democratic Education. In recent years there have been participants from Spain at IDEC conferences and today I know of an attempt to establish Spain's first democratic school near Barcelona.

Italy

Italian educators come to IDEC mainly from the school in headed by Francesco Codello, an extraordinary principal and educator, who takes his teachers on educational tours throughout the world to see various models of democratic education.

IDEC conferences have also had participants from France, representatives of two schools: the first, LAP in Paris, and the second in St. Nazaire.

In Turkey there are no democratic schools as of yet, but two conferences have been held in this area and there is considerable interest among academics and social activists.

The UK

In the UK, the situation seems static. Summerhill is presently in its fullest bloom since its establishment. The school has some 100 students and continues to be the most famous alternative school in the UK and perhaps in the world. In 2008, a TV series on the school was filmed by the BBC. In a few of my conversations with Zoë Redhead, A.S. Neill's daughter and headmistress of Summerhill today, she expressed her understanding of Summerhill's special standing in the world today and said that she is willing to take advantage of this special status in any possible way to promote the democratic education movement in the world.

In 1987 the Sands School was founded in Southern England by a group of English educators, among them teachers hurt by the closing of Dartington, which was established in 1922 and had been the main liberal school in the UK. Sands School was one of the first schools to participate in IDEC conferences.

The UK has a relatively large movement of homeschooling and small schools, which have recently shown interest in the ideas of democratic education.

Processes of democratization in public schools are also gaining momentum in the UK, under the heading of democratic education. In recent years, students and staff members of Summerhill have been involved in processes of change in public and private schools around the UK.

In the USA

The movement is large, its boundaries vague. In 2004, the first IDEC conference in the USA was held in Albany, New York by AERO. Since then, every year there is an AERO conference, which is declared as a meeting place for all alternative education in the USA. It is actually a meeting place for all those involved in democratic education in the USA and Canada. In addition, as I have already mentioned, since 1995 there has been the Sudbury Valley Conference, which unites all the schools belonging to that stream. It is interesting to note that despite the large number of democratic schools in the USA (about 100), the majority of them are private and have few students.

In parallel, many networks of different schools have developed in the USA, in the framework of public education. We can find in some of them the ideas of democratic education in their entirety or in part, in addition to new creations of fascinating models of education. An example is The Big Picture Company. This network of schools, headed by Dennis Littky and Elliot Washor, rapidly developing all over the USA, makes use of a school model based on every student's points of strength and fields of interest. The students choose areas of interest, and twice a week they study outside of school, in the community, guided by professionals in their chosen areas. This network, together with other networks of public schools, are taking part in the general revolution of the "small schools" going on in the USA today.

In my opinion, the greatest challenge facing American educators is to try and create democratic schools that will be recognized by the State as public schools.

Canada

In Canada there are some ten democratic schools, the most prominent of which is Windsor House in Vancouver, founded by Helen Hughes, which has about 170 students in ages four to eighteen. IDEC 2008 was held there; at the conference, which was organized by school graduates, students, volunteer parents and staff members, the atmosphere was pleasant and one could see the general good feeling of the school. Recently, Windsor House conducted a successful struggle for its right to recognition as a public school in Canada.

Another central figure in Canada is Matt Hern, who runs a center called Purple Thistle, which serves as an alternative to school. Children of all ages, but mostly youth, are invited to promote various kinds of projects there, to participate in the management of the place and to be part of a supportive alternative community. At the same time, Matt is an academic who has published several important books in the area of alternative education (the last one was *Everywhere, All the Time: A New Deschooling*).

In South America

Here, too, there is awakening, the center of which is in Brazil. IDEC 2007 was held in Sao Paolo, and was a peak event in a process that had begun to gain momentum throughout the continent.

Brazil

As far as my knowledge goes regarding the historical background of alternative education in South America, democratic education in Brazil began in 2002, with the establishment of the Lumiar democratic school in Sao Paolo. This venture was the product of an interesting partnership between the industrialist Ricardo Simler, the head of Semco, a concern which operates according to democratic principles, and Elena Singler, a leading educator in the area of democratic education in Brazil. Alongside the school, they founded the Institute for Democratic Education Studies, which later became the Institute for Democratic Education in Brazil.

The Institute helps in establishing democratic schools throughout the continent, as well as leading processes of democratization in regular schools. One of the most significant activities of the Institute was the establishment of some 85 schools in the democratic spirit operating along the banks of the Amazon (a story that could fill a book itself).

One of the many programs we were exposed to at the conference is called "a neighborhood as a school", the Aprendiz City School. We visited the area of this school's work in Sao Paolo and were amazed. The entire street, including workplaces, shops, restaurants, art galleries, a circus and sports facilities, all have become a part of the school.

Democratic schools have also been established in Colombia, Honduras, and other countries in South America, and attempts are being made to begin processes of democratization in Mexico, Uruguay, Argentina and Chile.

Africa

Ms. Sharon Caldwell runs the Nahoom Montessori School. It works according to the Montessori method and is trying to combine this method with ideas of democratic education. Recently we have received various applications from African educators interested in this area.

In the Arab World

Representatives of the Palestinian school "Hope Flowers" in Bethlehem have participated in IDEC conferences. Expansion of our activity in the Arab world is one of the most important challenges facing democratic education.

The Big Dance

In the last 20 years, in most countries of the Western world, laws have been passed on the subjects of children's and students' rights. At the same time, broad discussion is open on the question of education in a democratic world. Democratic education, which had been private and isolated, has come closer to public education and addresses broader and more varied publics. This is, among other reasons, because it serves as a good ground for developing working models of Life Long Learning. In a world of rapid change, pluralistic learning serves as a good platform for relevance and innovation.

Recently, we have witnessed the appearance of "centers for democratic innovation", which create connections among educational, public, industrial, cultural and the academic organizations (Ricardo Semler in Brazil, Dennis Littky and Elliot Washor in MET in the USA, Vicki Buck in New Zealand and the Institute for Democratic Education in Israel).

In my estimation, the international scene is still in its initial stages. The pioneers of democratic education are in a position of weakness as minorities in most countries of the world, but the international encounter could create a support group and serve as a major springboard for the development of ideas of democratic education. The encounter with the other is one of the important principles of democratic education, and I call it The Big Dance. This future development direction is made up of international networks connecting between "centers for democratic innovation", in whose framework students can choose schools in different places around the world (real and virtual), and experience choosing subjects and topics that they find fascinating. Adults who work at these centers for innovation, whether as educators, creators or academics, can also work or train in other centers around the world.

An additional development which I predict is the establishment of alternative academic centers (in the style of the "Incubator" at the Institute for Democratic Education in Israel and at Shura University in Japan), alongside "centers for democratic innovation", which deal with educational philosophy and other subjects of pluralistic learning and initiatives of democratic innovation. At these centers one can get professional training, at the highest international level. For example, a student (a graduate of a democratic school, a person interested in a career change or anyone else) can study for an academic degree or various kinds of certification. Studies would take place by staying and interning in several places around the world, to be chosen in accordance with areas in which the student wishes to specialize (it would be possible for someone to learn each semester in a different place). Such an encounter, with different cultures and world views, could give rise to true multi-culturalism, which would change the way people see each other, without the distorted spectacles of cultural stereotypes. In this way, a support network would be created for future initiatives of working models for "democratic culture" (see Chapter 3).

The Third Wave – Opportunities and Dangers

The awakening I have described thus far, happening in recent years in Israel and in the world, is the third wave of openness in education that one can identify in the last 100 years. The first wave came in the 1920's, centered in Europe. In this wave, there were prominent headings such as "progressive education" or "new education". The second wave came in the 1960's and 70's, centered in the USA; its prominent headings were "free education" and "open education". The present wave began during the early '90's, simultaneously all over the world, and its prominent heading is "democratic education".

Every one of the earlier waves influenced public education, which gradually increased the amount of freedom it gave to people in the education system – both students and teachers. A quick look through books describing the education system 100 years ago illustrates the long way that education and society have come towards democratization.

In this context, two main questions occupy my mind: First – In what way is this wave different from the previous ones? And second – Are we at the peak of a passing wave, or at the beginning of a fundamental change in the education system and in society in general?

Regarding the first question – the first waves acted as reactions to the concept of the "industrial school", which began to operate and gain power at the beginning of the 20th century (see Chapter 1). The present wave is fundamentally different, in that it operates less out of a motive to negate "old ideas in education" (this role is being successfully filled by educators working within the framework, academic researchers and dissatisfied parents), and more out of positive motives, in an attempt to answer the questions: "Which education system can best serve a democratic society?"; "How can education ensure the future existence of the world?"; or "How can we implement the ideas of democracy and human rights in the education system as well?"

In the second wave, the revolution focused on the child. Today in democratic education, the focus is on the relationship between the child and the adult, which operates within and outside the system, and on the ideas of Life Long Learning (see Chapter 5). The concept of the individual as part of society leads to the creation of a learning environment which is also connected to the public system, in a way that gives a unique response to every child.

As for the second question – the first two waves existed in parallel to the appearance of public schools all over the world. This wave grew and became stronger most impressively throughout the last 100 years. From the beginning of the 21st century, we see the decline, and perhaps the collapse, of the public education system. This crisis is expressed in academic research studies and in various commissions around the world, whose conclusions indicate that the old education system no longer works and is not relevant to this era, to the rapidly chancing times and fast pace at which we live, or to the challenges of society and culture facing us today.

The encounter between this rift and the wave of democratic education gaining its momentum, serves as an extraordinary opportunity. This is a unique situation, indicating that we are not in the midst of a passing wave, but rather in a process of changing stages or a quantum leap. If during the 19th century there was a period of "democratic ideas", such as in the USA, where there was democracy and equality, but not for women or blacks, and in the 20th century we see the emergence of democratic governments who used democratic procedures but continued to maintain "undemocratic cultures", in the 21st century an opportunity is emerging for a quantum leap that will be the harbinger of "democratic culture" (see chapter 3 and hereinafter).

The Emergence of Democratic Culture

Democratic culture is a culture which helps each individual to express his own uniqueness within the community. This is on the basis of principles of human rights and sustainability in various living environments.

It has two components:

One – the commitment of society to the creation of possibilities, frameworks and resources, which can help each individual discover and develop his uniqueness and express it in the community where he lives.

The second – the adherence to principles: commitment to a democratic culture means taking an activist standpoint. The citizen who is committed to democracy may be called upon to struggle for his rights, the rights of those around him, and those of individuals and societies throughout the world.

Democratic culture encourages the citizen towards active commitment to the advancement of social values such as equality, liberty and social responsibility, and towards active support of the implementation of human rights. An individual who adopts the principles of democratic culture will support cooperation between different people and will advance them, and will struggle for the possibilities of varied human life, while maintaining an intra-cultural and inter-cultural dialogue.

Democratic culture develops in stages:

The individual stage – whose goal is the self-realization of every individual in society. An individual who has experienced significant success can see the importance of the advancement of another; thus, it is important that this stage takes place during early childhood.

The interpersonal stage – support of another's growth. This means insight that an interpersonal dialogue is the best way and atmosphere for personal growth and for resolving interpersonal and intercultural conflicts.

The social-community stage – creating systems that will support the existence of democratic culture in the community in which I live.

The fourth stage – taking active responsibility in the areas of human rights and the environment, which are relevant to the future of all inhabitants of the earth. Seeing the entirety of humankind, the whole of the earth, and all its physical features, flora and fauna, as a single unit with shared interests; a unit whose protection is the responsibility of all the people living in it.

Conditions for Success

The different waves, in the past and the present, stemmed from strong social needs (in the first wave – a reaction to the ending of the First World War and the growth of socialism in Europe; in the second wave – the struggle for civil rights in the USA and opposition to the Vietnam War, and in this wave – the expansion of democratization and the information revolution throughout the world).

If we study the history of education in the world in depth, we can discover that the collapse of the first two waves did not come from external factors, but mainly from internal struggles and "murky waters" in the world of the adults leading the processes.

In order for the third wave to lead us to the safe havens of the emergence of democratic culture, several changes must occur in the various democratic education systems in all their components:

1. Recognition that the other – even if he is not a child – is an opportunity for growth

Many of those involved in democratic education make great efforts to convince adults to recognize every child as a unique individual, and to see the encounter with the other as an opportunity for growth. However, these same people find it very difficult to accept an adult who has different opinions. Many of them engage in bitter struggle to prove that they are right and the other is wrong. We have learned that developing dialogue with the other is possible, and what is more, effects growth.

2. Recognition that the truth is probably not "in our pocket"

The "keeper of the truth" has nowhere to grow. Creative ability cannot thrive in an environment of absolute knowledge. From my experience, the more open and honest dialogue I could generate with people who seemed far from me, without intentions of proving myself right – the more I grew and enabled growth.

3. Recognition of the fact that the other is sometimes called "the establishment", and that there are also people in the establishment

Too often, the establishment serves as a red rag in the eyes of people in alternative education. Censuring or fighting the establishment depletes the fuel and energy of our creativity. I have gradually discovered that it is possible to create dialogue with the establishment that is direct and enables growth. We have conducted, and are still conducting, an ongoing and fruitful dialogue with many of Israel's Ministers of Education. We have conducted experiments in cooperation with various departments of the Ministry of Education, such as the Department of Experiments: the Unit for Education towards Democracy; the Administration for Education towards Values; or the

Advancement of Youth, as well as experiments in the academic field with the Kibbutzim College of Education. During these experiments we found wonderful people, who saw opportunity in their encounter with us. None of the bodies mentioned completely adopted the viewpoints of democratic education, but I can say that through this encounter we discovered new things in our own thinking and activity. I believe that our partners in dialogue felt the same.

4. Recognition of the importance of self-criticism as a tool for growth

In traditional organizations, criticism is seen as a threat – a personal and an organizational threat. Critics are attacked and declared "traitors". Thus a situation has been created, in which criticism only comes from those with political or personal motives, while others learn that it is forbidden to "rock the boat you are in". Every system, and especially a democratic education system, must develop an organizational culture that encourages self-criticism, seeing all kinds of criticism as an opportunity for growth and not as a threat.

5. Taking democratic education outside the school

Since today we see a necessary connection between a school and its environment and community (see Chapter 2), and since the concept of a student (till age eighteen) has changed to a Life Long Learner, democratic education in general and pluralistic learning in particular must transcend the boundaries of the school. We speak of directions for adult development (as in a "personal Incubator"), development of organizational learning and learning in public and business organizations, promoting regional processes of a learning community, future centers, game development, connection to electronic media and other ideas as our imagination allows.

6. Connection to the Internet revolution – the Internet revolution is changing our lives entirely

The Internet as a tool bears within it many of the ideas of democratic education – a world of knowledge accessible to all and the abolishment of the old hierarchies (certain knowledge accessible only to certain people). The Internet enables us to create a new economic world, in which the main consumer product is the ability to create new ideas, the ability to think differently, not like everyone else. And to do this, one does not need a certificate, but does need many other things, such as creativity, expertise and mostly courage. Software programs of open code and tools such as social networks create huge possibilities for building a new education system. And in this place of new creation, democratic education has the advantage of 100 years of experience (accrued through all three waves). This is a golden opportunity for interaction – democratic education has developed tools over the years that can greatly help promote the Internet, and the Internet can open new fields to democratic education.

I will close this chapter with a quote from an article by Guy Rolnik in the Haaretz newspaper, where he describes an introductory tour of Google:

I conclude my visit in the small office of Stacy Savides Sullivan, who is the Chief Culture Officer of Google – in other words, the woman in charge of Google's cultural organization. Stacy's little room, the fact that she is wearing jeans and the informal and cheerful atmosphere, give no sign that she is one of Google's most senior employees.

'What kind of organizational culture do you impart to the workers?' I ask. 'I don't – the culture belongs to the workers, and my job is to see that it stays with them', she replies.

'And the managers? What is their job?'

'The managers' job is to help the workers realize their ideas.'

'So who's running the business?'

'We recruit people for Google who don't need to be run. These are people who manage themselves, who seek out their own challenges and assignments and initiate things on their own.'[20]

Indeed, I believe that this is the main question facing us – how do we create an education system that advances the students and enables them to become people who manage themselves, who seek out their own challenges and initiate things on their own, so that our world will be a better place to live in.

Chapter Eight

Democratic Education – The Journey towards a Sustainable Society

In this last chapter I would like to address the place of education in general, and of democratic education in particular, in the puzzle that is future humanity. To this end I shall attempt to imagine society as it will be in fifty to a hundred years from now.

This glimpse into the future liberates one's thoughts and offers a different and important perspective of the place where we are at present. In this future society, our children, grandchildren and great-grandchildren will live. If they are able, they will, like us, work, love, hate... but in one respect they will be completely different from us:

In this society each individual will have far greater capability than we have today – capability both for creativity and for destruction.

In the title of this chapter I have used the term "sustainable society", because the continued existence of the human race is not certain, nor can it be taken for granted.

People involved in education, as well as in the sciences, economics, culture, the environment, and all other areas regarding humankind, are forced today to address the question of how to create a society that can endure: A society that will overcome the immense obstacles waiting for it in the future, obstacles which stem from its very nature and conduct.

The naturalist Konrad Lorenz conducted an in-depth examination of the components of aggression in nature. He has determined, based on his research, that humans have reached a point at which their own aggressive impulses will destroy them, simply because they have acquired the ability to do so. "When a man invents a bow and arrow, these become from then on the property not only of his offspring, but of the entire society. And this property is no less stable than the various organs of his body", he writes.[21] In other words, it is sufficient that one person has the capability of creating weapons of mass destruction for these to become the property of the masses. This means that if technology continues to progress at its present pace, and at the same time the militaristic nature of humankind remains as it is – the end of human existence is closer than what we would predict.

On the other hand, there exists also the opposite aspect, that of creativity. The ability to build worlds is also the property of many individuals. If, in the past, few of us were exposed to information and few held the social power and the necessary means to carry out invention or creation, today many have this capability. We live in the "era of ideas", in which the distance between conceiving and carrying out is constantly decreasing. People can create or invent and inform the world of their achievements through a variety of technological means. Possibilities for creation and publicity, which in the past were the property of companies or wealthy individuals only, exist today in average homes: films and books can be published independently, new towns and settlements can be built, and unique enterprises initiated.

In the society of the future, our powers of both creation and destruction will grow immeasurably. In other words, every individual will be able to destroy the entire world – or to create new realities. Right now the scales are balanced; however the question is, which scale-pan will determine the future of humanity – that of destruction or of creation.

The Scale-pan of Destruction

How many people could a tribal leader of a cave clan kill? Several dozens, I would assume. Alexander of Macedonia achieved sufficient technological advancement to kill thousands. And Hitler? Hitler "succeeded" in killing millions. Now let us think for a moment about the average individual, not a leader. In the past, such a person could not obtain a rifle, as this was an expensive weapon, at the disposal of armies or leaders only. Today, there are children who own rifles. In the past, the average individual had no access to explosives, whereas today these materials are available, ready for distribution, obtainable on Internet sites. Is there even a chance that the same will not happen to weapons of mass destruction?

The factors that quicken the processes of destruction are rooted deep within our education and consumer systems. These two huge systems convey, each in its own way, a uniform message – that there is one reality, and that our duty is to adjust to it, and to integrate into it as well as we can. In order to do so, we must strive to be as much like everyone else as possible – to eat, drink and dress according to one order of fashion, which will make us "special" (like everyone), and at the same time, to reach agreed-on academic achievements, all at about the same age.

These two systems complement each other, so far successfully. Instead of being a varied, colorful democratic society, one which emphasizes the uniqueness of the people living in it, we have adopted the culture of consumption, or perhaps become addicted to it unintentionally. We are participants in the only game played on the field: the game of winners and losers.

A society in which many do not find their true place nor discover their unique talents, and do not know what their contribution is to creativity and to the future of humanity – such a society is a perfect recipe for creating unknown soldiers in the battle of destruction. Those people, who discover that all the creative places are taken by the "winners", and that the places vacant for "losers" are mostly concentrated in the service of the strong, find appropriate expression for their uniqueness through acts of destruction. On the other hand, the "winners" do not reduce the extent of their destructive activity, particularly in social and ecological spheres, because the negative results of their activity have no direct effect on them, but rather affect mainly the "losers".

And we as educators – where are we to go with the certainty that the world where our children and grandchildren will live will be a world with such potential for destruction? Do we examine what can be done today, to help the citizens of the future exist in a safe, growing democratic society?

I could say – and many present educators surely will say: We must reduce the potential power of the individual. We must reduce the access of the individual to knowledge, technology and science, and leave all these in the hands of "the people in charge". Perhaps this thinking was the rationale that served the developers of weapons of mass destruction (most of whom lived in democratic countries!) some 50 years ago. Today, this idea is ridiculous. There is no significance to the idea that the potential for destruction will "only" reach the hands of one billion people, and not of the other five billion. For, if destruction is accessible, it will be utilized.

Therefore, prevention through control will not succeed. The attempt to stop the process through the reduction of human capability will not prevent the destruction of the world. On the contrary, perhaps, the attempt to reduce the capability of the oppressed will just strengthen the energy of their anger and destruction, and will hasten the coming of what we wished to prevent.

It is in the aftermath of 9/11, 2001, that a one-of-a-kind opportunity has been created to effect great change. For a moment, almost all the inhabitants of the earth were able to realize that we are living on borrowed time. For that moment, we could see that military solutions are "more of the same", and do not offer a true solution for the roots of this process of destruction. An essential change is needed – one that requires far-reaching social and educational thinking.

There are those who say that we have already lost the battle – the powers of destruction have won. The future of the world has been decided. The scenarios for this are many and varied. But I believe the future has not yet been decided. It depends on us, and we must act under the assumption that we can prevail. We must ask ourselves, can we arrive at a world where people are not interested in destroying other people? Can humankind rid itself of the need for aggression that has characterized it since the beginning of time? It would seem to be mission impossible. But a negative answer will surely lead to the end of life on earth. Therefore, we have no choice but to cope with this challenge.

The Scale-pan of Creativity

I believe that democratic education marks a possible path for solving this existential conundrum. The proposal expressed in this book is the reinforcement of the powers of creativity of each and every individual – and finally – of society as a whole. Such reinforcement could significantly reduce the dimensions of destruction. At the same time, there must be recognition of the mutual interdependence that exists among all individuals in the world.

Children who are violent at school are those who have not succeeded in expressing their creative powers in the frameworks offered them, or whose creative efforts have not been recognized and appreciated. The level of violence decreases only when the entire education system changes, in order to express more fully the students' powers of creativity. The level of violence in democratic schools is much lower than in most other schools. Do children in the democratic schools have fewer violent impulses? Of course not. I believe the main reason is that the democratic school devotes its resources to the recognition of each and every child's unique creative powers – this is the key.

Erich Fromm, in his book "Escape from Freedom", writes about the relationship between violence and creativity:

"The will to live and the will to destroy are not independent and detached factors, but rather dependent on each other in inverse proportions. The more the will for life is frustrated, the stronger one's will for destruction. The more one's life is fulfilled, the weaker one's destructive power. Destructive behavior is the result of life that is not fulfilled. Living conditions of oppression lead to the lust for destruction, which creates, if one could use that word, the sources which feed the various hostile tendencies – towards others or towards one's self."

If the areas of creativity are not open to a person, he will turn towards areas of destruction: I destroy (others' creations) – therefore I am. This phenomenon is well- known in educational psychology. The child who feels rejected will turn to destruction in order to feel "recognized", to "show" his creative powers.

I agree that violence is a part of human character, and that we cannot create a society in which none of the individuals are violent. However, in our vision of future society, the education system must transfer the powers in the hands of humans from the scale of destruction to that of creativity. This will ensure the continuation of our existence on earth.

Sustainable Creativity: Creativity Focused on the Importance of Every Individual

The feasibility for an education system of coping with the empowering ability, awaiting future citizens, depends on two significant conditions:

First, we must create an education system which enables every citizen of the future to "herald" his existence through his unique creativity.

The second condition is the propagation of the understanding that one's unique creativity does not end with "I". "The other" is also gifted with unique capabilities, and there is a mutual interdependence among all the people in the world. This is not the dependence born of fear, like the dependence of a slave on his master or of an employee on his employer, but dependence born of recognition.

This is the important recognition that every person (and I really mean each and every one) brings something special to the world. Every individual has a new answer, a unique world, a personal proposal, energy, a new tune, an unusual ability. In this sense, we are all a part of a huge mosaic, and if any one part is missed, the whole loses out.

Ecologists tell us how important it is to prevent the extinction of plants, animals and rare species. They claim that even if we are not nature lovers, but only thinking of the human race, we must do all we can to prevent extinction. Today, we already know that certain species of plants have important medicinal properties, some as yet undiscovered. It is probable that the extinction of certain animals has kept vital information from humankind. This is even truer of humanity itself.

To a certain extent, there is already a partial understanding of "others'" ability to contribute to "us". Indian tribes, which were almost eradicated in North America, are being "rediscovered" by the white man as the bearers of important messages regarding medicine, life philosophy and the ecological approach to nature. People, who were defined in the past as "primitive" (and one must always ask – who is doing the defining?), are newly perceived as having significant insight on music, religion, and esoteric knowledge. The Chinese have offered their position regarding medicine, and it has been integrated into the knowledge existing in the West. The world has discovered that it is greater than the sum of all its parts.

Yet we have not yet been marked with the recognition that these things are true for each individual as well. Thomas Hobbs, in his book "Leviathan", claims that each human must protect and respect the other, so that he in turn will act similarly towards you; in other words, only in this way can you feel protected.[22] My perception is different: I believe that every one of us has an "asset" to offer the world, a unique gift, which, if lost, cannot be recovered. And so, we all have mutual responsibility to advance each person's journey towards finding his uniqueness. And this should not come out of fear, but rather out of hope that the discovery of these hidden treasures will allow for the creation of a better world. The mutual responsibility is not restricted only to educational pursuits, and it must have a response from social, economic and environmental areas. The unique gift of all of us must be enabled to exist and grow.

All for One, One for All

The working assumption of education thus far has been that in reality, as in football, there is only one game being played, and therefore some of the participants have to win, while the others have to lose (see Chapter 6). It is a world of one scale (see Chapter 3), of a uniform curriculum, of a necessary "foundation of knowledge". A world in which someone who does not succeed in his mathematics matriculation must feel he is a "failure", even if he is a talented artist. A world in which there is a right and wrong answer, "the world in the square", with a bell curve, a world in which 20% are successful and all the rest mediocre or losers – and they must constantly be made to feel this.

Looking at this working assumption, democratic education claims that there are many games in life, and that each person can choose the game most suitable for him, or can even create a new game. This is a critically important process. If we are playing in a field of varied opportunities, in which we can decide on the game that will enable us to "win" (or in other words, to create our personal special creation), the entire society can be changed into a win-win situation.

The understanding that each person bears a unique gift, which may be of help to me (even though I don't yet understand how), creates a very high level of mutual support among individuals.

One of the implications of this is that it is worthwhile for me to help each person find the unique gift that he bears. Not only because, in doing this, I can reduce the dangers of the world's potential for destruction, but also because perhaps, within his personal gift, lies the answer to the advancement of my own life and the life of humanity – Just like the rare flower we are trying to save from extinction.

Without the "One" there is No "All"

When I suggest the ideas underlying democratic education, as a means of promoting a sustainable society, I must emphasize the critical difference between democracy as essence and a democratic framework without essence. In places throughout Israel, and throughout the world, when people speak of "democratization" in the context of states, institutions or schools, they mean a procedural process. They see the framework of "voting rights" or a judicial system as a general characteristic of the democratic idea, and ignore the fact that democracy has an essence which is expressed in the protection of human rights.

We, at the Institute for Democratic Education, experienced an example of this in two different schools.

Several years ago, a process of democratization began in one of the most prestigious elementary schools in the center of the country. We were very proud of the process taking place in that school: A parliament was established, which enabled all the students and teachers to influence what went on in the school; a variety of committees for mediation were set up; unique programs were carried out for the prevention of violence; and elections were held. This was a "democratic celebration", although the curriculum of the school did not undergo any significant change. Whenever I was asked where one could see a school going through a successful process of democratization – I would send the inquirer to that school.

Three years passed. The principal of the school came to me, a very special woman with a charismatic personality, and asked me to help her get a job as a principal of a democratic school (which was founded as such).

"Listen, Yaacov," she said to me, when she saw how surprised I was, "you really don't understand what I'm going through."

"But I know your school well," I replied. "I ran workshops there; I know teachers and students…"

"You only see one side of the coin, the one we are interested in showing", she said, her eyes full of tears. "You don't know the other side."

She then suggested I visit the school for an entire day, to speak with the teachers individually, and as agreed, she gave them only one sentence of guidance: "Tell Yaacov the truth about your lives".

That was one of the most difficult days of my life. One after the other the teachers told me their painful stories. They told me how much strength they needed to get up to leave their homes and come to work in the morning; how they "put on their armor" as they arrived at the school; how frightened they were entering the classroom. They told me about children who threatened them; admitted that the interaction in class was frightening; told me about increasing, raging violence. Some told me about children who had hit them, while others related how they found themselves "stopping a child by force". They described life on a cruel battlefield. Most of them left the room in tears, leaving me more helpless and desperate than ever.

According to their descriptions, as the process of organizational democratization advanced in the school — so advanced the students' violence, which became almost intolerable.

And yet, as opposed to this story, there is the story of the Rogozin School in the south of Tel Aviv (as told in Chapter 6), which had been considered one of the toughest schools in Tel Aviv. In a gradual process, the structure of the learning program had been significantly changed, so that each student chose his own learning goals himself (with the help of his personal advisor) and realized them in the school. Homeroom classes were cancelled, and together with them all the old compulsory lessons. After the introduction of this change to the structure of the school and to the curriculum, the violence in the school decreased until it almost disappeared. The school's principal, in his own reports, could hardly believe it: from daily violence, including fistfights, throwing bottles, and gang violence, the violent episodes in school became very rare. Not only that, but there was a decrease in violence in the surrounding area (of youth who did not attend the school).

What, then, was the difference between the two schools? Why had one become a complete failure, and the other a great success?

The difference is between a democratic framework and a democratic essence, between form and content. In the first school, the process of democratization had included only the framework: elections, a parliament, appointing committees – including a mediation committee to prevent violence. At Rogozin, on the other hand, the process included the essence as well. As soon as we changed the very structure of the studies, and allowed every individual to express himself and his own personal essence without force; as soon as the teachers became personal advisors (and as such – more caring, close and personal towards the students) – from that moment on, the extent of the violence changed as well.

Is this the reason why in democratic countries there is so much violence at the personal level? Is it that when people believe they have no real outlet for self-expression, they direct the democratic energy towards society – and turn to violence?

The Vision and the Invitation

Abraham Maslow, one of the founding fathers of humanist psychology, presented the model of the pyramid, which shows the hierarchy of the individual's needs in society. At the pyramid's base are the physiological needs. Above them come the security-related needs and the need for love. Above those, in a relatively small area, we see the need for appreciation, and above it, the need for self-fulfillment.

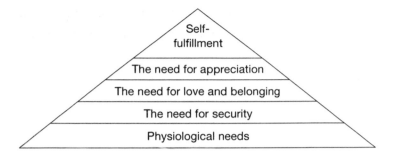

Maslow's main idea was that a person can engage in meeting a particular need only after the needs below it have been fulfilled. He estimated that only about 2% of the population reaches the stage of self-fulfillment.[23]

I believe that this is the very essence of the danger to humanity. If our present situation means that 98% of the people of the world do not have the right to find their own self-fulfillment, this explains the violence surrounding us and the future danger to the fate of humanity.

Facing this bitter reality, democratic education offers a new way. This way will "reinforce" the citizens of the future and turn the pyramid into a rectangle. (I use Maslow's pyramid as a convenient example, but this is true for any concept which describes society as a pyramid.)

First I wish to focus on the revolution done by democratic schools: I begin with the appreciation stage, mainly because it is there where most of the school's activity takes place nowadays, and to my opinion, the change must come from the core subjects of the education system (later I will return to Maslow's basic stages and demonstrate how I believe changes can be made in them too).

The stage of appreciation is parallel to "finding one's areas of strength" in pluralistic learning. According to Maslow also, in order to reach self-fulfillment we must first have positive experiences of success and appreciation, in order to be empowered. Maslow divides this stage into two: external appreciation, and after that, internal self-esteem.

The conservative learning system ignores the important role of the stage of appreciation in the strengthening of the child, and in his preparation for the stage of self-fulfillment. It deals only with the so-called description of the "objective" situation in the square, by assessing the students as strong, mediocre and weak, with no connection to the child's internal world at the time of assessment, and with no goal of enabling each child to experience success. This approach builds the pyramid and perpetuates the situation in which few can successfully cross the stage of school appreciation, and arrive at the stage of self-fulfillment.

Democratic education, on the other hand, is directed towards finding the special skills and areas of strength of each and every individual. Assessment also focuses on these areas. Even when the child's achievements are tested against others', it is in the areas of his strength.

In this way, he can experience and even prove success. In addition, democratic education also concerns itself with the other part of this stage, which is self-esteem. It is achieved through the examination of the child's inner world, through his own and his advisor's eyes, verbally, in conversations or in writing. This approach greatly increases the child's chance to receive the appreciation he needs and to be strengthened for the next stage, that of self-fulfillment.

This stage, in Maslow's pyramid, is parallel to the "area of growth" in pluralistic learning. As I have already detailed (in Chapter 3 and at other opportunities), this is a difficult stage of searching, falling, engaging in one's desires and interests, and not necessarily in one's proven ability. Therefore, in order to be in this stage, much strength and self-confidence are needed, that were acquired in the previous stage. In the framework of democratic education, this stage is possible to achieve. For everyone. Both due to the appreciation acquired in the previous stage, and because failure and setbacks are perceived as positive and educational experiences.

And here is the main message of democratic education to the world and to the future of humanity: it offers a way for all, not only for a selected few, to reach self-fulfillment.

As the number of people reaching the highest stages grows, the triangle will become a rectangle:

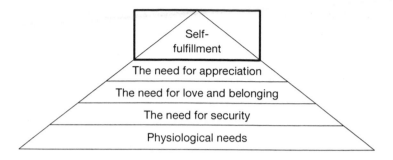

If indeed a large proportion of the population (and not just 2%) would reach the area of growth, self-fulfillment and creativity, this will completely change the path in which humanity walks. Violence will decrease considerably and the forces of destruction will be defeated.

I know that this vision may sound imaginary and without basis to some of the readers. I suggest they visit a democratic school, spend time in the yard and speak with the children.

Returning to the pyramid, we can ask how can this change in perception of the concept of assessment on the part of the education system, lead to a society that sees as its basic commitment the fulfillment of everyone's most fundamental needs.

I believe that such a change is currently taking place in new frameworks of democratic-social education, operating in areas where the socio-economic conditions are weak (see Chapter 6 – the Givat Olga Democratic

School and the Bat Yam personal education program), and it is moving in two directions:

1. A change in the status of the educator – Only an educator who can see the uniqueness of the student can create a relationship that is not dependent on systematic comparison between him and other students around him or compared to the average for his age. Only this educator can see the unfulfilled needs of the student in their place among the basic needs, according to Maslow. True, such an educator is sometimes found in traditional education systems, but democratic education offers a convenient platform for the activity of this kind of educator.

2. A connection between systems of education and of welfare – The new educator will serve as the liaison between the student, his family and his community. The educator will be able to motivate and navigate processes of support for the unfulfilled needs of the student and his family, either on his own or by operating various professional elements in the community.

Democratic education also proposes a long-term change. A change in the structure of education systems in international proportions will bring about meaningful change in the function of society and the family unit as well. Graduates of the democratic education system, who have achieved self-fulfillment, are equipped with the understanding that each person, and not just an elite minority, can bring his uniqueness to the world. These graduates (and their parents and teachers, who were partners in this process) are motivated to create change in society, which will lead to meeting the basic physical and security-related needs of every child and adult, with no differentiation. In a recent study at the Institute for Democratic Education, we discovered that by any standards, a large proportion of graduates of democratic schools (72%) are involved in some sort of social activism.

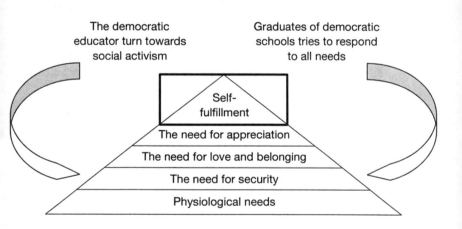

The family unit, built by graduates of democratic schools, also will not see children as a tool for meeting the parental needs, but will give them the freedom to develop their unique powers of creativity and will provide them with the love and security they need. The pyramid will change – as most people reach self-fulfillment.

The possible vision:

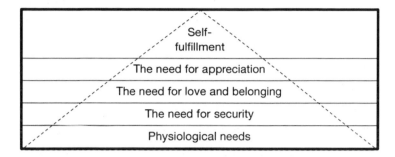

Is everything to be found in education? Is a change in the education system sufficient to cause social change? Politics, economics, society and the judicial system – all these play central roles in democratic thinking. But in this book, my goal has been to examine the connection between education and life in a democratic society.

In my opinion, most of human society is in processes of democratization – political, economic and social processes. The education system, which was supposed to support the creation of a democratic society (see Chapter 3) in order to complete the picture, did not undergo the desired parallel change. In this way, a dangerous tension was created between existing democratic frameworks and a hobbling democratic culture. Today, we live with a democratic mechanism which lacks the rudder of values that democratic culture should produce.

Democratic education and pluralistic learning have great importance in the process of creating a democratic culture. I refer not only to schools, but also to the broader context of the need for Life Long Learning and education.

"The learning person", and not "the knowing person", is our chance for life in a democratic culture. "The learning person" will work in the "democratic learning organization", which can be a school, a different workplace, or a new organizational structure, which transcends the known boundaries and creates an organization of interdisciplinary cooperation and partnerships. This is not an organization which reconstructs its own activities, but rather re-invents itself, examines its activities and their outcomes in the past and the present, and in accordance with its learning, changes towards the future (see Chapter 6).

In my more distant vision, people will live in learning democratic communities. I believe that a deep connection between the individual, his family, his workplace and his community, whose goal is to enable everyone to reach his creative and productive potential – this connection will cancel out the need for destruction.

Every member of the community will bear responsibility on three levels:

First, self-responsibility – to bring to expression the unique property which each and every one bears in his body and soul.

Second, responsibility for the other – since the other, too, has a unique gift, which is irreplaceable.

Third, responsibility for all humanity – including the various societies and groups within it, and the physical environment in which we live. This environment also bears unique properties, which contribute to the continuation of life on earth.

I believe that we can overcome the forces threatening the existence of our planet. And beyond survival – I believe that we can create a wondrous human society, which will see the age of wars as a period in distant history, a period which will serve as a warning sign against the image of humans as perceiving the other as a threat rather than as an opportunity.

How do we create this society? I do not know, but I am in the midst of an intensive search for the answer.

Bibliography

1. Neill, Alexander S. 1996. *Summerhill School – a New View of Childhood*. New York: St. Martin's Griffin.

    Additional information about Summerhill:

    Alexander Neill's books:

    *   Neill ,Alexander S.1960. *Summerhill – a Radical Approach to Child Rearing*. New York: Hart Publishing Company. (Forward by Erich Fromm).
    *   Neill ,Alexander S. 1966. *Freedom – Not Licence!*. New York: Hart Publishing Company.
    *   Neill, Alexander S. 1967. Talking of Summerhill. London: Gollancz.
    *   Neill ,Alexander S. 1973. *Neil! Neil! Orange Peel! A personal view of ninety years*. London: Weidenfeld & Nicolson.
    *   Neill, Alexander S. 1996. *Summerhill School – a New View of Childhood*. New York: St. Martin's Griffin.

    Books about Summerhill:

    *   Croall, Jonathan. 1983. Neill of Summerhill – the Permanent Rebel. London: Routledge & Kegan Paul.
    *   Croall, Jonathan (Ed.). 1983. All the Best, Neill: Letters from Summerhill. London: André Deutsch. (A collection of letters by Neill to people like H.G. Wells, Bertrand Russell, Henry Miller, Wilhelm Reich, Paul Goodman, Homer Lane, and others.)
    *   Sims, Hylda. 2000. Inspecting the Island. Ipswich (UK): Seven-Ply Yarns. (A novel by an ex-Summerhill pupil.)

- Various authors. 1973. Summerhill, For and Against: Outstanding Writers in Education, Sociology and Psychology Evaluate the Concepts of A.S. Neill. Sydney; London: Angus & Robertson.
- Walmsley, John. 1969. Neill and Summerhill: A Pictorial Study. Baltimore: Penguin.

Summerhill's website offers information on the school, its institutions and its history, and contains different studies concerning the school; it also enables contact with the school for different purposes, from a tour in the school to job possibilities: http://www.summerhillschool.co.uk

2. Watzlawick, Paul, John H. Weakland, and Richard Fisch. 1974. *Change: Principles of Problem Formation and Problem Resolution*. New York: Norton.

3. Senge, Peter M. 1990. *The Fifth Discipline: the Art and Practice of the Learning Organization*. New York: Doubleday/Currency.

4. Korczak, Janusz. 1996. *Writings: How to Love a Child, Pedagogical Moments, Child's Right to Respect*. (Yonat and Alexander Sened, Trans.) Tel Aviv: Hakibbutz Hameuhad. (In Hebrew.)

Additional books by Januscz Korczak:

- Korczak, Janusz. 1970. *Pedagogical Writings*. (Dov Sadan and Shimshon Meltzer, Trans.) Tel Aviv: Hakibbutz Hameuhad. (In Hebrew.)
- Korczak, Janusz. 1998. *Writings – 4th Volume*. (Uri Orlev, Trans.) Jerusalem: Beit Lochamei Hagetaot & Yad VaShem (In Hebrew.)

Studies concerning Korczak's educational doctrine:

- Various authors. 1987. *Studies of the Heritage of Januscz Korczak – a Collection of Articles*. Jerusalem: Beit Lochamei Hagetaot & Haifa University (In Hebrew.)
- Regev, Menachem (Ed.). 1996. *Touching the Person – the character and thinking of Januscz Korczak as reflected in his*

and others writings. Jerusalem: Academon (In Hebrew.)

5. **Sudbury Valley School's website** offers theory and practice concerning the school, photos from the school's routine, admission procedures, articles about the school's ideology and references to other schools in the spirit of Sudbury: http://www.sudval.org

Books about Sudbury:

- Greenberg, Daniel. 1985. *The Sudbury Valley School Experience.* Framingham, Mass: Sudbury Valley School Press.
- Greenberg, Daniel. 1987. *Free at Last: The Sudbury Valley School.* Framingham, Mass: Sudbury Valley School Press.
- Greenberg, Daniel, and Mimsy Sadofsky. 1992. *Legacy of Trust: Life after the Sudbury Valley School Experience.* Framingham, Mass: Sudbury Valley School Press.

6. Rogers, Carl R. 1969. *Freedom to Learn: A View of What Education Might Become.* Columbus, Ohio: Charles E. Merrill Publishing Company.

7. Babylonian Talmud, tractate *Avodah Zarah.* p. 19, sheet 1. (In Hebrew.)

8. Goleman, Daniel. 1995. *Emotional Intelligence.* New York: Bantam Books.

9. **Books by Mihaly Csikszentmihalyi:**

- Csikszentmihalyi, Mihaly. 1990. *Flow: The Psychology of Optimal Experience.* New York: Harper & Row.
- Csikszentmihalyi, Mihaly. 1996. *Creativity: Flow and the Psychology of Discovery and Invention.* New York: Harper Collins Publishers.
- Csikszentmihalyi, Mihaly. 1998. *Finding Flow: The Psychology of Engagement with Everyday Life.* New York: BasicBooks.

10. Abbott, John, and Terry Ryan. 2000. *The Unfinished Revolution.* Visions of education series. Stafford: Network Educational

Press.

11. Korczak, Janusz. 1996. *Writings: How to Love a Child, Pedagogical Moments, Child's Right to Respect*. (Yonat and Alexander Sened, Trans.) Tel Aviv: Hakibbutz Hameuhad. (In Hebrew.)

12. Gribble, David. 1998. *Real Education: Varieties of Freedom*. Bristol: Libertarian Education.

    Other books by David Gribble:

    • Gribble, David. 2005. *Lifelines*. Bristol: Libertarian Education.

    David Gribble also runs the website of IDEN, the International Democratic Education Network, which offers information on people and organizations belonging to the international democratic education community and publishes news related to the field. The website's address is: www.idenetwork.org

13. Dewey John. 1966. *Democracy and Education: an Introduction to the Philosophy of Education*. New York: The Free Press.

    Other books by John Dewey:

    • Dewey, John. 1938. *Experience and Education*. New York: Macmillan Co.

    • Dewey, John. 1956. *The Child and the Curriculum & The School and the Society*. Chicago: University of Chicago Press.

    • Dewey, John. 1948. *Reconstruction in Philosophy*. Boston: The Beacon Press.

    The Center for Dewey Studies website: http://www.siuc. edu/·deweyctr

14. Greenberg, Daniel. 1985. *The Sudbury Valley School Experience*. Framingham, Mass: Sudbury Valley School Press.

15. Miller, Alice. 1983. *The Drama of the Gifted Child & The Search for the True Self*. London: Faber & Faber. *P 226*

16. Fromm, Erich. 1941. *Escape from Freedom*. New York: Farrar & Rinehart, Inc.

17. A description of the method and its applications can be found in the following book:

Cunningham, Ian, Ben Bennett, and Graham Dawes. 2000. *Self Managed Learning in Action: putting SML into practice*. Aldershot, Hampshire, England: Gower.

18. Tom Peters website: http://www.tompeters.com

Books by Tom Peters:

- Peters, Tom. 1994. *The Tom Peters Seminar: Crazy Times Call for Crazy Organizations*. New York: Vintage Books
- Peters, Tom. 1997. *The Circle of Innovation: You Can't Shrink Your Way to Greatness*. New York: Knopf

19. Hurn, Christopher J. 1978. *The Limits and Possibilities of Schooling – an Introduction to the Sociology of Education*. Boston: Allyn & Bacon. P 316

20. Rolnik, Guy. 3/12/2007. Taking Stock: Me, You, Larry and Sergei will Change the World. An article in *Haaretz* newspaper. Available at: http://www.haaretz.com/hasen/spages/930354.html

21. Lorenz, Konrad. 1952. *King Solomon's Ring – New Light on Animal Ways*. New York: Crowell. P 359

22. Hobbes, Thomas. 2007. *Leviathan*. Radford, VA: Wilder Publications.

23. Maslow, Abraham. 1954. *Motivation and Personality*. New York: Harper.

Feldenkrais, Moshe P 171
Watzawick, Weakland + Fisch
"Change" P 205
Mahen, Ronald 22 ?
UN Bill of Human Rights P 250
Hern, Matt "Everywhere all e one time" P 344

CPSIA information can be obtained at www.ICGtesting.com
Printed in the USA
BVOW040741040112

279753BV00001B/2/P